CULTURE SHOCK!

Ukraine

Meredith Dalton

Graphic Arts Center Publishing Company
Portland, Oregon

In the same series

Argentina	Ecuador	Laos	Sri Lanka
Australia	Egypt	Malaysia	Sweden
Austria	Finland	Mauritius	Switzerland
Belgium	France	Mexico	Syria
Bolivia	Germany	Morocco	Taiwan
Borneo	Greece	Myanmar	Thailand
Brazil	Hong Kong	Nepal	Turkey
Britain	Hungary	Netherlands	UAE
California	India	Norway	Ukraine
Canada	Indonesia	Pakistan	USA
Chile	Iran	Philippines	USA—The South
China	Ireland	Saudi Arabia	Venezuela
Costa Rica	Israel	Scotland	Vietnam
Cuba	Italy	Singapore	
Czech Republic	Japan	South Africa	
Denmark	Korea	Spain	

Barcelona At Your Door	Paris At Your Door	A Student's Guide
Beijing At Your Door	Rome At Your Door	A Traveller's Medical
Chicago At Your Door	San Francisco At Your	Guide
Havana At Your Door	Door	A Wife's Guide
Jakarta At Your Door	Shanghai At Your Door	Living and Working
Kuala Lumpur, Malaysia	Tokyo At Your Door	Abroad
At Your Door	Vancouver At Your Door	Personal Protection At
London At Your Door		Home & Abroad
Moscow At Your Door	A Globe-Trotter's Guide	Working Holidays
Munich At Your Door	A Parent's Guide	Abroad
New York At Your Door		

Illustrations by TRIGG

© 1999 Times Editions Pte Ltd
© 2000 Times Media Private Limited
Revised 2001
Reprinted 2000, 2001, 2003

This book is published by special
arrangement with Times Media Private Limited
Times Centre, 1 New Industrial Road, Singapore 536196
International Standard Book Number 1-55868-632-0
Library of Congress Catalog Number 99-60172
Graphic Arts Center Publishing Company
P.O. Box 10306 • Portland, Oregon 97296-0306 • (503) 226-2402

All rights reserved. No part of this publication may be
reproduced, stored in a retrieval system, or transmitted,
in any form or by any means, electronic, mechanical,
photocopying, recording or otherwise, without the prior
permission of the copyright owner.

Printed in Singapore

To the good people of Ukraine
and to those expatriates genuinely dedicated
to a better Ukraine
a better life for Ukrainians
a better world
peace.

CONTENTS

Doing Business and Surviving Ukraine 265

ACKNOWLEDGMENTS

Although my heritage includes no Slavic blood, something about Slavic culture seized me many years ago in John Bowlt's art history classes in Austin, Texas. In 1996 while living in Kyiv, a Ukrainian interpreter and dear friend told me that I was half-American, half-Ukrainian. At the time I wished it were so. My little brother once described himself as three-eighths Irish (true, although I always preferred the one-third joke), half Southern, and a quarter Okie, plus some Nordic percentage (of which, like Slavic, we Daltons possess none). John, a veritable math scholar, couldn't get his proportions to add up. I, too, am intrigued by national identity, ethnicity, and multiculturalism—the world's as well as my own. At the same time, all of us are aware of the tragic consequences of insisting on a particular lineage.

Today I view myself as a sort of collector of places; the topographical features range from the mundane to the elegiac. But in the end it is the people whom I have met that have individually and collectively colored my perceptions. Like those American crazy-quilts that I have loved since my youth, my impressions of Ukraine have been molded through interactions with fellow American, Canadian, Ecuadorian, English, Irish, Belgian, French, German, Swiss, and other expatriates who shared their own observations and experiences with me. Ukrainian friends and colleagues, likewise, have indelibly shaped my experiences.

Special thanks to the following Ukrainians and expatriates; I apologize for any significant omissions: Jim Asher; Mark Baillie; Jennifer Baker; Cynthia Bakle; Igor Bandarenko; Amanda Barley; Betsy Bassan; Marco Berchtold; Joe Bidnez; Lesia Bihun; Carrie Braxton; Len Brockman; Zakhar Bruk; Andrey Cheban; Evgeny Chernyak and Irina, Natasha and Oleg; Bohdan Chomiak; Jim Davis; Lena Davis; Roger Dean; Geoff Elkind; Bob Evans; Gary Fickemeyer; Igor Fotiev; Randy Fortenbery; H³; John Helmuth; Dwight Hewitt;

Laura Hoover; Ty Jagerson; Myron Jarosewich; Kathy, whose kids attend New Hope School; Patricia Koch and Brian Foster; Marta Kolomayets; Andrey Kolomiets; Peter Koshukov; Nikki Lemley; Tom Lemley; Allison Lynch; Carlyse Marshall; Shannon Matthews; Joe MacFarlane; Tim McQuillin; Nigel Mukherjee; Igor Musiyuk; Boris Najman; Andrew Pearson; Hugh Patton; Meagan Plagge; Ron Prescott; Randy Regan; Linda Rogers and Jeff Berstein; Jeff Rosenberg; Hermanito Willie Salinas Zambrano; Skip Sayer; Kevin Scallan; Dick Shriver; David Snelbecker; Doug Stephenson; Kathryn Stevens; Nick Stevens; Aleksei Strelnik; Annelise Tarnstrom; Kristi Tarnstrom; Tanya of Coopers & Lybrand; Glenn Tasky; Pavel Ustimenko and Valentin, Lena and Olga; Harry Walters; Greg Welling; and Sasha Zinchenko.

Additional thanks go to my dear friend Jacqueline Curzon Price, who shared her photographs after so many of mine were stolen last year, and to my little sister Catherine, whose photographs proved invaluable (and superior to mine). I love you, Twin. Special thanks to Clifton Warren, who is consistently available to me and whose heart is huge; to Lori and Andrew for opening their home and hearts to me in the 13th hour, and to Keith Bowden of the University of Central Oklahoma who helped me with Photoshop in my time of need. Special thanks to Olena Czebiniak for converting my Russian into Ukrainian. Thanks also to the editors at Times Editions, who encouraged me without overwhelming me. It's a harder task than most people realize.

As always, thanks to my loving and supportive family; to Tia and Cuz, and to all my friends who genuinely encouraged me. This includes Alyssa, Andrew, Karen, Eve and many others—not only do I know who you are, I also know where you live (that's more than you can say for me!)

Thank you, one and all.

— *Chapter One* —

INTRODUCTION TO UKRAINE

On the last day of November 2001, a Ukrainian friend drove in from Kharkiv to Kyiv to see me before my departure for the United States the following morning. (He also likes, whenever we meet, to remind me that Kharkiv is really Kharkov, but more on that below.) The actual date is not so important; what mattered most was that I had had another opportunity to revisit my Ukrainian friends and a country very dear to me. I also saw Kyiv's flurry of construction activity and the new monuments erected in honor of Ukraine's 10th anniversary of independence, celebrated on August 24, 2001.

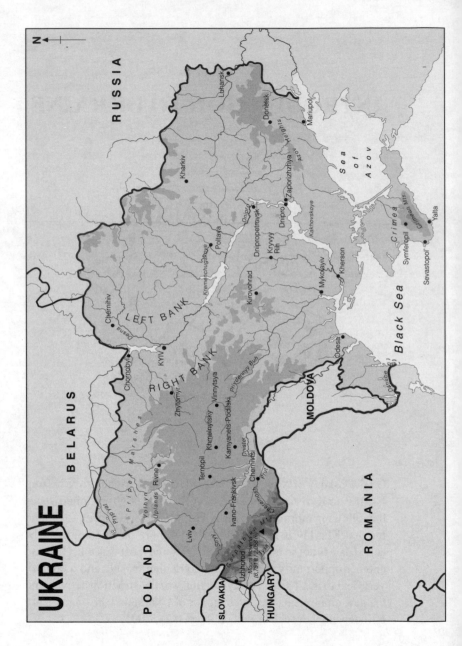

Evgeny's car has Kharkiv plates, and Kyiv's dreaded DAI—the notoriously corrupt street police—pulled us over about 12:30 am. We had finished a late dinner and were looking for, you guessed it, a bottle of good Ukrainian vodka or, more accurately, *horilka*. Evgeny had asked me to deliver this gift to my father in Oklahoma.

The DAI does not need a reason to pull you over. They can simply choose you because they don't like the car you drive, your car tags, or your haircut. But one of the big changes in 2001, favorably noted by many in the expatriate community, is that the DAI can no longer issue on-the-spot fines. Some people still pay bribes to get the DAI off their back, but today you don't have to have cash on you for paying fines. (And when you paid fines in the past, where exactly did that money go?)

The DAI had pulled us over, it turns out, because Evgeny's driver was driving too slowly. What next happened did my heart good. My dear friend asked the DAI officer where we might find a nice bottle of vodka at that hour. The policeman perked up and told us to drive forward two blocks, turn right, and go another two blocks. Evgeny thanked him, and we sped off into the cold November night.

Most visitors to Ukraine are quick to observe the hospitality and generosity of Ukrainians. Outside of Ukraine, the country is perhaps best known as the breadbasket of the former Soviet Union and for its rich soil; as the site of the world's most horrific nuclear accident in 1986; for its post-independence disputes with Russia over Crimea and the Black Sea Fleet; for its delicious *borshch*, Ukraine's national soup that was subsequently adopted by other Soviet republics; for Kyiv Dynamo, the celebrated football team; for its unique peppered vodka called *horilka z pertsem*; and for fine, native handicrafts, including beautifully decorated Easter eggs that predate the Christian era. But Ukraine is much more than this—and far more complex.

UKRAINE AT THE CROSSROADS

Ukraine's strategic position marks an ancient crossroads between the Black Sea, the Sea of Azov, and the Baltic Sea. This same location between modern-day Germany and Russia proved particularly inauspicious during World War II, as a disproportionate number of battles was fought on Ukrainian soil.

Today Ukraine is an independent nation, at times divided by language, history, and religion. The Dnipro River reflects a physical and cultural demarcation between eastern and western Ukraine. Left-Bank (or eastern and southern) Ukraine was traditionally Russian-speaking and generally favored Russia, whereas Right-Bank Ukraine spoke Ukrainian and was sometimes staunchly nationalistic.

These distinctions are somewhat changing as Ukrainian, once described as a language for peasants and the intelligentsia, is now the official language used by the government and in schools. In practice, Russian has been the dominant—and most practical—language for business, as historically more Ukrainians spoke Russian than Ukrainian and Russian was the official language of all Soviet republics. Also, Russia is Ukraine's primary trading partner. But the popularity of the Ukrainian language is steadily growing and influencing Ukrainian attitudes.

One major difference, however, from the Soviet era is that Ukrainians today don't discriminate against Russian-language speakers. The Soviets vehemently discouraged any displays of Ukrainian solidarity or culture—especially language, as it was considered the most important component of nationality. However, the roots of Russification in Ukraine were not a distinctive Soviet feature but may be traced to the Russian Empire during the mid-18th century.

For centuries Poland and Russia fought over Ukrainian soil, and their influences and territorial divisions have ramifications today. The Ukrainian Uniate Church in western Ukraine is essentially a hybrid of Ukrainian Orthodoxy with Catholic Poland's influences. Ukraine's Orthodox churches are further divided and even antagonistic. The fate of Ukraine's Jews is another bloody chapter in Ukraine's turbulent history, and discrimination against Jews remains one of the Soviet Union's legacies. However, the roots of Ukraine's anti-Semitism clearly predated the communist era. Lastly, Kyiv's Tatar population, who had settled in the Podil district, received permission from President Kuchma and built a mosque in the capital in 1998. There are also Protestant, Jewish, and Muslim minorities in Ukraine.

The lack of information available on Ukraine during the Soviet era was striking, and Ukraine is still often relegated to the back sections of books on Russia. Many outsiders erroneously believe that Ukraine is today a part of Russia. The histories of the two nations are inextricably connected, and in fact Ukraine, Russia, and Belarus all trace their roots to the great state of Kyivan Rus that emerged in the 9th century. But let us mince no words here: Ukraine is not Russia.

Among Ukraine's most infamous chapters in recent history was the forced collectivization of farms and Soviet dictator Joseph (Iosif) Stalin's deliberate starvation of some six to 10 million Ukrainians in the early 1930s in an effort to break the Ukrainian spirit. Stalin failed, but his actions must be considered among the foremost factors that have molded modern-day Ukrainian identity.

Like its megalithic neighbor Russia, Ukraine is today undergoing a period of vast and small changes. Historically, it has been difficult at times to unravel where Russian and Ukrainian cultures overlap or diverge. Chauvinism and its associated handicaps are prevalent in both cultures, and isolated reports by outsiders in recent years have suggested that Ukraine could be on the verge of ethnic combustion. The broad consensus is that this view is unreasonable.

A more legitimate concern in the wake of the disastrous financial crisis of 1998 was that, without additional help from foreign financial institutions, Ukraine's financial straits might force the country back into Russia's expanding sphere of economic and political influence. Three years later, Ukraine is clearly holding its own and has now managed to curb inflation. This is not to say that all is well in Ukraine, and the presidency of Leonid Kuchma has been fraught with controversies. Moreover, life outside Kyiv is considerably different from life within. But it does seem especially unlikely that Ukraine would ever relinquish its hard-earned independence from Russia.

There is not a single definition for "Ukraine." According to many sources, the name "Ukraine" originates from a Slavic word meaning "borderland." "Little Russia" and "South Russia" were two former names for the region that have since been rejected for their derogatory implications. Today, Ukrainians prefer the English name "Ukraine" to "the Ukraine" for reasons given later. Like their Slavic brothers, Ukrainians are proud people and generous hosts. Their national anthem, *Ukraine is Not Yet Dead*, underscores a bittersweet history and strong national character.

GEOGRAPHY

With an area slightly larger than France, Ukraine is today the largest country completely within Europe. The Ukrainian Soviet Socialist Republic was the third largest of the 15 Soviet republics after Russia—now the world's largest country—and Kazakhstan.

To Ukraine's north lies Belarus, the former Soviet republic called Byelorussia or White Russia. To the east (and northeast) is Russia. West of Ukraine are Poland, Slovakia, Hungary, Romania, and Moldova, formerly the Soviet republic called Moldavia. Ukraine's southern border lies along the Black Sea and Sea of Azov and includes the Crimean Peninsula.

CLIMATE AND TOPOGRAPHY

Most of Ukraine is gently sloping steppes, and its moniker "the breadbasket of the Soviet Union" stems from the fertility of its celebrated black soil. Ukraine's northern steppes, bordering on

Belarus, are forested, providing sources for food, fuel, and building materials—as well as excellent hiding places from past invaders and difficult rulers. On its western border, Ukraine is flanked by the Carpathian Mountains, where opportunities exist for downhill skiing and hiking expeditions.

Crimea in the south has a Mediterranean climate and is known for its vineyards, spas, and health resorts, along with a spectacular coastline. The Russian or Ukrainian Riviera refers to this peninsula.

The capital Kyiv is slightly above the latitudes of Frankfurt and Prague. It is generally known for its warm summers and mild winters, but it can still get quite cold. The disposition of its residents appears to change with the arrival of spring thaws. Outdoor life rebounds quickly as Kyiv's café culture unfolds in its streets.

ETHNICITY AND IDENTITY

The Cyrillic letters resembling CCCP in English are actually SSSR; they stood for the Union of Soviet Socialist Republics (USSR). In Russian, USSR referred to the Ukrainian Soviet Socialist Republic. (If all this is confusing, study the Cyrillic alphabet in the chapter *Humor and Language*.)

The Ukrainian SSR was the second most populous republic after Russia. Ukraine's population is now about 49 million, and slightly declining each year due to emigration, high mortality, and declining birth rates.

Ethnic Ukrainians represent 73% of Ukraine's population; ethnic Russians comprise 22%. More Ukrainians today speak Russian than Ukrainian, although the majority of the population is bilingual. These numbers will continue to increase in independent Ukraine, because the official language is now Ukrainian.

Jews are considered a distinct nationality in Ukraine. Ukraine's Jews comprise less than 1% of the population, now estimated at somewhere between 300,000 and 400,000. This still makes Ukraine home to one of largest Jewish communities in the world. More than

200,000 Jews have emigrated to Israel, Europe, or North America in the past 10 years. There were frequent concerns that there could be no Ukrainian Jewish population in another 10 years, based on current demographics. Half of Ukraine's current Jewish population is over 50 years old, and the young have tended to emigrate more than their elders.

Unlike Poland, however, there are Jews today in the smaller towns, although the bulk live in urban areas. While Jews have been distressed to watch as their numbers thin out, an incipient Jewish revival is garnering support in Ukraine. More than 70 Jewish schools, including day schools and Sunday schools, have now opened in numerous cities.

Other minorities in Ukraine today include Belarusians, Poles, Hungarians, Romanians, Moldovans, Slovaks, Bulgarians, and Gypsies. Where applicable, these ethnic minorities tend to live near the borders of their ancestral homelands. Consequently, with the notable exception of the Belarusians, most minorities live in western Ukraine. Similarly, the bulk of ethnic Russians live in Ukraine's more populous eastern and southern regions.

Five Ukrainian cities today boast populations of over one million citizens: Kyiv, Kharkiv, Dnipropetrovsk, Odesa, and Donetsk. Zaporizhzhya, an industrial town in southeastern Ukraine, boasts a population of nearly 900,000. Each of these cities is predominantly Russian-speaking, and all but Odesa are located in Left-Bank Ukraine. Odesa is about 75 miles west of the Dnipro, which is why one often hears references to "Left-Bank Ukraine plus Odesa."

The Dnipro River (Dnepr in Russian) roughly halves the country in a sort of yin-yang fashion. Right-Bank Ukraine is comprised of western and central Ukraine, whereas Left-Bank Ukraine includes the eastern and southern regions. The Dnipro's physical division also reveals a psychological demarcation.

Right-Bank Ukraine is predominantly Ukrainian-speaking and home to some of Ukraine's most ardent nationalists. The unofficial capital of western Ukraine is Lviv, a city with a particularly Central European feel. Activists here spearheaded the independence movement. Because of this, and also because Lviv is the largest city in western Ukraine (about 800,000 people), there is a tendency to mistake the people of Lviv as a prototype for western Ukraine. However, Lviv and its immediate surroundings were not ruled by Moscow prior to 1939. As a result, its wayward populace never fully succumbed to the Soviet stronghold in Moscow. Also, between 1941 and 1944, Lviv was occupied by the Germans. When the Red Army seized control of the city in 1944, things did not necessarily improve for Lviv's residents, many of whom were accused of collaborating with the Germans.

The emergence of Ukrainian nationalism is often associated with the art and writings of Ukraine's national hero, Taras Shevchenko, born into serfdom in 1814. Shevchenko was responding in part to the suppression of Ukrainian culture (and later language), traceable to the mid-18th century. Ryszard Kapuscinski, a contemporary Polish journalist, has observed that nationalism cannot exist in a conflict-free environment; there will always be grudges and claims. Consequently, whenever nationalism does surface, there will be an immediate reaction on the part of the group's enemies. Not surprisingly, Ukrainian nationalism was illegal under the Soviets.

By contrast, Left-Bank Ukraine (plus Odesa) speaks Russian and at times favors Russia, although a 1998 motion to join the proposed Russian-Belarusian union was dismissed. Of Ukraine's 10 million ethnic Russians, some 80% live in the eastern and southern regions. President Leonid Kuchma, elected in 1994 largely by Ukraine's Russian-speaking populace, has learned Ukrainian and now delivers all speeches in the country's official language. Native Ukrainian speakers nonetheless scoff at his grammar. Compare this, however, with a Communist Party meeting in 1939 where the Georgian-born Stalin made a Russian grammatical error; every speaker who followed him repeated his error out of fear.

Ukraine's sequential domination by other peoples, further complicated by its history of changing borders, helps explain Ukraine's personality complex. It is important to recognize the coexistence of pro-Ukrainian and pro-Russian factions; equally important is recognizing current ethnic tensions without exaggerating them.

Ukraine also perpetuates many of its chauvinistic traditions. Ethnic minorities in Transcarpathia today complain of discrimination. Prior to 1945, this region was part of Hungary, and many here still set their watches back one hour to Hungarian time. Some also insist that Subcarpathia is a more accurate name than Transcarpathia. Crimea, with its ethnic Russian majority, and Tatar minority, is marked by external and internal divisiveness. Ethnic tensions in neighboring Moldova in the Transdnistr region also continue to affect Ukraine.

In the light of these ethnic tensions—and further scuffles within Ukraine's ethnic mix are conceivable—there are those who would have you believe that independent Ukraine is a pressure cooker, another Yugoslavia waiting to happen. It is not.

Ukraine is Not Russia

It is not possible to speak of Ukraine without addressing Russia at length, as their Slavic histories are inextricably linked. But they are now two distinct countries, and it is incorrect to lump Ukraine as a part of Russia.

On August 24, 1991, Ukraine's Supreme Rada (equivalent to Russia's Duma or parliament) adopted a declaration of independence, dependant upon a national referendum. December 1, 1991, saw an unprecedented voter turnout of 84% with 90% voting for independence.

Ukraine, Russia, and Belarus all trace their origins to Kyiv, which you hear called the "mother of Russian cities" or, more correctly, "the mother of all Rus cities." This is because Kyiv was once the capital of the great state of Kyivan Rus. All three Slavic countries have separate, but related, languages, although Belarus under its president Alexsandr Lukashenko has scrapped Belarusian for Russian as its official language.

Despite shared elements of history and Slavic culture, many differences between Ukrainians and Russians are more subtle than church authority and language issues—and sometimes far more inflammatory. An understanding of Ukraine's history of colonization by Russians and Poles (and earlier Lithuanians) helps to explain the unique character of Ukrainians. For centuries, Ukrainians have viewed their country as the underdog, and this was naturally reinforced through years of suppressing Ukrainian culture; in 1876 the Ukrainian language was banned in schools and in all publications. In more recent history, Stalin clearly targeted Ukrainians, but he didn't necessarily spare other Soviet peoples.

Similarities with Russia and Poland

Ukraine is distinct from Russia in that there are two dominant languages, three Orthodox churches, and, for centuries, the nation was dominated by outsiders. Culturally, Ukraine shares more traditions with its Eastern Slavic brothers, the Belarusians and Russians, than with its neighboring Poles, although much of its cuisine falls somewhere in between.

The so-called Russian soul is really the Slavic soul, and Ukrainians and Russians alike have strong predispositions toward mysticism and superstition. The role of vodka traditions among the Eastern Slavs is historical and significant: both Russians and Poles claim to have invented the intoxicating elixir. Drunkenness and alcoholism are unfortunate corollaries attached more to Ukrainians and Russians than to Poles. The Eastern Slavs also share a tendency toward fatalism that is often linked to their excessive drinking.

Graft and corruption are also legitimate concerns for those traveling to the former Soviet Union or establishing business relations there. Seventy-plus years of communism, including some 25 years under Stalinist absolutism, have molded Soviet citizenry and individual character in different ways from communist rule in Eastern Europe.

Ukraine's financial woes are acute, but the country possesses vast mineral wealth. Ukraine's ultimate wealth, however, is its people, and outsiders who fail to recognize this should look to other countries for their international exploits.

What's in a Name?

An overview of the origins of the name "Ukraine" summarizes aspects of Ukraine's changing borders and its self-perception as inferior to Russia.

The name "Ukraine" or *Ukraina* (say *ooCRYeena*) originates from the Slavic word meaning "borderland." From the 12th to 15th centuries, "Ukraine" meant "borderland," "bordering country," or "country." Continuing into the 16th century, documents made references to various Ukraines, Galician Ukraine and Kyiv Ukraine among others, but over time "Ukraine" came to mean the Cossack territory stretching along both sides of the Dnipro River, then part of the Polish Commonwealth. In the 17th century the concept of Ukraine was extended farther east to include not only eastern Ukraine but also territory of the Muscovite state of Slovidska Ukraine, which attracted Cossack settlers. After Hetman Bohdan Khmelnytsky's successful uprising against the Poles in the mid-17th century, "Ukraine" referred to the rise of a Cossack state in central Ukraine. This was not its official name, but the Hetman territory was usually known as Ukraine in both Ukrainian and Polish sources at this time.

The 1667 and 1668 partitions between Muscovy and Poland interrupted the evolution of Ukraine as a unifying concept. Indeed, this period sowed the seeds for much of the east versus west conflict encountered in Left-Bank and Right-Bank Ukraine. The former, then a Muscovy protectorate, was transformed into a province of the Russian Empire; it became officially known in Russian as Malorossiya or Little Russia. It was also sometimes called Southern Russia.

The larger part of the Ukrainian territories was unified with the Russian Empire during the Partitions of Poland between 1772 and 1795. This paved the way for the concept of Ukraine as Ukrainian national territory, as well as the emergence of Ukrainian nationalism in the 1840s. Only Ukraine's far western territory, the region around Lviv, was excluded; this went instead to the Hapsburg Empire.

Taras Shevchenko associated "Ukraine" with a proud Cossack past, whereas "Malorossiya" reinforced national humiliation and colonial status. From the mid-19th century, "Ukraine" at last displaced all other names for this territory.

The years following the Russian Revolution and World War I were chaotic and unstable, and civil war broke out and lasted until the early 1920s. This was really a prolongation of revolution. In 1918, for example, there were at least 30 governments in what had been the Russian Empire. After 1920, parts of western Ukraine were divided between Poland, Romania, and Czechoslovakia. In 1921, the Bolsheviks gave formal recognition to Ukraine's independence; then in 1922, Ukraine was seized and incorporated into the newly formed USSR as the Ukrainian Soviet Socialist Republic.

In its 1991 declaration of independence, the new state adopted "Ukraine" as its official name. The name in English is not "the Ukraine" as it was formerly called in English. In fact, the articles "the" and "a" do not exist in the Ukrainian, Russian, or Belarusian languages. The larger issue, however, is that "the Ukraine" suggests to Ukrainians a geographical region when, in fact, Ukraine is today an independent country.

Language and Identity: Kyiv, Kyyiv, or Kiev?

Years of practice have meant that "Kiev" still appears more frequently in print than "Kyiv." Nevertheless, the sentence "Kiev is the capital of the Ukraine" neither sounds nor looks correct to me.

The traditional English spelling of Ukraine's capital city was a direct transliteration from the Russian "Kyyiv," and was proposed as a more accurate Ukrainian transliteration but this never really took hold. Independent Ukraine has now adopted "Kyiv" as the official English spelling for its capital. The stress in all cases is on the first syllable. In practice, it falls somewhere between *KEYyiv* and *KAYyiv*.

In the post-Soviet era, Russian remains the language for most business, and more people in the capital still speak Russian than Ukrainian. But street signs, storefronts, and billboard advertising are in Ukrainian. For example, you'll see the abbreviation *vul.* in Ukrainian for *vulytsya* (meaning street) whereas you might hear the Russian *ulitsa* spoken. This gets confusing at times, but such is life in contemporary Ukraine; many speak a mixture of both languages.

The situation is further complicated because so many of the Soviet names have been replaced, sometimes reclaiming the pre-revolutionary name. Not all cities have adopted new names for communist ones. For example, Kharkiv's Karl Marx and Lenin Streets remain unchanged, whereas Kyiv's have been renamed. Skeptics claim that changing the communist names is merely window-dressing.

In Ukrainian and Russian, the names of many Ukrainian cities and towns are slightly different. For example, the Ukrainian transliteration for Odessa (on the Black Sea) is Odesa; because the dominant language here is Russian, you will encounter the Russian transliteration far more often. Slightly more confusing is nearby Mykolayiv (the Ukrainian name), called Nikolaev in Russian. Kharkiv in the east and only 25 miles from the Russian border is a "Russian" city; to many, it seems more appropriate to use its Russian transliteration of Kharkov, thereby respecting the wishes of the majority of Ukrainian citizens living here. Officially, however, the city is now Kharkiv. (My friend Zhenia jokes that that's like telling someone that I was raised in Oo-klahoma.)

Go to Lviv (Lvov in Russian, Lwow in Polish, and Lemberg under the Germans and the Hapsburgs), and you will find that the people speak Ukrainian, or perhaps Polish, but not Russian. The rest of western Ukraine speaks Ukrainian. Kyiv's international airport is "Boryspil" in Ukrainian but still Borispol to the world at large. A few English transliterations of place names are the same as the local names, such as Donetsk and Lutsk.

Below is a list of places whose Ukrainian and Russian differ:

Ukrainian name	Russian name
Boryspil	Borispol (Kyiv's international airport)
Chernivtsi	Chernovtsy
Chernihiv	Chernigov
Chornobyl	Chernobyl
Dnipropetrovsk	Dnepropetrovsk
Dnipro (River)	Dnepr
Ivano-Frankivsk	Ivano-Frankovsk
Kamyanets-Podilski	Kamenets-Podilsky
Kharkiv	Kharkov
Khmelnytsky	Khmelnitsky
Kirovohrad	Korovograd
Krivy Rih	Krivoy Rog
Kyiv	Kiev
Lviv	Lvov
Luhansk	Lugansk
	(the Soviet name was Voroshilovgrad)
Mariupol	(the Soviet name was Zhdanov)

23

Mykolayiv	Nikolaev
Odesa	Odessa
Pochaiv	Pochaev
Rivne	Rovno
Ternopil	Ternopol
Uzhhorod	Uzhgorod
Vinnytsya	Vinnitsa
Zaporizhzhya	Zaporozhie
Zhytomyr	Zhitomir

See the chapter *Humor and Language* for a more detailed discussion on language.

The Crimean Question

Crimea is predominantly Russian, with 63% of the population, although it was officially given to Ukraine in 1954 in recognition of Ukraine's 300 years of unification with Russia. Moscow time is no longer observed in Crimea. Rather, all of Ukraine is today united in the same time zone, which is GMT +2, with Moscow one hour ahead. The first attempt in 1997 to unite all of Ukraine under one time zone failed quickly, and Moscow time resumed in Crimea. A second recent attempt proved more successful.

Tatars ruled Crimea before the 18th century, when Russians occupied the peninsula. Following World War II, the Soviet dictator Stalin accused the Crimean Tatars of collaborating with the Germans during the latter's three-year occupation. Stalin banished the entire Tatar population of some 250,000 to Central Asia, with the largest numbers deported to Uzbekistan. Nearly half died en route. His successor Nikita Khrushchev said later that Stalin would have deported far more Ukrainians, but their numbers were too large.

Since independence, some 250,000 Tatars, out of a population of 400,000, have returned to their ancestral homeland. In 1998 and 1999, violent protests erupted when repatriated Tatars were not allowed to vote in elections. This was because most of Crimea's Tatars did not possess a passport, having relinquished citizenship rights when they left former Soviet states. For those holding Uzbek passports, efforts have been made to simplify the process for obtaining Ukrainian citizenship. Tatar leaders have since called for similar measures to ease naturalization for repatriated Tatars banished to other countries in the Soviet Union.

Crimean Tatars are today allowed to own land and to open their own schools. They have also fought hard for the recognition of their language as a state language, arguing that it would otherwise be lost. During the Soviet era, the Tatar language was, of course, forbidden.

Repatriation for Crimea's Tatars is not the region's only issue. In 1995, Ukraine declared Crimea's separatist constitution and presidency under Yuri Meshkov invalid. Crimea had declared self-rule in 1992, which Ukraine did not recognize. For a time, war between Ukraine and Russia seemed a possibility. Ukraine was clearly wise in having never sent troops to Crimea; for its part, Crimea recognized that tourism, unlike wheat and iron ore production, does not continue during wartime. Because tourism was its foremost priority, Crimea withdrew its claims for independence, and further conflict was averted.

Crimea is the one autonomous republic within Ukraine. As such, it has been allowed to speak Russian and mostly do as it pleases—so long as it continues to wave the flag and doesn't try to break away.

The Crimean mafia has its own reputation. I heard of a businessman who sold tractors to farmers throughout Ukraine, many of whom later defaulted payment on these $130,000 pieces of equipment. Some ex-police types (read thugs) came in and said that for $20,000 they could get the equipment back. To the businesman, this seemed like a better deal than losing the entire amount. The caveat? Tractors sold to Crimeans would not be repossessed.

Transdnistr

In 1994, Moscow signed a peace agreement with Moldova in which Russia agreed to close its 14th Army base in Moldova's separatist Dnistr region. In late 1998, the Ukrainian and Moldovan presidents were still urging Moscow to withdraw its troops as agreed. Russia now says that all troops will be removed by the end of 2002.

In 1990, pro-Moscow forces in Transdnistr proclaimed independence from Moldova. Historically, this sliver of land between the Dnistr River and Ukraine's western border was part of Ukraine until 1939, when it was ceded to Moldova. Moldova has never recognized independence in Transdnistr. Moldova's population of 4.4 million is primarily ethnic Romanian, whereas in Transdnistr, ethnic Slavs with a population of 750,000 outnumber Moldovans two to one. The fear, then, was that Moldova would seek to reunite with neighboring Romania.

In 1992, a brief war was fought between the separatists and Moldova. The separatists were armed with weapons from the former Soviet 14th Army. A ceasefire was brokered by Aleksandr Lebed, then the base's commanding general and now a prominent Russian politician. Although tensions between the Dnistr separatists and the Moldovan government have since abated, neither side has budged on its stance. In 1998, Ukraine began insisting on its right to send peacekeepers to Transdnistr, with Russia somewhat uneasy about this Ukrainian presence.

Romania, Ukraine, and Moldova have all expressed interest in establishing a Lower Danube Free Economic Zone for the shipment of Caspian oil through their countries. Part of Ukraine's interest in Transdnistr stems from weak border controls. In 2001, the Moldovan president asked for Ukraine's help in tightening border controls around Transdnistr because of alleged wide-scale smuggling in the area. Ukraine is also concerned about potential border and visa issues with Poland and Hungary, both of which have applied for European Union membership.

ENVIRONMENT AND ENERGY

Under the Soviet system, the republics were marked by different specialties. Uzbekistan, for example, was celebrated for its cotton production; Minsk in Byelorussia concentrated on domestic appliances; and Ukraine, with its rich soil and large population base, emphasized agriculture, as well as chemical and heavy industry, including metallurgy, machine-building, energy-intensive manufacturing, and nuclear missile production. Consequently, Ukraine attained dubious distinction as the most industrialized of the Soviet republics. In Soviet terms, this also means that today it is among the most contaminated, as widespread environmental pollution accompanied all Soviet industrialization. Improper disposal of toxic wastes and a general lack of ecological controls in mines and industrial plants wreaked havoc on Ukraine.

The Donetsk region is exceptionally rich in coal deposits. This coal, along with Ukraine's rich iron ore deposits, is used in the steelmaking process and as an energy source for much of Ukraine's strong manufacturing base. Coal is highly polluting and has contributed adversely to Ukraine's already daunting environmental legacy.

Since independence, the government has enacted environmental protection laws in an effort to halt additional pollution. Still, Ukraine lacks the financial resources to repair the widespread damage sustained during the communist period.

Further, under the Soviet paradigm, end users paid virtually nothing for energy, and waste was rife. Moreover, increasing demand ostensibly signaled a more powerful country. Today, Ukraine's tradition of wastefulness, combined with gross inefficiency, is further complicated because the country possesses inadequate natural energy reserves. As a result, Ukraine has racked up huge debts to Russia in recent years. One solution for drawing down Ukraine's debt has been the exchange of Ukrainian wheat for Russian oil and gas. However, these barter transactions, in which no money exchanges hands nor are the transactions taxed, has never come close to solving the mounting debt problems that strained relations between the two

27

countries. Ukraine also hopes to restructure its gas debts with Turkmenistan.

In late 2001, Ukraine and Russia at last reached an agreement, whereby Ukraine will pay Russia more than $1.4 billion in natural gas debts over a 12-year period. To do this, Ukraine will issue corporate debt, and a three-year grace period was granted. That up to 90% of Russia's exports to Europe are piped through Ukraine was surely in Ukraine's favor. However, Ukraine must also prove itself more responsive to Russia's accusations that Ukraine has been siphoning off some of these gas exports.

Chornobyl

April 26, 1986 marked a black day in world history. The explosion at the Chornobyl power plant in Ukraine was the world's worst nuclear disaster. The then Soviet government deliberately downplayed the gravity of the situation. The accident at Chornobyl and its tragic aftermath underscored the pernicious nature of government actions and, in this case, inaction on the part of the former Soviet government. For many, it came to symbolize all that was wrong with the Soviet Union.

In the face of upcoming Labor Day celebrations on May 1, the Soviet government didn't want panic to disrupt the annual event. After all, May Day and October Revolution Day were important vehicles for commemorating the triumph of the Soviet system.

The foreign press reported the incident before the Soviets did. Swedish scientists recorded high radioactivity levels, which the United States then traced via satellite to the radioactive plume above Chornobyl. The deliberate delayed response on the part of the Soviets effectively lost time in containing the contamination, contributing to greater radiation exposure and the loss of more lives. This complicity on the part of the government irrevocably altered the history of the Soviet Union; some say that it ultimately cost the Soviet Union its existence.

Chornobyl is located 60 miles (97 km) north of Kyiv and very close to the Belarusian border. Belarus suffered more than Ukraine due to prevailing wind patterns; estimates are that nearly one-quarter to one-third of Belarusian soil was seriously damaged. Parts of western Russia were also severely contaminated. Ukrainians and Belarusians contend that had this tragedy occurred on Russian soil, or closer to Moscow politics, the response would have been swifter.

Many Ukrainians are scared of having children in the wake of Chornobyl. Ten years after Chornobyl, my friend in Kyiv remarked that his sister-in-law had miscarried in Ukraine and subsequently given birth to a healthy child in New York. This was de facto proof to him that the 1986 tragedy was a contributing factor in the loss of the first child.

A sizeable increase in vodka and red wine consumption followed the Chornobyl catastrophe, based on the belief that these drinks help to flush radiation from the body. Ostensibly the liquidators (Chornobyl's cleanup crew) were given vodka rations for this reason; however, it is more likely that vodka was needed to mollify fears of contamination.

Access to iodine in the days immediately following Chornobyl was grossly inadequate. When it was available, many people drank it without proper instruction, burning their throats and stomachs. Fearing a panic, the government deliberately curtailed its availability at one point. Used properly, iodine attaches itself to the thyroid; otherwise, radioactive iodine will. If there is no space available for the radioactive isotope, it will be flushed from the system as an unneeded nutrient. Reports of thyroid damage, especially among children, are staggering. Similarly, bones latch onto calcium—and radioactive strontium. After Chornobyl, inadequate supplies of "clean" milk also put children at greater risk of strontium poisoning. In any case, radioactive cesium can find many hosts in the human body and is not easily flushed out.

An Incomplete Summary of Facts about Chornobyl
Chornobyl's explosion was the result of a failed experiment. Engineers had advised Moscow that they would perform a test on the morning of April 26, 1986, but Moscow didn't respond. The Ukrainians opted to proceed with the experiment. They wanted to know what would happen if some of the systems failed, so they intentionally shut down part of the reactor.

The problem lay in the reactor's design. Calls to eliminate all such RBMK reactors were widespread. Specifically, in slowing down these systems, other functions were actually sped up temporarily. The plant itself had been hastily constructed to substandard specifications. Defective metal was used so that construction could stay on schedule. Also, a lot of cement had been stolen during construction; sand was then added as filler, resulting in adulterated cement.

In cesium levels alone, Chornobyl has been described as equivalent to 300 Hiroshimas. A problem arises, however, in comparing the victims of Chornobyl to Japan's World War II atom bomb casualties. Chornobyl victims had been exposed to small doses of radiation over a long period prior to the 1986 explosion, including regular releases of radioactive steam in order to prevent a sizeable buildup of noxious contaminants. Scientists and medical specialists have confirmed that the Soviet and Japanese nuclear incidents don't correlate well.

The Soviet government repressed its scientists, physicians, and journalists after Chornobyl. Doctors were forbidden from linking illnesses and deaths to radiation exposure. The government intervened in the press to pinpoint the Chornobyl engineers as scapegoats rather than the fallible reactor design itself. Also, when acceptable levels of radiation rocketed off the scale, the scale was changed to accommodate amounts 20 times the originally acceptable levels.

For some communities, maps of irradiated areas were not drawn until years after the explosion. Some evacuations were planned for as late as five years after the accident. Four radiation zones were mapped with Zone One being the most contaminated and unfit for human habitation; this didn't prevent some elderly people from later moving back there. Some claim that all of Kyiv is in Zone Four with Zone Three hot spots. But Zone Four residents are exempt from taxation, and Kyiv could not survive without its already limited tax revenues if it were classified as Zone Four.

The evacuations were puzzling. Some began within a few days, quietly out of fear of widespread hysteria. While high-ranking government officials were sequestering relatives, most adults and children were unaware of the burgeoning cover-up. Many recall an unseasonably warm May Day parade during which children marched in the Kyiv streets with bare legs, unknowingly kicking up radioactive dust. Later, the government had these same schoolchildren rake all the leaves and bury them. All mutant animals were destroyed, as were evacuees' pets. In other cases where people weren't evacuated, their farm animals were seized but not necessarily destroyed.

People who wanted to leave contaminated areas were prevented by law from moving. In the Soviet era, and until quite recently, citizens could not relocate simply because they wanted to live elsewhere. (See the next chapter's discussion of internal passports and the *propiska* registration stamp.) Others later returned to their contaminated homes. Thieves also raided contaminated homes and sold the furniture to unsuspecting buyers.

In some contaminated areas millions of rubles were spent to dig ditches to bury radioactive soil, which soon regained its high levels of radioactivity. So-called clean homes were built in areas where the residents should have been relocated altogether. In other cases, people were relocated to contaminated areas.

Subsidies—colloquially referred to as "coffin money"—were offered to members of certain villages, while neighboring villagers received nothing. The system was arbitrary at best, and even though some people were offered clean milk and tinned meat, supplies of clean provisions were always inadequate. Consequently, many were forced to consume their own irradiated milk, cattle, fruit, and vegetables; irradiated wood was burned for heat. Because of the subsidies, people wanted to be reclassified for additional benefits. The government dispersed much of the contaminated products throughout the Soviet Union, declaring that some should be diluted with uncontaminated products. In this way, it was hoped that no single community would be overloaded; instead, contaminated products were offered to Soviet citizens at large.

In Bryansk, one of Russia's western regions hardest hit by Chornobyl, locals insist that Moscow ordered planes from the Bryansk and Oryol military bases to fire cloud-seeding missiles, causing rain to fall and thereby diverting radioactive clouds from Moscow.

Chornobyl was not the first major nuclear catastrophe in the Soviet Union, but it was its last. *Glasnost* (openness) and *perestroika* (restructuring) may have been the new Soviet buzzwords, but to many Soviet citizens Chornobyl's tragic unfolding showed how little these were put into practice. Mikhail Gorbachev's appearance on national television more than two weeks after the explosion marked the first time in history that a Soviet premier had admitted an error, and this was a grave one. The growing cynicism was strengthened by the government's egregious behavior and cover-up. Chornobyl's aftermath also sparked an environmental movement that addressed issues beyond nuclear problems.

The subsequent breakup of the Soviet Union means that the mass of information on Chornobyl, clandestine and public, is no longer part of the Soviet Union. Whose information is it? Alla Yaroshinskaya, a Ukrainian journalist who has studied the subject extensively, is convinced that without the failed coup of August 1991 we would have far less information. Still, no records were kept on the liquidators, many of whom had helped to build Kyiv's metro but were then relocated throughout the Soviet Union.

The cover-up was extensive and, by all rights, criminal but this fact is really moot now. The bigger issue is the ongoing waste in the name of humanitarian aid. Millions of dollars have helped to line the pockets of bureaucrats, while Chornobyl's victims have rarely seen the 12% social tax collected on all paychecks. For several years there have been discussions about reducing this tax, or even scrapping it altogether, because it has been regarded almost universally, since its inception, as a sham.

Travel Advice for Chornobyl

Western experts generally agree that today's visitors to Ukraine need not worry about Chornobyl's residual effects. However, do observe some basic precautions. For example, although locals do it, you might think twice before swimming in the Dnipro River in the vicinity of Kyiv; some of the silt was contaminated by radioactivity and then carried downstream. This also means drinking local water is not advised. If you must, make sure you boil it first. Also, while Ukrainians love their wild berries and mushrooms, avoid them if their origin is uncertain. Other foods are not generally specified.

For those who want to visit Chornobyl, there are now tourist agencies specializing in "ecological" tours there. You can also make your own arrangements, but the tour agencies will handle all the necessary paperwork, which sounds like a real bonus to me. You will still need approximately one month for clearances. Once you reach the Chornobyl checkpoint, 11 miles (17 km) from the site, you will be transported in a vehicle that never leaves the contaminated zone. Still curious? Contact New Logic at (044) 462–0462 or Sam Travel at 264–1184.

Nuclear Energy and Missile Technology

Ukraine is today one of the largest recipients of international aid, in part because of its history of nuclear energy and missiles.

Ukraine currently depends on its five nuclear power plants for roughly half of its energy needs. These reactors will reach the end of their safe life span around 2010. One significant drawback is that Ukrainian nuclear power plants exclusively use Russian-made (and low quality) nuclear fuel.

In 1995, Ukraine signed a memorandum with the Group of Seven economic alliance of countries to close down Chornobyl by the end of 2000, which it duly did. In exchange Ukraine received aid to construct two new nuclear reactors to replace Chornobyl's lost capacity. There have been continuing debates about these two new reactors at Rivne and Khmelnytsky, which by late 1998 were 70% complete. By December 2001, one year after Chornobyl was permanently shut down, these two reactors were still not yet complete. The European Bank for Reconstruction and Development has offered a loan, but they also proposed that Western firms do the work. President Kuchma turned to his Russian counterpart Vladimir Putin, who has agreed to help Ukraine in an effort aimed at meeting Ukraine's energy needs.

During the Soviet era, Ukraine was also a center for producing nuclear missiles. The United States paid Ukraine's nuclear fuel bill through 1998 in exchange for Ukraine relinquishing its Soviet-era warheads—the world's third largest arsenal—to Russia in 1996. The United States also contributed money to completely destroy the missiles and silos that once housed the warheads. The last of these was destroyed in October 2001. The one remaining problem is that Ukraine still lacks an effective method for reprocessing the highly toxic solid fuel that was used in the missiles.

SNAPSHOTS OF HISTORY

Early Beginings
The ancient chronicles refer to the kingdom of Kyivan Rus, the Eastern Slavic state that was the precursor to modern-day Russia, Ukraine, and Belarus and whose capital was Kyiv. At its height it

stretched from the Danube to the Volga and from the Baltic to the Black Sea. Its prosperity grew in large measure to its trade route along the Dnipro River. In 1982, Kyiv observed its 1500th anniversary; Moscow celebrated its 850th birthday in 1997.

Ukraine's early history essentially concerns several important and competing clans. Most significant were the Scythians and Varangians.

The Scythians were Central Asians who settled the steppes north of the Black Sea around the 7th century B.C. The Scythians distinguished themselves as horsemen and gold craftsmen. Warriors were encouraged to drink the blood of the first enemy killed and to make chalices out of enemies' skulls. Ruthless toward their enemies, they valued friendship and loyalty above all else. Their civilization was based on commerce, and they established contacts with Greeks from Asia Minor who had settled along the Black Sea coast around the same time. By the 4th century B.C., the Greek coastal cities were booming and continued to do so until the 2nd century B.C. The Greeks and Scythians intermarried, and both groups crafted many of the famous Scythian ornaments and decorations characterized by animal motifs. The finest examples of Scythian art in Ukraine can be seen in Kyiv's Monastery of the Caves.

With the exception of Crimea, the Scythians were defeated by the Macedonians in 339 B.C.; a century later, they were overwhelmed and assimilated by the Sarmatians, an eastern nomadic group. The Sarmatians dominated this area for the next 400 years.

In the 2nd century A.D., Germanic Goths arrived from what is today northern Poland; they set up a state covering most of modern Ukraine. Around A.D. 370, the Huns, a nomadic tribe originating in Mongolia, drove out the Goths; the empire established by the Huns potentially threatened the Roman Empire.

The migrations of the Slavs, the direct ancestors of Ukraine's current population, had begun early in the Christian era, no later than the 2nd century A.D.; but the big migrant wave did not come until the

6th and 7th centuries. The Slavs were able to spread throughout the region while the Huns focused on other territories. Linguistic and cultural differences mark the Western Slavs—forerunners of today's Poles, Czechs, and Slovaks—and the Southern Slavs—forerunners to the Bulgarians, Macedonians, Serbians, and Croatians—from the Eastern Slavs, ancestors of the Ukrainians, Russians, and Belarusians. By the 7th century, the Eastern Slavs were based on the right bank of the Dnipro.

Trade among the Eastern Slavs was poorly developed. In the 8th century, the Khazars, nomadic Turkic and Iranian tribes from the Caucasus, penetrated much of Ukraine. The Khazars, who adopted Judaism in the 9th century, built an empire based on their military and equestrian strengths as well as their Iranian and Jewish trading skills: they were both conquerors and traders. Their capital was then near the mouth of the Volga, but Kyiv proved to be an important trading base, helping to bridge the Arab and Byzantine peoples.

The Slavs were valued by the Khazars for their honey, wax, furs, and slaves. But many conflicts with the Arabs and encroachments by the Turkic Pechenegs weakened Khazaria; meanwhile, the Varangians began appearing with increasing frequency and force. The Varangians were Swedish Vikings who, beginning at the end of the 5th century, had set up a southern outpost in Kyiv. In the 6th century, they set up trading posts east of the Baltic.

The Varangians, seeking further profits, continued to move southward and, in 860, raided Constantinople, prior to fighting the Khazars.

The etymology of "Rus" has been a matter of historical debate with some contending that the Slavs called the Varangians "Rus." In any case, there is consensus that the Scandinavian impact on Eastern Slavic language and culture was minimal. The rise of Kyivan Rus was the result of a complex interrelationship of ethnic peoples.

In 882, Oleh of Novgorod proclaimed himself ruler of Kyiv. Twenty years before, when he first established himself in Kyiv, he

Photo: Meredith Dalton

The founders of Kyiv, according to legend: brothers Kiy, Shchcek, and Horiv, and sister Lybid.

declared it would become "the mother of all Rus cities." Kyiv and Novgorod were now successfully united as the main depots on the "Greek" trade route. The highlight of Oleh's rule was when he attacked and pillaged Constantinople in 911.

After Oleh, the reign of Ihor was much less successful. Ihor's wife, Olha, ruled from 945 to 962 after Ihor was ambushed and killed for repeatedly forcing his subjects to pay tribute. Olha was depicted in the chronicles as beautiful, crafty, and wise. She recognized that the arbitrary collection of tribute had to be changed and instituted the first reforms in Kyivan Rus, specifying certain tributes at certain intervals. Her foreign relations were marked by diplomacy, not war, and she went to Constantinople to negotiate with the Byzantine emperor.

Finally, Kyivan Rus expanded in the later 10th century under Svyatoslav. After crushing the Khazars, the greatest competitors for hegemony in Eurasia, Svyatoslav conquered the northern Caucasus. All of the Eastern Slavs came under Kyivan rule. The problem was that the Khazars had kept eastern nomadic tribes, such as the Turkic Pechenegs, from advancing along the Ukrainian steppes.

In 968, Svyatoslav agreed to help the Byzantines against the powerful Bulgarian kingdom. With a huge army, the rich cities along the Danube were captured. Svyatoslav's empire now stretched from the Volga to the Danube, and he preferred the Balkans to Kyiv. Byzantium worried about its aggressive neighbor and turned against him in a brutal campaign. Forced to return to Kyiv in 972, his army was ambushed by Pechenegs, and Svyatoslav was killed.

Ukraine's Christian Origins

In 988, Volodymyr (Vladimir in Russian) accepted Christianity from Constantinople, thereby strengthening the role of Byzantine culture, with its art, education, literature, and imperial authority, within Kyivan Rus. Christianity had arrived in the previous century (Olha had converted circa 955), but Volodymyr is recognized for introducing Christianity to his realm on a significant scale. According to legend, Volodymyr forced a large part of Kyiv's population to be baptized in a mass ceremony in the Dnipro River, despite freezing temperatures. His reign was marked by the annexation of what is now western Ukraine, thus setting the scene for the centuries-long struggle against the Poles. As a result of his conquests, Volodymyr's realm became the largest in Europe.

After his death, Volodymyr's eldest son killed three of his younger brothers; two of them, Borys and Hlib, were later canonized by the Orthodox Church. The second son, Yaroslav the Wise, defeated the eldest brother, then split the realm with yet another brother to avoid bloodshed. Yaroslav received the land west of the Dnipro, and Mstyslav won the east. Kyiv was too valuable to divide.

Yaroslav's reign is usually considered the high point of Kyivan Rus. He continued to expand his empire and won back lands that had been lost to the Poles. He also successfully destroyed the Pechenegs. In gratitude for winning this battle, Yaroslav built Sofiyivskiy Sobor (St. Sofia's Cathedral) between 1017 and 1031; it was dedicated in 1037. St. Sofia's is named and modeled after the Hagia Sofia (Holy Wisdom) in Constantinople. In addition to its religious role, St. Sofia's was the seat of the metropolitan and a center of learning, culture, and politics in Kyivan Rus. It housed the first school and library of Kyivan Rus.

Yaroslav the Wise is considered by some to be the "Peter the Great" of Kyivan Rus, although Yaroslav looked southward, not westward. Ukrainian nationalists have nonetheless balked at this analogy. The construction of churches was very important to Yaroslav; during his rule, Kyiv boasted over 400 churches. Yaroslav is also noted for his codification of the legal code. Finally, in an effort to prevent the internecine fighting that had arisen among his brothers, he divided his territories among his sons before his death and established rules of seniority and rotation. Problems arose, however, whenever one of the sons died; often sons of the deceased ignored the rules of rotation and instead fought against their uncles, who now had seniority for that territory.

Political fragmentation contributed to the decline of Kyiv as more and more principalities split off and Kyiv lost its wealth, population, and territory. Kyiv became a principality like all the others. At the same time, Kyiv's assets had always been its liabilities. Whereas Khazars and Slavs had successfully exploited Kyiv's favorable location to make it the strongest and richest town on the Dnipro trade route, it also meant that Kyiv attracted marauders. At the same time, other trade routes opened up, making the Dnipro less important. The pillage of Constantinople in 1204 by the Crusaders was a blow to Kyivan commerce. The final blow came in 1240 when the Mongols, called Tatars by the Eastern Europeans, sacked Kyiv and its inhabitants fled.

The Cossacks and Bohdan Khmelnytsky

The Mongol sacking of Kyiv effectively ended the Kyivan Rus empire, and its power base moved north and west. In the mid-14th century, parts of western Ukraine were absorbed into Polish and Lithuanian kingdoms, and eastern Ukraine was held by Russia. Sovereignty changed hands repeatedly.

The Cossacks (*Kozak* in Russian and Ukrainian) were originally refugees who fled serfdom, beginning in the 15th century, to hide out in what was then the borderland, now Ukraine. The name "Kozak" is probably derived from a Turkish word meaning "free man" or "adventurer," although some maintain the name may be related to the Cossacks' celebrated horsemanship skills. Later its meaning was broadened to include Ukrainians who went into the steppes to fish, hunt, and practice other trades, such as beekeeping. The Cossacks are today lauded for winning independence from Poland and for establishing the state that made up the central part of modern Ukraine. The western part remained with Poland.

The Cossacks were the most militant of the Ukrainian population. They set up democratic military communities whose elected leaders were called hetmans. The most famous of these was Bohdan Khmelnytsky (1595–1657), who gained fame for leading the Ukrainian people in the war of liberation against the Poles. One Khmelnytsky method of achieving liberation was striking an alliance with the traditional enemies of the Cossacks, the Crimean Tatars. Khmelnytsky is also recognized for his ability to mold unruly peasants and Cossacks into powerful and organized armies. Further, Khmelnytsky instilled pride and self-confidence in a group that had previously lacked a sense of identity, and he repeatedly stressed that defending Orthodoxy was a major goal of his revolt. According to some historians, he succeeded in building the platform for Ukrainian statehood; however, the Ukrainian nationalist poet Taras Shevchenko and others have criticized him for bringing Ukraine into Russia's sphere.

Photo: Catherine Isabel Dalton

Kyiv's arch, colloquially called by some "The Yoke." This monument is dedicated to the 1654 unification of Russia and Ukraine.

Sovereignty didn't last, and central Ukraine was quickly annexed to Russia. As a result of Khmelnytsky's efforts toward unification with Russia, Ukraine was essentially divided during the late 17th century, with Poland controlling the western half and Muscovy controlling the eastern part. Western Ukraine remained with Poland for another century, until the Partitions of Poland between 1772 and 1795 transferred much of Polish Ukraine to Russian hands. By now roughly 85% of Ukraine had fallen under Russian control. Only the far western region of modern Ukraine around Lviv remained with Poland; this fell under the reign of the Austro-Hungarian Empire after 1867. With the decline of the Polish kingdom, the Cossack period also ended. This new period marked the beginnings of Russification and the suppression of Ukrainian culture.

That Khmelnytsky is regarded as a hero by many is a source of great tension for some Ukrainians. As many as 200,000 Jews were slaughtered during his reign; thus Jews and Poles universally hate him. Furthermore, according to the Soviet interpretation of history, Khmelnytsky's greatness lay in his understanding that the salvation of Ukrainians lay only in unity with the Russian people. Some have predicted that he, like many communist-era heroes, may later be relegated to oblivion, in part because he signed the treaty of unification with Russia. At the same time, his achievements have been compared to the impact of Oliver Cromwell on England, in that despite his unpopularity, his impact on Ukrainian history is irrefutable.

A monument to Khmelnytsky on a rearing horse—frozen mid-gallop and with mace drawn and pointed towards Moscow—was erected in 1888. The site is where Kyiv residents welcomed their triumphant hero more than two centuries earlier. After independence, this square, formerly called Khmelnytsky Square, was renamed Sofiyivska Square. At the same time, neighboring Lenin Street was renamed Bohdan Khmelnytsky Street. The mace is a Ukrainian symbol of authority, with both Cossack and anti-Russian implications. Wooden versions are for sale in all the souvenir shops.

Collectivization and the Faked Famine

In the late 1930s, Stalin targeted his purges against the intelligentsia and Communist Party itself. In 1932, Stalin's response to the peasants opposing collectivization was to demand grain deliveries that were impossible to achieve. His scheme was ruthlessly enforced; people starved to a slow, hideous death—there were even tales of cannibalism—while Stalin's henchmen were dispatched throughout the countryside to unearth hoarders of grain. People who were not visibly starving were suspected of stealing. The sentences for all manner of crime were rarely confiscation of property or minimum 10-year prison sentences, execution was far more common.

While grain producers in regions bordering Ukraine were included in this hysterical sweep, the Ukrainian peasants were the actual target, precisely because they were more fiercely resistant than the

Russians. Ostensibly, it was the kulak class that was the most hated. Kulak comes from the word for "fist," and it was a derogatory reference to the so-called rich farmers—these were very often peasants with no more than one or two cows to their name. This "famine" was a mad attempt to break the independent spirit of the Ukrainian peasant and to destroy the kulak class.

Estimates range from six to 10 million deaths as a direct result of this famine, sometimes called a drought in Soviet history books in which the dates were also changed. Actual truths about the famine were unspeakable for many years; with 10-year prison sentences and even executions the price for such talk, long after the terror famine was over. Only in 1988–1990 was the hideous truth fully revealed, although people had been quietly making reference to it for years. Prior to the *glasnost* period, there was no official mention that the famine was premeditated. Of all the Soviet falsifications, this was perhaps the most massive lie.

Some Ukrainians have told me that whatever horrific deeds were committed in the name of war, the far greater insult to the Ukrainian people was this deliberate famine engineered by the megalomaniac Stalin. To the Soviet population at large, Stalin was responsible for thinning the intellectual ranks, and he targeted nationalities and minorities without compunction or conscience. These same friends tell me that Stalin was worse than Hitler ever was, as Stalin directed his purges against his own people. He destroyed the best of the best. While I don't want to split hairs over who was the greater evil, this ugly piece of Ukrainian history helps to explain why Ukrainians view their agricultural and peasant traditions as separate from Russia's agricultural experience.

De-Stalinization

The aftershocks from Khrushchev's 25,000-word "secret speech" in 1956 denouncing Stalin were sensational, and thus the period of de-Stalinization was launched. The cult of Stalin was partially resurrected during Leonid Brezhnev's leadership (1964–1984) with plans for a full rehabilitation of his name in 1969 and 1979; in both cases rehabilitation was only narrowly averted thanks to foreign communist leaders and prominent Soviet intellectuals.

It is interesting that Khrushchev's speech focused on repression against high Communist Party officials and crimes committed following the celebrated murder of Leningrad Party leader Sergei Kirov in 1934. The exclusion of Stalin's crimes of collectivization distressed Gorbachev, whose own family came from Russian "middle peasant" stock (as opposed to the vilified kulak class). Russia's middle peasantry was often swept away in the anti-kulak hysteria, as were many kulaks who were not particularly wealthy. Gorbachev was not in attendance during Khrushchev's historic speech, but Khrushchev's focus on violence against the upper Communist Party echelons, to the exclusion of mass terror, struck some party members who were present. Khrushchev's public denunciation was nevertheless a remarkable feat.

UKRAINE'S REPUTATION ABROAD

Ukraine has been hailed as the breadbasket of the Soviet Union,

Eastern Europe, or simply Europe. Its rich, black soil called *chornozem* ("black earth") produced one-quarter of the wheat and much of the sugar beet for the USSR. Livestock, rye, sunflowers, and flax were also important. Today, agricultural production is roughly one-half of its highest Soviet levels due to the high cost of energy and agricultural inputs, languishing equipment, and general mismanagement. Moreover, the state is unable to relinquish its long-standing tradition of market interference. Grain bans occur on a regular basis, sometimes couched in new rhetoric but with the same results—grain that is contracted for sale but not yet delivered is effectively seized by regional and *oblast* (state) administrations in an effort to supply local needs. The old days of state control are, sadly, not old enough.

In agriculture and in all areas of industry, stultifying bureaucratic obstacles abound, and corruption is rife. These are not distinctive features of post-Soviet life: Author Nikolai Gogol (who was born in Ukraine) satirized bureaucratic inefficiencies over 150 years ago, and corruption (and crime) was a growing problem under the Soviets, particularly in the later Brezhnev years. Only during Stalin's reign was corruption kept to a minimum.

Soviet salaries were always maintained at very low levels, but housing and energy costs were practically free, and education and pensions were guaranteed. It was not a cashless society, but access and influence were generally more powerful and more valuable than money. Today's officials continue to receive such low wages that bribes are often perceived as necessary income supplementation (by the payee) or as a cost of doing business (by the payer). Indeed, people with ordinary amounts of cash can buy off officials at reasonable rates, although your company or employer might have other ideas about such practices.

The Soviet system also laid the foundations for today's enormous and expanding barter economy. One of its features is the absence of tax revenues. While the Ukrainian government is working hard to improve its collections, the prohibitively high tax rates mean that even those who want to work within the law are often forced to maneuver around it. For other Ukrainians, avoiding taxes is considered a matter of national pride, and tax collectors are universally regarded as among the most corrupt and despicable government officials. In general, people also vehemently mistrust the *militsiya* (police), and many rely on the protection provided by their "security firm" a.k.a. mafia protection. After all, they are paying for it, aren't they?

Both the crime and corruption of the later Brezhnev era have escalated since independence. In 2001, Ukraine was dishonored by being named on an international list of noncooperative money laundering countries. Like Russia, Ukraine is today stigmatized for its problems with the mafia, although that same Organisation for Economic Co-operation and Development list removed Russia temporarily for its recent efforts to combat money-laundering problems. The international press is filled with tales of mafia infiltration into practically every business venture. Violent crime, while far more common in Russia, is negatively impacting on Ukraine's incipient democratic struggle. Western businessmen are by no means immune to the mafia's actions, but at the end of the day most of them can pack their bags for home if they so desire. There are isolated stories of foreigners who have lost their lives in mafia turf wars. By all accounts the situation is serious and goes well beyond the repeated tales of ineffective police—many of whom are reputed to be in cahoots with the mafia—the labyrinthine bureaucracy, and inbred governmental corruption.

From a foreign perspective, constantly changing tax laws, including retroactive ones, may prove unmanageable. Visibility here extracts a much higher cost than elsewhere, for with it often comes numerous inspectorates looking for baksheesh. One critical lesson for surviving Ukraine, according to some foreigners, is to consciously separate the actions of the government from its citizenry. Suffice it to say that the more you get to know Ukrainians, the more you will marvel at their ability to carry on as well as they do.

Freedom of the Press?

The rise of so-called "hate journalism" has been a legitimate concern for former Eastern European and Soviet countries. The communist tradition of using the media to denounce enemies of the state is being reworked to new, propagandistic ends: manipulative journalists are capable of arousing ethnic strife among rural and less educated people; they are also encouraging voters to turn against the intelligentsia.

Allegations that President Kuchma may have directed the September 2000 murder of journalist Heorhiy Gongadze threatened to bring down Kuchma's government in 2001. Gongadze is only one of many Ukrainian journalists killed, assaulted, harassed, or censured in recent years for openly criticizing the government. Gongadze published an Internet newspaper, so it was much more difficult for the authorities to tamper with its distribution. At the time of his abduction, he was being harassed for reporting regularly on corruption among Kuchma's advisors; he had also noted voting irregularities when Kuchma was campaigning to curtail parliamentary authority.

A RELIGIOUS MELTING POT

The Orthodox Churches Today

The Ukrainian Orthodox Church, Moscow Patriarchate was formerly called the Russian Orthodox Church in Ukraine. This name was officially changed in 1990, in part because the church was concerned that it was losing ground to the resurgent Catholics, linked with the reviving of national consciousness in Ukraine's western region. Allegiance is to the Moscow patriarchate, with Metropolitan Vladimir based in Kyiv.

The smaller Ukrainian Orthodox Church, Kyiv Patriarchate is headed by Metropolitan Filaret, who claimed Kyiv authority in 1992. Filaret was excommunicated the following year by the Russian

Orthodox Church. There has been much ill will between these two Ukrainian Orthodox churches.

The year 1990 also marked the second reemergence of the Ukrainian Autocephalous Orthodox Church or UAOC. In 1686, the Patriarch of Constantinople forced the Ukrainian Orthodox Church to recognize authority from the Russian Orthodox Church. In 1921, the UAOC emerged for the first time during a brief flowering of national identity following the Russian Revolution. By 1930, however, the "self-governing" church was forced underground again. Today all services are in Ukrainian and allegiance is to the Ukrainian patriarchate in Kyiv.

Of Ukraine's 14,000 Orthodox parishes, 8,000 fall under the jurisdiction of Moscow's patriarchate and the remaining 6,000 under Kyiv's.

The primary contender to Orthodoxy in Ukraine is the Ukrainian Catholic (also called Greek Catholic or Uniate) Church, which follows Orthodox rituals but recognizes the Pope in Rome as its leader. (Uniate priests are the only Catholic priests allowed to marry.) This church principally exists in Ukraine's western, Polish-influenced half. It dates back to 1596, when many Orthodox leaders in the region were being pressured by their Polish Catholic rulers; they pledged allegiance to the Vatican but kept the Eastern rites. Catholics, and especially Greek Catholics, were persecuted under the tsars and most brutally under Stalin. In 1946, their church was abolished and all of its property was seized. Parts of it were handed over to the Russian Orthodox Church. Like the UAOC, the Ukrainian Catholic Church was thus forced underground and did not resurface until the late 1980s. This was when the independence movement was garnering support in Right-Bank Ukraine.

Much fanfare surrounded the 2001 visit by Pope John Paul II to Ukraine. The Pope came to celebrate the rebirth of the Greek Catholic church. He also hoped to ease religious tensions with the Ukrainian Orthodox Church. (The rift between Roman Catholicism and Eastern Orthodoxy dates to the Schism of 1054.) However, Kyiv is a particularly sensitive destination for Eastern Orthodox believers, because this is where Prince Volodymyr was converted to Christianity in 988. Kyiv itself is viewed as the cradle of Russian Orthodoxy. Leaders of the Ukrainian Orthodox Church as well as Patriarch Aleksei II, head of the Russian Orthodox Church in Moscow, strongly urged the Pope not to come. For his part, the Pope hoped that this visit might pave the way for visiting Moscow.

The Pope's reception was reportedly cool in Kyiv, but he was very well received in Lviv. In a mass service attended by 1.4 million people, the Pope beatified (paving the way for sainthood) 28 Greek Catholic martyrs, 27 of whom were Ukrainian, and one Russian. Many ordinary Orthodox believers came out to see the Pope, at times defying the leaders in their own church.

Kyiv's Pecherska Lavra

St. Sofia's Cathedral and Kyiv's Pecherska Lavra (say *peCHERska LAvra*) or Monastery of the Caves are World Heritage sites. They are also Ukraine's most important religious sites. The Lavra's origins date to the 11th century, and this was a monastery of the highest order.

St. Sofia's was badly damaged by the Mongols in 1240 and suffered further damage by the Poles and Lithuanians. By the late 17th century, it lay in ruins until its reconstruction early in the 18th century on orders of Russian Tsar Peter the Great (1672–1725).

During Peter's reign, the Lavra was an important pilgrimage site. In the mid-18th century, the monastery owned some 80,000 serfs, and there were three glassworks on the grounds.

The Lavra bell tower was completed in 1745. This was built to replace the one that had burned in 1718 along with the cathedral. At 315 feet, it was the highest bell tower in the country and the tallest structure in the Russian Empire before St. Isaac's Cathedral in St. Petersburg surpassed it. The tower was so high that the monks were

49

Photo: Catherine Isabel Dalton

Kyiv's Pecherska Lavra (Monastery of the Caves). This fascinating site dates back to the days of Kyivan Rus.

afraid it would collapse and refused to pay the architect for his work. The architect, J.G. Schedel, had to sue the monastery for his fee.

Uspenskiy Sobor (Assumption Cathedral) was the centerpiece of the Lavra architectural ensemble. The most revered relics were cherished here, and Kyiv princes (and later prominent religious people and high-ranking military) were buried here. In 1941, during the German occupation, the cathedral was blown up. Some sources still charge the Nazis with this act, although it was later said to be the work of the Soviet Red Army attempting to trap the German forces.

Without the cathedral the focus of the Lavra was lost. Assumption Cathedral was restored and its consecration celebration in 2000, commemorating nine years of Ukrainian independence, escalated the ongoing conflict between the two divided branches of the Ukrainian Orthodox Church. The Moscow Patriarchate claims ownership of the cathedral, which is located on the grounds of the Lavra, owned by the Moscow Patriarchate. The Kyiv Patriarchate said the cathedral is the only true Ukrainian church, so it is rightfully Kyiv's.

Since independence, the Kyiv Patriarchate has complained of harassment in predominantly Russian-speaking eastern Ukraine, whereas the Moscow Patriarchate says that the government has allowed the Kyiv Patriarchate to appropriate their churches in Ukrainian-speaking western Ukraine. For its part, the government intends to claim Assumption Cathedral as its own in order to not further aggravate the conflict between the two churches.

The Caves

The story of the *pechery* (caves) began in the mid-11th century with a monk who settled in the caves to pray. More monks chose to go underground and eventually they turned their attention to the construction of the Assumption Cathedral.

The tradition of burying monks in the catacombs continued until the 17th century. During the 14th century, monks presumably discovered that dead bodies in the catacombs do not decompose, so the corpses were put into coffins and displayed for visitors as the relics of saints. In 1643, Metropolitan Petro Mohyla canonized 69 monks buried in the catacombs.

The near caves, where the bodies are better preserved, contain 73 coffins, and the far caves have 45. You can tour the caves for the price of a candle, which will help you to see your way through the short but claustrophobic maze. Visitors should dress conservatively out of respect for the monks; I've also heard not to look at monks unless their palms are turned upwards.

The monastery was closed and converted into a museum in 1927, with the caves gifted to the Museum of Historical Treasures of Ukraine. This is one of several museums housed on the monastery grounds. Jewelry dating from the 6th century B.C. to the 19th century A.D. is exhibited, as are golden ornaments made by the Scythians and other master craftsmen of Kyivan Rus. The state returned the caves to the church in 1987, and a year later it recognized the 1000th anniversary of Kyiv's mass baptism.

Other museums of note on the grounds include the Museum of Microminiatures and the Ukrainian Museum of Folk and Decorative Art. During the Soviet era, there was even a Museum of Atheism on the grounds. It was housed in the refectory, and among its displays was a mummified rat. The curators explained that climactic conditions had preserved the rat, which, like the mummified saints, had no religious value!

Jewish History Prior to World War II

Kyiv historically boasted one of the world's most important Jewish communities. The center of Kyivan Rus was a commercial crossroads between Central Asia and Western Europe, attracting itinerant Jews and later settled communities. The Jewish population tried to convert Prince Volodymyr to Judaism. Volodymyr's first choice was presumably Islam until he learned that alcohol was forbidden.

Jews in Ukraine were intermittently persecuted and expelled, only to return again. At times, Jews could reside in the city; sometimes merchants could only enter the city for business but had to be out by day's end; at other times, they could not enter at all. Bohdan Khmelnytsky massacred Jews in his efforts to free Ukraine from Poland's yoke and to defend Orthodoxy. When eastern Ukraine was subsequently annexed to Russia, the ban on Jewish settlement was renewed. Eastern Ukraine did not have a Jewish community again for another century, when the Polish Partitions of the late 18th century brought in half a million Jews. These Jews were confined to the occupied lands: present-day Ukraine, Belarus, Lithuania, and eastern Poland comprised the "Pale of Settlement."

The notion of a "Jewish problem" grew in the 19th century. In 1835, Jews were expelled once again from Kyiv, but they continued to enter the city as tradesmen. In the 1860s, the city districts of Podil (Podol in Russian) and Lebed were assigned for Jews with residency permits. With the exception of the German occupation years, Podil has been the center of Kyiv's Jewish life ever since. Prior to World War II, one-fifth of Kyiv's population (or 175,000) was Jewish, whereas Lviv was one-third Jewish. Odesa boasted the highest Jewish percentage of all: a century ago half of its population was Jewish, and it was one of the largest Jewish centers in the world.

In Ukraine, generalizations can be made about urban dwellers and villagers. The cities were typically populated by non-Ukrainians, notably Jews and Russians, who were closely associated with urban growth and industrial expansion. To a Jew, the Ukrainian represented the backward, ignorant villager; to a Ukrainian, the Jew represented that foreign, exploitative city element, who bought his produce cheaply and sold all goods at high mark ups.

Pogroms occurred in 1881 and 1905, but Jewish life and culture flourished in Kyiv. The University of Kyiv attracted more Jews at the turn of the century than any university in the Russian Empire. The possibility of further large-scale pogroms arose after a Jew assassinated Russian Prime Minister Pyotr Stolypin in 1911. The same year, Mendel Beilis was charged with the murder and mutilation of a 12-year-old Christian boy in Kyiv. Beilis, a Jew, had supposedly killed the boy for his blood, which was to be used for ritual purposes. Police actually traced the crime to a gang of thieves, but Beilis was nonetheless imprisoned for two years before his trial, where he was acquitted.

In the earliest years of communism, Kyiv was a major center of Jewish culture with its Yiddish schools, newspapers, literature, and theaters. Many Jews fought in the Russian Revolution with its promises of religious tolerance. Revolution leader Leon Trotsky (born Lev Bronstein) was a Ukrainian Jew, although he later denied it. Beginning in the 1930s Jewish culture was systematically destroyed throughout the Soviet Union.

Babi Yar and Its Monument

In August 1941, the Germans captured or killed over half a million Soviet troops in Kyiv. On September 21, the Germans captured Kyiv. They were to occupy the city for nearly 800 days, until the Red Army retook the capital on November 6, 1943.

On September 24, 1941, the Soviet Army started fires in downtown Kyiv in reaction to the fascist invaders, and on September 26, Nazi retaliation was planned. On September 29, Jews were ordered to report to the designated site with their documents and warm clothes; those who did not show faced execution. Germans spread rumors that the Jews would be relocated to ghettos or labor camps. The posters appearing in Russian, Ukrainian, and Yiddish gave unclear instructions about the meeting place; however, the general proximity to a rail station appeared to bode well for relocation.

Instead, more than 33,700 Jews were killed by the Nazis in a two-day period after being stripped of all their belongings. Their bodies were then dumped into a ravine: Babi Yar means Granny's Ravine. (Babi Yar is "Babyn Yar" in Ukrainian, but the Russian is the more familiar name.) Over the next two years, the total killed at this site reached 100,000; some estimates suggest the total was closer to 200,000. Those executed were primarily Jews, but some were Ukrainian partisans and nationalists, prisoners of war, and Gypsies. Evidence shows that Ukrainian guards were willing participants in the massacre.

Babi Yar will live on in infamy as a powerful symbol of Jewish suffering. For years, Soviet authorities refused to acknowledge that most of the victims killed in this Kyiv ravine were Jews. To erase this horrific memory, the government even tried to build a housing project at Babi Yar in the 1960s; the project was canceled when Jews and non-Jews protested.

In 1959, a monument was erected on the site of a wartime German prison camp. This was several hundred yards from the ravine. The monument referred only to "fascist occupiers" and "citizens of

Photo: Catherine Isabel Dalton

The monument to the Jewish massacre at Babi Yar, Kyiv.

Kyiv." The only hint that the vast majority of victims was Jewish was that one plaque to the "citizens of Kyiv" was in Hebrew. Also in 1959, a plaque was erected at the home of Sholem Aleichem on Red Army Street. Aleichem is one of the great Yiddish writers, best known for capturing the Ukrainian Jewish experience; *Fiddler on the Roof* was derived from his Tevye stories. Aleichem's Jewish origins were acknowledged on the plaque, thereby betraying cracks in the official anti-Semitism. However, this plaque was replaced a year later by another that did not mention his Jewish roots. In 1992, the three-story building built in the 1880s was gutted, presumably to make way for a museum, a project that now appears to have stalled. However, a monument to Aleichem was erected in 1997 on Basseina beside Bessarabskiy Rynok.

In 1961, Yevgeny Yevtushenko, the internationally renowned poet, wrote his most celebrated poem, "Babi Yar," lamenting the absence of a monument and acknowledging the murdered Jews. Dmitri Shostakovich set this to music in his 13th Symphony in 1963.

On September 28, 1991, the 50th anniversary of Babi Yar, an explicitly Jewish monument (with menorah) was dedicated closer to the site of the killings. Representatives from the Soviet and Ukrainian governments, Israel, and the United States attended the ceremony. The sanctioning of this memorial was one of the last official acts of the Soviet Union, which collapsed less than three months later.

There are further plans today to create a museum and archive dedicated to all Ukrainian Jews killed during World War II. A list of those killed at Babi Yar is also being compiled.

Jews Today

Many Jews returned to Kyiv after World War II despite the continued suppression of Jewish life. The infamous "Doctors' Plot," concocted by Stalin, accused nine doctors—including six Jews—of planning to murder communist leaders. Their public executions were planned in Moscow to be accompanied by a massive anti-Semitic campaign and deportations of Jews. Stalin's timely death in 1953 spared their lives.

During the 1970s and 1980s, the Soviets allowed emigration from time to time. Since independence, emigration has continued steadily, and Ukraine's Jewish population is estimated to be half of what it was just 10 years ago. Anti-Semitism survives, although the Ukrainian Nationalist group RUKH has staunchly supported a Jewish role in independent Ukraine. Many Jews still express a desire to emigrate, but there is also a Jewish revival under way, and this is having a positive impact for Jewish Ukrainians who do not wish to emigrate.

Historically, Ukrainian Jews spoke Russian (and Yiddish), not Ukrainian. Since independence, a number of Hebrew schools have opened. In the immediate years following independence, these schools were mostly preparing the younger Jewish population for emigration to Israel and elsewhere. Today, Jewish Ukrainians who are not intending to emigrate are studying Hebrew. There are also current efforts to revive Yiddish, the historic Ukrainian-Jewish tongue.

Kyiv's Great Synagogue (Brodsky Shul) on Shota Rustaveli was built in 1898. After 1926, religious practices and education were forbidden by the government. Properties were seized and used as archives, libraries, theaters, and sports centers. Kyiv's Great Synagogue housed a famous puppet theater until the end of 1997. In 2000, the Great Synagogue was rededicated. There are plans to create a Jewish community complex around Shota Rustaveli, the area that was once home to Kyiv's wealthiest Jews.

During the late 1990s, Kyiv's Podil district began undergoing a revival. People especially like that it retains much of the flavor of the early 20th century. By contrast, 90% of Warsaw was destroyed during World War II. Kyiv's synagogue on Shchekavytska Street was opened in 1894. It has been in continuous use except when the Nazi occupiers used it as a stable.

NATIONAL ICONS

Ukraine's National Hero

Taras Shevchenko is the beloved national hero of Ukraine. Shevchenko distinguished himself equally as a great artist and poet. While the fate of so many Lenin statues throughout Ukraine is uncertain, Shevchenko's monuments are secure. The most recent one in Kyiv was erected on Independence Square in 2001.

Born into serfdom in 1814, the prominent Russian artist Karl Bruillov, whom Shevchenko met and impressed in St. Petersburg, helped Shevchenko purchase his freedom. Shevchenko then became a leader in the fight against serfdom and promotion of Ukrainian nationalism. After his arrest in 1847, he spent 10 years in internal exile. He was released in 1857 but never returned to Kyiv. He was frail in his final years and died in 1861 aged 47. His home in Kyiv is now a museum filled with his drawings, paintings, and manuscripts.

More Heroes

Lesya Ukrainka and Ivan Franko are names you'll frequently hear in Ukraine. Ukrainka was a famous poet; Ivan Franko was the writer for whom Lviv's university is named. Franko is considered second in stature to Shevchenko. Author Isaac Babel was born in Ukraine as was Nikolai Gogol. While Gogol distinguished himself in St. Petersburg, he greatly admired and recorded Ukrainian folk tales and carols. *An Evening at Dikanka* (first published under the pseudonym Rudy Panko, Beekeeper) reflects his strong Ukrainian roots.

Aleksandr Pushkin lived in Odesa for a while, and Anton Chekhov enjoyed Crimea, the leisure destination of heads of state and wealthy people. Josef Conrad was born in present-day Berdichev. In the early 20th century, the so-called Russian avant-garde included Ukrainian artists Aleksandra Exter, Iosif Chaikov, and the Burliuk brothers, David and Vladimir.

Photo: Meredith Dalton

The monument in Lviv to the Ukrainian writer Ivan Franko, for whom Lviv's university is named.

Mikhail Bulgakov was Ukrainian; you can visit his house on Kyiv's winding Andriyivskiy Uzviz, which served as inspiration for the *White Guard*. His most celebrated work is *The Master and Margarita*. The 1995 English translation by Diana Burgin and Katherine O'Connor is excellent.

Popular Ukrainian heroes today include the boxing Klitschko brothers, the soccer star Andriy Shevchenko, and Yulia Tymoshenko, the former deputy prime minister especially popular among young women as a high-ranking government role model. Tymoshenko fought hard to reduce widespread corruption in Ukraine's energy sector, but she was fired from her post in 2001. It is unlikely to be the last we will hear of her.

"Motherland" and Other Monuments

In Kyiv you cannot escape the Defense of the Motherland Monument. You'll hear her called simply the Motherland, Mother Russia, or the Iron Lady. This gaudy, oversized 236 feet (72 metre) stainless steel monument, dedicated to the Defense of the Motherland, is criticized for its imposing, static design. Note that the sword is disproportionately small—it looks as if it were cut off in space. In fact, the monument's design had to be altered so that it wasn't higher than the bell tower at the Monastery of the Caves. To many locals, this monument exemplifies the wasteful spending of the Brezhnev era.

Two museums are located at the site. One of them is dedicated to the Afghan War, the Soviet Union's tragic nine-year war that has been compared to the United States's Vietnam. The other is the Ukrainian Museum of the Great Patriotic War (World War II), which focuses on children and their suffering.

The Arch of Unification, or "the Yoke" as some locals call it, is a monument to Ukrainian and Russian unity. Whatever you call it, this monument, like Mother Russia, is remarkable if only for its sheer size.

Yaroslav's Golden Gate Zoloti Vorota (say *zoLOtee voROta*)

was the main entrance to Kyiv, which in Yaroslav's day was surrounded by a high defensive wall. Like St. Sofia's, this gate, built in 1037, was inspired by Constantinople's Golden Gate and was famous throughout Europe. It was covered with gold and precious metals and topped with a tiny church. Destroyed in the 1240 Mongol-Tatar raid, it was presumably covered with earth about 1750. This stone and wood structure was rebuilt in honor of the city's 1500th anniversary in 1982. Minor renovations have since been done, and a monument to Yaroslav was erected on the grounds in 1997 (based on a 1899 model).

The Soviet Union was renowned for its monumental and public sculptures, and Kyiv and other Ukrainian locales are no exception. Lenin still stands in Kyiv facing Bessarabskiy Rynok, although there was a hot debate about his survival a few years ago. My personal favorite public sculpture from the Soviet era is what Kharkiv citizens call their Five Men Carrying a Refrigerator monument; once you've seen this Socialist Realist ensemble, it's hard to think of another name. Its official title is Monument in Honor of Proclaiming Soviet Power in Ukraine.

Post-independence monuments and churches

One thing that hasn't changed since independence is the tradition of erecting public sculptures and monuments. If anything, recent activity has been at a fevered pitch. In 1996, several monuments were erected to commemorate five years of independence. This included in Kyiv the Olha Monument (which also includes saints Andriy, Cyril, and Methodius) on Sofisky Square and Archangel Michael on Independence Square. Lviv joined the monument-building spree in 1996 with a tribute to Taras Shevchenko, along with the accompanying 40-foot Wave of National Revival momument.

More remarkable changes were seen in Kyiv in 2001, again centered around Maidan Nezalezhnosti (Independence Square). New monuments to the founders of Kyiv and to Shevchenko were installed here, but the most remarkable addition was the towering column entitled Victory to Ukraine. Sadly, many Ukrainians told me that these monuments were one of the better ways to launder money, because no one knows how much a monument costs. Or as one Ukrainian stated: "This is how to turn black money into white." The results are visually stunning—although I understand that folks outside of the capital city are less than impressed with the city's remarkable facelift.

Rebuilding former churches has also received post-independence priority. Apart from the rededication of Assumption Cathedral in Kyiv, another reconstruction project included Mykhaylivskiy Zolotoverpkhiy Cobor (St. Michael's Golden-Domed Cathedral) near Mykhaylivksa Square.

The Tryzub

Whereas the troika (with its three horses abreast) has long been associated with Mother Russia, the *tryzub* (trident) is the official coat of arms of Ukraine. It is seen on state buildings and on currency notes. During the Soviet era, it was outlawed as a nationalist symbol—and immediately reintroduced after independence.

The *tryzub* has its roots in Kyivan Rus, and there are various theories about its origins. One theory is that the trident is a symbol of Poseidon, the Greek god of the sea. The oldest examples found on Ukrainian soil date to the first century A.D.; it was later stamped on the coins issued by Volodymyr, who may have inherited this symbol from his ancestors. Later rulers chose a two-pronged version as their coat of arms, and in the 12th century, the state emblem was the Archangel Michael, but the trident continued in usage as a dynastic coat of arms until the 15th century. It was also used as a religious symbol.

Nearly 200 variations on the medieval trident have been uncovered. Prince Volodymyr's was adopted by the short-lived Ukrainian National Republic. In February 1992, the Verkhovna Rada selected the trident as the chief element in the state's coat of arms. You will see this prominently displayed on government buildings throughout Ukraine.

Various versions of the trident are also used, for example, by the Ukrainian Catholic Church and other nationalist organizations.

The Flag

The Ukrainian flag is divided into two equal horizontal bands. The top is azure, and the bottom is golden yellow. Most believe that the top band represents a blue sky, and the yellow represents Ukrainian wheat or sunflowers. In the past, however, these colors have been reversed.

Flags became popular with the arrival of heraldry in medieval Europe. The standard flag in Kyivan Rus was predominantly red with a golden trident or bident, but there were others. One flag of the Galician-Volhynian period in western Ukraine was azure with a golden lion. The symbol of Lviv is the lion, from which its name is also derived.

There were many banners and variants on flags within the Ukrainian territories. Archangel Michael appeared on Kyiv flags of the Lithuanian-Polish period; a two-headed eagle is another symbol of this period. In the Cossack period, there were two hetman standards: one was the Archangel Michael; the other had the coat of arms of the individual hetman. Red was the predominant color for both.

With the annexation of central and western Ukraine by Russia and Hapsburg Empire, the various flags disappeared. The Russian Empire had no territorial flags, whereas western Ukraine had three: a golden lion on azure, horizontally striped yellow-azure, or azure-yellow. The order of colors was not fixed. There was also a Soviet Ukrainian flag with a hammer and sickle, a five-pointed star, and Cyrillic initials.

The National Anthem

Before delving into some Ukrainian characterizations, it is noteworthy that Ukraine's national anthem is entitled *Ukraine is Not Yet Dead.* Ukrainian history helps to put this title in perspective. The anthem evokes a mixture of hope and desperation; it is poignant and befitting for this nation that has collectively suffered and labored hard for independence. It proclaims that not only is Ukraine not yet dead, but neither is its glory nor its freedom. "Luck will still smile on us brother-Ukrainians."

Like the trident above, this anthem was adopted by the short-lived Ukrainian National Republic at the end of World War I. This was naturally replaced during the Soviet era and adopted again after Ukraine's independence.

— Chapter Two —

UKRAINIANS AND THE FOREIGNERS WHO MAKE IT THERE

FIRST IMPRESSIONS

Ukrainians, Russians, and Belarusians share Slavic roots and Soviet inculcation. However, to simply lump them together as Slavic peoples (or Russians, as is more often the case) and to ignore historical differences is naive at best. So how are we to fairly characterize Ukrainians? In ethnic and linguistic terms, Ukrainians most closely resemble their Eastern Slavic cousins, the Russians and Belarusians. For historical reasons mentioned in the previous chapter, Right-Bank Ukrainians share traits with the Western Slavs, particularly the Poles, but don't mistake the people of Lviv as a prototype for the rest of western Ukraine. Further, the transition to a market economy has been far easier for Poles and other Eastern Europeans than for the Ukrainians who struggled for the 70-plus years under the Soviet yoke.

In temperament, Ukrainian tendencies toward spirituality and fatalism elicit comparisons to the Russian, or more aptly, Slavic soul. The Mongols or Tatars, who sacked Kyiv in 1240, ending the Kyivan Rus kingdom, are credited with staving off the expanding states of Poland and Lithuania, and their Catholic intentions, from Russia. However, along with protecting both the region and the Orthodox Church, the Mongols cut off Western cultures and contributed to the region's backwardness.

Specifically, neither the Renaissance nor the Protestant Revolution ever reached Russia or Left-Bank Ukraine, meaning that neither did the spirit of individualism or free inquiry. The collective spirit that survives today in Russia (slightly diluted in Ukraine) derives in part from Mongol autocracy and the institution of state service, wherein every member of the group has a paramount obligation to that group. In Ukraine, however, the situation is complicated because Right-Bank and Left-Bank Ukraine were divided during this critical period in Europe's history. The Renaissance and Reformation did infiltrate Poland's sphere, which in turn influenced Right-Bank Ukraine. The net result may have contributed to the recalcitrance of the Ukrainian peasantry that Stalin strove to destroy.

Ukrainians are especially superstitious and yet well educated. Ukraine boasts a strong tradition of higher education, and the Soviet educational system maintained high standards for educating (and indoctrinating) its youth. In theory, a schoolboy studying at a particular location within the USSR should have been able to pick up his studies on the following day, in any other Soviet location, at the precise point where he had left off. One negative aspect of Soviet education was limited exposure to certain problem-solving skills. Because the system patently discouraged its citizens from thinking critically or questioning their superiors, today's newfound freedoms offering unprecedented choices can be overwhelming. The educational system that stressed rote memorization above all else did not encourage active decision-making. Older people especially complain that it is difficult to adapt to society's accelerated (and often unwanted) changes.

Time and again, Ukrainians distinguish themselves as gracious hosts and generous folk. Ukrainian women are very attractive and make great efforts to maintain stylish dress. They are generally submissive in this patriarchal society, which is both sexist and racist. Men show their age more quickly, often ravaged by excesses of alcohol and cigarettes. Attitudes toward work and money are clouded by seven decades of communism, just as issues of privacy were informed both through Soviet legacy and years of communal living. Society (and consequently business relations) is clearly based on relationships rather than contracts, and petty to excessive bribery and corruption are aspects of the culture.

The increasing stranglehold of the mafia as a post-independence phenomenon is especially alarming. Many view the scourge of homelessness, prostitution, and pornography that has blighted Ukrainian society in recent years to be a byproduct of the past decade's democratic reforms. One early response in this new age of lawlessness, poverty, inflation, and worthless pensions was the strengthening of pro-communist sympathies. Advocates of communism argue that turning back the clock will help to repair society's ills, and that individual freedoms should be sacrificed for the collective good. However, 10 years after Ukrainian independence, the chances for a communist comeback appear to be at an all-time low. The economy has rebounded since the 1998 financial crisis and 2001 was a record year since independence. Likewise, observers noted that the communist protesters marching on November 7, 2001 to commemorate the anniversary of the October Revolution of 1917 were at record low levels. News articles reported that some of the younger protestors had been paid to join in the assembly.

New stereotypical profiles have emerged in independent Ukraine. Today's strata of society, including pensioners, bureaucrats, the

New Rich (or New Russians), the mafia, young entrepreneurs, and an incipient middle class, are distinctive from their Soviet forebears. A reasonable question might be, what happened to the Soviet stereotypes of the late Brezhnev era? Specifically, the *apparatchiky* (civil servants), the *nomenklatura* (elite members of the civil service), the military, the intelligentsia, and dissidents.

One overriding observation distinguishes for me the Ukrainian national character, if there is such a thing: Ukraine is not for the meek. This is true for the expatriate community, in very different and deliberate, ways, but more importantly for the Ukrainian people. Their history is a troubled one, and personality traits have emerged from their collective experiences. In contrast to Americans who take very seriously their right to "the pursuit of happiness," Ukrainians aggressively pursue their right to survival.

KYIV VERSUS THE REST OF UKRAINE

The coexistence of pro-Russian and Ukrainian nationalist factions, helps to describe various Ukrainian profiles today. While extreme nationalist factions do exist, the vast majority of Ukrainians lies somewhere between the two poles, and indeed much of what is said about Ukrainians at large is also applicable to East Slavs. Nevertheless, a 1998 proposal to unite Ukraine, Belarus, and Russia as one Slavic state was promptly rejected by Ukraine's parliament. Ukraine had fought too hard for independence to relinquish it so easily, whereas Belarus's leadership favored union with Russia.

Ukraine's capital appears to be a good indicator of mildly changing perceptions toward national identity and pride since independence. Most Kyivans are politically moderate as opposed to staunchly nationalistic. In Yaroslav's day, Kyiv was considered too valuable to split between east and west factions; now its physical location and political stance provide a good keel for the nation. Its 450-member parliament is populated with centrists, nationalists, and communists of varying intensities. Historically, most Kyivans spoke

Photo: Catherine Isabel Dalton

A typical scene along Kyiv's main thoroughfare of Kreshchatyk.

Russian as a first language and still prefer it. Many are now relinquishing their former strong opposition to Ukrainian, which is good because it is now the language of government and schools. More Ukrainian is heard today in the streets than a couple of years ago, and some are embracing the national language, although Russian remains the language for most business dealings.

It is nonetheless necessary to differentiate Kyiv when assessing Ukraine as a whole. While it is true that the cities were more successfully Russified (and Sovietized) than Ukraine's rural counterparts (with the exception of Lviv), Kyiv stands apart. To the visiting foreigner, the city has verve, albeit nothing like the frenetic energy of Moscow or the stateliness, grandeur, and dark, bone-chilling winters of St. Petersburg. Kyiv is large, yet retains its provincial feel. Granted, those foreigners who spend more of their time outside of central Kyiv, and this includes exploring the capital's farthest regions, will surely be reminded that they are in the former Soviet Union. But Kyiv is an eminently livable city. Expatriates here often state that they deliberately chose Kyiv over Moscow's chaos. Against the backdrop of the steady flow of the Dnipro, it's hard to beat the history and architecture of the Ukrainian capital.

Ukrainians outside of Kyiv often dream of moving to the capital to find better jobs. In the past, foreigners in Ukraine typically chose Kyiv because of job opportunities and governmental access, but this is beginning to change. After the financial collapse of 1998 many foreign companies brought their expatriate staff home, with those positions permanently filled by Ukrainians. Of course, some smaller companies closed shop altogether.

Ten years after independence, the expatriate community is very different from just five years ago, just as Ukraine and Ukrainian business practices have changed significantly during this period. Today there are far fewer aid workers and development types. A diehard corps of diaspora that came to Ukraine early on still remain. It's not uncommon to hear of Ukrainian-Canadians and Ukrainian-Americans who have been in Ukraine for five (and often more) years. Then there are the expat mavericks—young and mid-career entrepreneurs—some of whom came to Ukraine only for a short stint, but they were seduced by the country, its challenges, opportunities, and excitement (and often by the beautiful women). Their success today, and certainly their survival, means they cannot allow Ukraine's daunting bureaucracy and corruption to turn them into cynics and drive them home. These entrepreneurs are an unusual breed, in part because they lack the larger support system of their home governments or of large corporations—or even the language and cultural ties uniting the Ukrainian diaspora. The most successful of these businesspeople are genuinely trying to adapt their Western ways to the new Ukraine, rather than the other way around.

Another observable change within Ukraine's expatriate community relates to the changing face of Kyiv. As Ukraine's capital, Kyiv has been the recipient of most of the post-independence spoils. Kyiv's remarkable facelift marking 10 years of independence included the spectacular new train station and the renovations along Kreshchatyk and especially around Independence Square, the likes of which were not seen on any small scale throughout Ukraine. It is becoming increasingly difficult to keep track of the new monuments erected throughout the city.

Expatriates in Kyiv were formerly attracted to the capital city, even if few would say it, because of its restaurants and its collegial expat community. The latter has changed partly in response to the expansion of the former. The expat community has become more dispersed, as there are simply too many restaurant options now available. There are always the current hangouts, of course, and I recommend seeking these out early on. This applies for all the cities, not just Kyiv.

While many of Kyiv's restaurants are often pricey, sometimes outrageously so, there are also reasonably priced alternatives. Moreover, their quality and variety has improved steadily. Until recently, this seemed to have more to do with expatriate than local demand, but the case is now reversed. Not surprisingly, economic recovery was slow after the 1998 collapse. In 2000 the economy improved, and 2001 marked an economic boom in many respects, as the economy recorded a positive growth rate for the first time since independence. Year-end figures have suggested anywhere from 9 to 14%, which is remarkable, especially in comparison with the European and United States economies during 2001.

For shopping convenience, Kyiv now has supermarkets, in addition to its "Western grocery stores," which have been around for many years and are more like "mom-and-pop" enterprises. It is now easy to find food from Western Europe, often sold at Western European prices. Locals generally cannot afford to pay these high prices, but neither are they spending their cash on outrageous rents or on favorite pricey restaurants. Also, visitors to Ukraine in the past were virtually assured that, whatever their location, they would not spend a lot of money on clothes (unless they shopped exclusively at Benetton). Wealthy Ukrainians continue to travel abroad to buy clothes, but the choices for clothes shopping have skyrocketed during the recent economic boom.

In short, the division between Kyiv and the rest of Ukraine remains the same now as in the recent past, if not more pronounced. One possible exception is Odesa: the second largest port in the Soviet Union has long been regarded as Ukraine's most international city and has attracted a large number of Britons, Germans, and other Europeans. In 2001, the five-star Kempinski hotel was opened overlooking the Black Sea. Odesa's milder climate has always made the city especially attractive, and it boasts a reputation all its own for humor.

The other cities boasting populations of over one million: Kharkiv, Dnipropetrovsk, and Donetsk, as well as Zaporizhzhya's 900,000 are less Westerner-friendly, which has its own rewards.

THE SOVIET LEGACY

Popular accounts of Soviet life made frequent reference to shortages, queues, excessive alcohol intake, and communal living, all of which were valid generalizations. Today, the shortages and queues seem largely a thing of the past in the larger cities, except when adverse financial news in Ukraine or from Russia creates a run at money exchange points. This point is not to be taken lightly, as witnessed in the wake of the 1998 financial crisis. The fact that three years later both the Russian and Ukrainian economies had bounced back, and even expanded, bodes well for the survival of these newly independent states. But it's easy to let the meteoric growth of their capital cities cloud the harsher realities of economic conditions in outlying regions.

Some say that now you can find anything in Ukraine that you want—as long as the price is right. I used to say, when shipments were irregular and mercurial, if you find something today that you think you might want tomorrow, buy it now. My advice today hasn't changed much; certainly Ukrainians are used to stocking up whenever they find a good deal.

Outside the larger cities, the shelves were never well stocked, and most local residents couldn't afford to buy the products if they were. Yet Ukrainians are survivalists and exemplify the concept of "getting by." For most, the *dacha* (country cottage) is more necessity than luxury. The idea that Ukrainians escape to their village sounds like a great weekend getaway, but there is much work to be done at the *dacha*. Under Brezhnev, each family was entitled to one hundredth of a hectare for private use. This strip of land, or *sotka*, continues to grow many of the vegetables that will tide the family over during harsh winters and often harsher economic times.

Problems stemming from excessive alcohol intake continue to plague Ukraine. Vodka (and moonshine) consumption rose in the years following independence. Recently there is a rise in beer consumption, and Ukrainian breweries are aggressively improving and expanding their product lines to attract consumers. These attempts have been successful, and vodka consumption has declined slightly. However, vodka is still very much a part of Ukrainian culture. Drinking vodka is part of a long tradition; and drinking too much vodka is a source of national embarrassment. (The chapter *Socializing, Food, and Drink* discusses vodka and its associated traditions in detail.) Suffice it to say here that people coming to Ukraine for an extended period should be prepared to drink toasts; if you have an alcohol problem before you arrive, you should reconsider your decision to come at all.

Ukrainians are accustomed to communal living. Private ownership of apartments is a distinguishing feature of independent Ukraine, yet, for economic and practical reasons, communal living remains very much a part of Ukrainian culture. Communal living exacts a high price on family relations and marriages. Living in cramped quarters is not conducive to easy relationships, and the divorce rate in Ukraine is high. Some divorced couples continue to live together out of necessity. Alcohol-related problems disrupt home life as well.

PUBLIC DISPLAYS OF AFFECTION

Often Ukrainian couples are more outwardly affectionate than Americans. They enjoy holding hands and kissing in public. For young couples whose communal apartments provide no privacy, park benches may be the best alternative. The street is often their only space; while not private, it is away from their cramped living quarters. None of this means, however, that their elders approve.

Cold weather does not drive people from the streets; many bundle up and continue to stroll, even if their expressions at times seems to match their somber clothes. Nevertheless, when the chestnut trees lining Kreshchatyk Avenue bloom in the spring, Kyiv takes on a different feel. The streets are far livelier, smiles are evident, and brighter colors and miniskirts return. Molded white plastic chairs and tables sprout alongside kiosks, with Coca-Cola and Pepsi umbrellas competing for visibility. Women stroll together arm-in-arm or holding hands, as do men to a lesser degree—sometimes in the spirit of camaraderie, sometimes hanging onto each other after too many toasts.

Except for the New Rich, dining out is reserved for special occasions. Ukrainians share a love of dancing with their fellow Europeans, and dancing is often a part of an evening out on the town. In hotel dining rooms there is a dance floor, often next to large, blown-out speakers that play sentimental music, such as "Kakaya Zhenshchina," too loudly for those trying to have a dinner conversation. Synthesizers are popular instruments for live music in the hotels.

Flower vendors were among the first privatized businesses in Ukraine and are commonly situated near metro entrances and in the underground passageways. Women buy flowers for themselves, or men buy flowers for them. Watch out for even numbers! They signify death. Often you will see couples strolling or sharing an alcoholic drink on a public bench; the woman in each case holds a single rose.

PRIVACY AND PERSONAL SPACE

During the Soviet era, the unspoken idea was that if you needed privacy you were hiding something. There were no phone books to locate those lucky enough to have phones installed, so these people were also lucky in having privacy. While residential phone numbers for Kyiv are now available online, the waiting list for a new phone (at reasonable cost) remains lengthy. Moreover, different regions throughout even the central part of the city vary widely in the quality of their telephone lines.

The popularity of cellular phones is understandable, even if those who have them often sport them in obnoxious ways. (A largely ignored sign posted outside one of Kyiv's early expat haunts asked patrons to kindly turn off their phones before entering.) Now as in Soviet times, you need to keep track of your friends and their phone numbers—especially because it seems like people are always changing apartments here!

Dark and dingy entrances to apartment buildings are overwhelmingly the norm; this tends to discourage people from wandering where they aren't invited, but it isn't the reason. In the Soviet days there was often a *babushka*—an old woman who often wore a scarf—posted near the elevator. This is called the *lift* (say *leeft*) and pay attention to whether it breaks down often—you may prefer to walk up flights of stairs if yours breaks down frequently. The job of this woman was to watch the comings and goings of people in the building. Today no one stands guard, and hallway lights burn out (or are stolen) and are not replaced. Sometimes, in the hallways, you can't escape the smell of urine. (For more about the *babushka,* see later in this chapter under Respect for Elders.)

Front doors to apartments often hide a second door inside. The ones you'll see may be padded brown nawgahide and covered with buttons resembling a vertical mattress pad; others are wooden or steel. Most are uninviting. In noting down addresses, always ask your friends not only for their apartment and floor numbers, but also which building entrance to use, and whether there is a (working) front door code. Wandering in the dark can be creepy.

Another interesting phenomenon pertains, I can only surmise, to crowd control. Building entrances often have several sets of double doors. Naturally, in winter these should be closed to retain the heat. Sometimes many windows are then opened because the heat is cranked too high and can't be adjusted. But even at other times only one set of doors will be operable, and only one of the double doors will open. Traffic in both directions will thus use the same door. McDonald's on Kreshchatyk is a good example of this.

Metro stations stand apart with their separate entrance and exits; their heavy, dangerous swinging doors have been called "widow-makers." Still, you rarely get the sense of people rushing to catch the metro, although there is shoving when standing in a line for something. Maybe this is because metro riders know a very long escalator ride (or two) separates them from the next train. It's especially hard to pass through the tight crowds of people with their bulky winter clothing and shopping bags in tow.

The invasion of personal space seizes the attention of many foreigners. First, there is the practice of standing close in lines or standing a bit too close when speaking to you. Cutting in lines and even shoving in crowds, while never personal, is common. Moreover, no one would ever apologize for this. (If you do, they'll know right away that you are foreign, but they probably already know.) For those with claustrophobic tendencies, the metros can be a harrowing experience. I personally dislike the metro when people start shopping for the holidays.

In Ukraine, I am most reminded of the luxury of privacy when the loudspeakers on Kreshchatyk fire up for holiday celebrations or a bit of political grandstanding (which is really the same thing). Both were part and parcel of the Soviet propaganda machine, and these loudspeakers never fail to transport me to another place in time. On overnight trains, too, if you're not already awake, a loud piped-in radio will serve as your alarm for the last hour before arrival.

One cold December night in 1995, I returned to the Hotel Rus after an exhausting trip. Once installed in my new room, I discovered that I was unable to turn off (or down) the hidden radio—the one which I heretofore didn't know existed. Exasperated, I tried unsuccessfully to pry it from behind the heater. I muffled it with an extra pillow and bedspread and even my overcoat but to no avail. Miserable, I conceded defeat and rode the elevator to the lobby where I demanded a change of room. The Soviet-schooled receptionist replied dispassionately that all the rooms were the same: they were testing the fire alarm and I needed to wait—for as many hours as it took.

This story seems foolishly minor in retrospect, and Ukrainian hotel staff have vastly improved, but it is times like these (especially when you are exhausted or maybe homesick) that will test your ability to live in Ukraine. You will be assaulted frequently by things that seem incredible or inane. You will also hear expatriates ranting about Ukrainians and everyday absurdities. Heed my previous warning: Ukraine is not for the meek. That includes us.

Other cultural surprises for me were the screaming matches, replete with profanities, between Ukrainians in our office. Emotional outbursts and florid excesses (as in compliments, flowers, hospitality, and drinking) are not uncommon, while self-expression and alternative lifestyles are not openly accepted, although this is somewhat changing. Still, in Ukraine, you also need to be prepared for those times when racism or anti-Semitism rears its ugly head. Virulent stereotypes are ingrained, and this is where outside observers may wish to impose their worldly views. When provoked, remember that your views are not welcomed, and, in any case, patronizing attitudes never help.

Many foreigners observe an abruptness in Ukrainian behavior. Cards are slammed on the table during a friendly card game, and *nyet* (meaning *no* in Russian) or the Ukrainian *ni* (say *nee*) is more emphatic than in English. Again, according to Western standards, people appear less courteous and less appreciative in part because niceties like "thank you," "you're welcome," and "please" are not spoken with the same frequency. It is not unusual when misdialing a residence to have the person hang up on you without a word, simply because he or she was not the person you were calling. (There are the occasional others who will want to talk even after you've discovered your error.) Service-without-a-smile was once the norm—certainly off the expat trail, but this is steadily changing, particularly for those businesses that are facing competition or trying to adapt to Western models.

STARING IS NOT IMPOLITE

Staring is culturally acceptable in Ukraine, and foreigners are often recipients of such unwanted attention. I experienced it mostly from elderly Ukrainians or in places away from city centers where foreigners were less common, and consequently more visible, in the community.

In general, younger Ukrainians are attracted to the West and want to see Western business practices adopted. By contrast, today's elderly were taught throughout their lives to mistrust all foreigners. Those few foreigners who visited during Soviet times were an oddity and their movements were both limited and highly scrutinized. Separate apartment houses were formerly designated for foreigners, and Soviet citizens were explicitly warned not to mingle with expatriates. To some Ukrainians, the expatriate population represents capitalism's evils that Soviet propaganda had railed so hard against.

It is difficult, if not impossible, to comprehend the vast changes Ukraine has undergone since the days of *glasnost* and *perestroika*. Today's pensioners are financially and psychologically exhausted, having lived their whole lives under a regime with certain known quantities. They worked, not necessarily too hard because the Soviet system did not reward those who worked hardest, but they played by rules that guaranteed a pension upon retirement. What they expected, of course, was that it would provide for their needs, as opposed to the practically worthless pensions that are the reality today.

While foreigners are by no means credited with destroying the pension system, their increased presence in Ukraine coincided with changed attitudes. It is no wonder that a percentage of Ukraine's population, especially elderly citizens with their inadequate retirement income, yearn for the glory days of communism. Some argue that things weren't especially good then, but at least they knew what to expect.

RESPECT FOR ELDERS

English dictionaries give "a woman's scarf" as one definition for *babushka* (say **BAbooshka**). When you hear the term, in all probability the speaker is talking about "grandmother" or simply the ubiquitous older woman who often wears such a scarf knotted below her chin. *Babushky* often come across as humorless and dour. (I generally assume that most are widows and struggling to survive on paltry pensions.) They view themselves as a mouthpiece for morality and have no qualms about scolding a stranger. For example, Ukrainian babies are well wrapped, even suffocatingly so, despite the heat. Pity the mother whose baby's legs are exposed to a passing *babushka*!

Respect for elders is very much a part of Ukrainian life. My Ukrainian assistant once told me that we could not easily reprimand the office housekeeper for poor performance, as she was older than we were. I had to politely disagree with this. For the record, this housekeeper was neither a pensioner nor especially old.

My assistant voiced similar concerns when I complained to my landlady that removing furniture from my apartment without giving me prior notice was not acceptable. I certainly had no intention of being disrespectful, but I also wanted to make a point that we had a signed contract, including clauses about what furniture would be provided and how much advance warning (72 hours according to our lease) the landlady would give me before entering the premises. The larger issue for me was that any unplanned disappearance of furniture from my apartment might be construed as theft.

CONTACTS, NOT CONTRACTS

Ukraine is very much a society based on relationships rather than contracts. As elsewhere, the coexistence of relationships and contracts is hardly mutually exclusive, but in Ukraine the relationship always takes precedence.

Now as in the Soviet era, people are heavily reliant upon friends and family to provide them with food and other necessities during difficult times. Similarly, you will often—without asking—be offered the names of cousins and friends who can provide whatever service you may be needing. Westerners tend to be more cautious in recommending an individual in case the latter's poor performance damages their own credibility. This is not the case in Ukraine, where doing a favor for a friend, or even bringing two new parties together, is the primary consideration.

For your part, you need to make certain about the person with whom you are dealing. The law does not provide adequately for contract compliance, and many view a contract as simply another piece of paper. Clearly, for those looking to do business in Ukraine, it is imperative to understand that you cannot simply fly into town, meet some folks, sign a deal, shake hands, and hop back on a plane. You need to be prepared for a long-term investment in time and relationship building. The relationship is the linchpin in all business transactions, never the contract.

Similarly, you will find that as soon as you land in Ukraine you will need to link up with a good translator and driver, and probably a lawyer and accountant who can assist you through the byzantine Ukrainian business world. Expats will also provide you with a wealth

of knowledge, suggestions, and shortcuts. I highly recommend an early trip to O'Brien's Irish Pub, The Golden Gate, Arizona Barbecue, or whatever the latest hot spot is—it won't be hard to find out—for a beer and some relationship building. Contacts, both foreign and local, can often provide shortcuts along the miles of red tape that you will inevitably encounter during an extended stay in Ukraine.

Greasing Palms

Ukrainians also need a technique for surviving their country's red tape, in addition to the bribery, corruption, and crime that were rising during the late Brezhnev era and have escalated since independence. Only during Stalin's reign was bribery less of a problem, and that was out of fear. The Soviet concept of *blat* roughly translates as access, pull, or connections that is always more powerful than currency, which in any case you can only spend once. A related term is *svyazy* meaning connections and strings, which is not the same as *vzyatka*, meaning kickback or bribe. Today, *blat* and *svyazy* remain enormously valuable and *vzyatka,* enormously pervasive.

Ukrainians have a strong tradition of helping friends and family. Skeptics argue that even family members can never be fully trusted, but this is a perception from Stalinist days when the system encouraged people to turn in family and friends for actions against the state. There is the famous story of Pavlik Morozov, the 14-year-old Ukrainian who denounced his own father for hoarding grain in the early 1930s. Many Soviet monuments were erected to this little hero-martyr whom the villagers had killed for his betrayal. Evidence shows that Stalin privately thought him "a little swine" for denouncing his father, but turned his example into a useful political weapon. Today it is comforting to be able to rely on others to help you get what you need, information or otherwise. Even more so than in Soviet times, many Ukrainians remain perpetually financially strapped while their costs for food and apartments have rocketed.

Unlike *vzyatka*, *blat* and *svyazy* do not involve the exchange of money or bribes, although small gifts may be given. This is what I sometimes call "tipping in advance." People talk about the value of a bottle of beer or a box of chocolates in easing a sticky relationship, or as a show of kindness or gratitude. (An old folk saying: "If you don't oil, you cannot start your journey.") One English friend in Moscow remarked that the occasional packet of cigarettes to the parking attendant meant his car didn't get nicks in it—in contrast to the unhappy experiences of his friend, who assiduously refused to play the game. There's a joke that when *blat* dies there will be no funeral: where would we find the coffin or nails?

Early on, some of the younger and good bureaucrats jumped ship, while the older ones in place tended to abuse their position by demanding bribes to supplement their paltry income. And the size of the bureaucracy has soared since Ukraine gained its independence. Foreign entrepreneurs said that by late 2001 the hierarchy of bribes has been slightly altered. There are now generally two levels at which bribes are being demanded, whereas formerly there was really only one. Now the bribes are for smaller amounts, but the net result in some cases is the same or slightly higher.

An old Soviet curse, "May he live on his salary!" applied equally to ordinary citizens as to governmental officials; the difference was that the former opted, if possible, to moonlight for its supplemental income. Today you will find that many of the kiosk vendors and street sellers of books and postcards were trained as engineers or earned doctorates; they turned to selling because they needed to earn money. Some argue that in another decade these corrupt officials will be retired, and a younger generation, eager to emulate Western Europe, will not tolerate the current rampant abuses in the system.

Sometimes Europeans single out Americans for their puritanical views toward petty corruption, but none will dismiss the detrimental impact of coming into contact with Ukraine's mafia. The world is clearly watching to see how the Ukrainian government will rein in this accelerating problem. The widespread allegation that the police are involved with the mafia's activities is especially disheartening to ordinary, law-abiding citizens.

BARTER

Barter has long been a way of life for Ukrainians. The increased number of items available for barter since independence has, if anything, strengthened this practice. Naturally, barter has its greatest appeal when what you genuinely want what is bartered. Yet learning to barter has become a survival necessity, as there are endless stories of people being paid in potatoes and used car tires. While they can eat potatoes, they might not need tires.

One presumed advantage to bartering is that these transactions are not taxed. However, economic studies have shown that the hidden taxes associated with extralegal activities—which are activities outside the law because one cannot afford to be legal, and thus should be differentiated from illegal activities—are more costly than paying taxes. Why? Because extralegal activities attract illegal practices. In Ukraine's case, the bureaucrats and the mafia are the recipients of these hidden taxes, while the state's coffers remain empty.

Barter has obvious repercussions for the state, which is in dire need of tax revenue. Reforming the tax code is a constant discussion in Ukraine's parliament. Inadequate tax collection means that preventive maintenance of infrastructure is mostly postponed until a crisis occurs. We've all heard stories about miners striking because they haven't been paid in months, and factory wages in arrears are hardly unusual. A Ukrainian colleague quit the army because he hadn't been paid for months; he is the lucky exception because he jumped into a high-paying job.

The corporate worlds in Ukraine and Russia have embraced bartering on a grand scale, both out of necessity and the desire to avoid heavy taxation. It was estimated that in 1992, 6% of corporate revenues in Russia came in the form of barter. By 1998, that figure had mushroomed to 70% or 80%, according to news reports. Ukraine's figures are presumed to be in line with Russia's. Not surprisingly, good barter negotiators command high salaries today.

The tradition of barter, like the *dacha*, exemplifies Ukrainian flexibility, industriousness, and creativity. I am reminded of a joke about two Ukrainians who meet to strike a business deal. The first wants a cartload of sugar, for which the second demands a fair price. The deal is settled and off they go in opposite directions: the first to locate some cash, and the second to locate some sugar.

Make no mistake, Ukrainians are survivalists, and their ability to "get by" is a distinguishing feature of the Ukrainian personality.

NEKULTURNIY/BEZKULTURNIY

What does it mean to be *nekulturniy* (say **neecoolTOURnee**) or *bezkulturniy* (**say beescoolTOURnee**)? Literally, these means "uncultured" or "without culture," and they are quite derogatory. An egregious error is not checking your coat at the opera, nightclub, or restaurant, although restaurants are relaxing this requirement. Elsewhere, they won't admit you inside unless you check your coat, so you can generally avoid that damnation. If you worry about being cold in the restaurant, just remember that the other guests won't have their coats either. The travesty of centralized heating is that chances are just as likely that the heat will be higher than you'd like.

Many coats do not have loops for hanging them sewn into their lining. If you own such a coat, you may hear sighs of frustration when you check it at restaurants. With the increase of foreigners, coat-checkers will probably become better psychologically equipped to deal with the absence of loops. But beware the opera houses. The coat-checkers there can be downright mean! I've even read suggestions that international students traveling to the former Soviet Union sew in these loops in advance of a winter visit!

Other *nekulturniy* behavior includes sprawling or slumping in a chair. Sitting with your ankles crossed is a sign of unnecessary assertiveness or hostility, especially to older people.

SUPERSTITIONS GALORE

Ukraine is marked, as elsewhere, by its own blend of superstitions, health concerns, home remedies, and rules of etiquette. For example, sitting on cold stone steps is considered bad for one's health and also inappropriate behavior. As a rule of thumb, follow the example of locals in unknown situations. The phrase "when in Rome..." tells only part of the story; the Slavic spin seems more the better one here: "In private do as you wish but in public do as you are told."

An open window in my office was often an invitation for unsolicited comments from staff members. That the window was open presumably explained why my back hurt or why I still had the remnant of a cold. There are strong beliefs that sitting on cold surfaces or drinking from cold cans will cause colds. And if you already have a cold, you will be reminded endlessly not to touch a glass of cold juice. Leaving the house with wet hair or exposure to any sort of draft is considered further invitation to catch colds. Tea, never coffee, is imperative in the recuperative stage. Garlic is well known for its magical and medicinal values; it has even earned the nickname "Russian (or Ukrainian) penicillin."

According to some, superstitions help to explain life's inequalities and unpredictability, including the randomness and capriciousness that marked the Soviet era, particularly under Stalin. Yet the superstitious nature of the Eastern Slavs was entrenched long before the communists arrived; rural communities have long been marked by the popularity of folk wisdom, home remedies, and superstitions. The popular Russian saying, *"Khuzhe byvaet,"* translates as "It (or things) could be worse." There is a resigned quality to Ukrainians that boggles and frustrates foreigners, but this too is about survival.

One popular superstition pertains to women sitting at the corner of the table (I must have done this too many times) as it means not getting married for seven years. Whistle inside a building and you will whistle away your money. Knocking on wood for good luck (or as a preventive against bad) appears universal, and a black cat crossing your path never bodes well. Ukrainians will also symbolically spit over their left shoulder, just as they will toss three pinches of salt over that the same shoulder if they spill some. This is because the devil sits over your left shoulder, an angel over your right.

Borshch made on a Thursday signals that the devil himself will bathe in it, and a pot left unattended on the stove can mean trouble for your whole family. If you count *varynyky* (dumplings) as you make them, they will overcook and their fillings will seep out. An empty bottle on the table could mean depleted food reserves, so move it just to be safe. (This is why empty vodka and beer bottles are quickly removed.) If a knife falls to the floor, a male will visit; a spoon, a female; and if a coal falls from the stove, expect a guest from far away. If you want to catch a witch, wrap a piece of cheese in a cloth and tie it to your shirt during Lent. On the Saturday before Easter, witches will appear and beg for the cheese.

The cat must be the first to enter a new house, so death will take the cat and not your grandmother. If you put your clothes on wrong, adjust them immediately or people will beat you. A cultural statement could be inferred from this last one, but it's probably better not to read too much into superstitions.

If you leave something behind unintentionally, this means you will come back. For example, a foreigner who forgets a pair of shoes when returning home will eventually revisit. For shorter journeys, one should sit awhile before leaving the house. If you forget something when you leave, you should not go back for it. However, if you must, look into the mirror (or don't). If some superstitions sound a bit contradictory, they are. This is one of the great things about them!

ON GENEROSITY AND ETIQUETTE

Ukrainians are very generous and hospitable. General rules of etiquette dictate that you should always offer to share snacks and cigarettes with those around you, including strangers. You'll find that fellow travelers in your train compartment will offer you bread, sausages, bottled water, vodka, and whatever they have with them. Sometimes it's hard to refuse. An elderly woman on the train absolutely insisted on making my bed for me; she then instructed that a man in our compartment, a high-ranking military official whose driver was meeting him, give me a ride once we reached our destination. He was on a tight schedule, but she was his elder, so he said yes. (See Safety Precautions in the chapter *Settling Down* regarding accepting drinks and food from strangers.)

Like whistling indoors, standing with your hands in your pockets when meeting someone is impolite, because you are supposed to shake hands. Keeping your hands in your pockets is a form of disrespect, although close friends won't mind.

In Orthodox churches, skirts are more appropriate for women, but traditions are changing. Women should at least cover their head with a scarf or hat, and men should remove their hat. I once made the mistake of forgetting my scarf when a throng of people had congregated for the all-night Easter service bearing baskets of foods to be blessed. Traditionally, even non-practicing Ukrainians attend this service, and everyone carries a white candle. Like all Orthodox services, there is standing room only, and the scent of incense is pervasive. Imagine my surprise when I discovered that a foul burning smell was actually my hair on fire!

Never shake hands across the threshold of a door; this is very bad luck as it forecasts a quarrel. You should pay close attention to this for all business and personal introductions. Also, always take off your gloves before shaking hands. Expect to check your coat, umbrella, briefcase, and baggage at the entrance of most upscale restaurants and the like.

Universal rules of etiquette dictate that on public transportation you should give your seat to the elderly and handicapped, as well as to pregnant women and mothers with small children. Never place your feet on train seats or on tables. Chewing gum in public is not considered polite, but neither is spitting, which is nonetheless more common than you are probably used to seeing.

GESTURES

Ukrainians are not known for their hand gestures. But there are a few worth mentioning. One is the way in which Ukrainians count using their fingers. A clever story, surely apocryphal, was that one way to catch spies in the old days was to watch their use of fingers.

My favorite gesture is that of flicking one's neck for a drink. There is the story about a man who saved Peter the Great's life (or did some great favor for him). In return, the tsar gave the man a document that stipulated free drinks for life. The man needed only to present this at a tavern to receive his drink. Perhaps after a night of excessive booze, the document was misplaced, whereupon the man had his neck tattooed with the tsar's decree. Thereafter, when he desired a drink, he merely flicked this tattoo. Today, minus tattoo, the gesture of flicking one's neck is still related to drinking. Often it is the response to the question "Where were you last night?" a flick would mean "I was out drinking" or "I drank too much." Flicking one's neck can also mean, "Let's go have a drink."

A Swede once asked me the meaning of a Russian painting entitled "Waiting for a Third." It showed two men on a park bench with a bottle of vodka. While the subject was Russian, it could have been Ukrainian. The title refers to the tradition that vodka be drunk in groups. *Na troikh* means "for three." A gesture that relates to this entails holding the middle and index fingers together horizontally. This indicates that the person is waiting (or looking) for a third.

Two fingers over your shoulder (indicating military stripes) means a KGB man. Pointing to an imaginary chandelier means this room is bugged. A curved index finger as eyebrow symbolized Brezhnev, noted for his bushy brows.

Finally, don't put your thumb between your index and middle fingers. This is a particularly rude gesture.

BEAUTY'S CURSE

Ukrainian women are quite good-looking. Expatriate men certainly comment on this a lot, and even the Beatles sang their praises in "Back in the USSR"—*Well, the Ukraine girls really knock me out. They leave the West behind.*

Ukraine is prime hunting ground for discovering female models these days. Long legs, Slavic cheekbones, beautiful blondes à la Poland, and stunning brunettes attract the good, the bad, and the ugly. The good include expatriate men who come to Ukraine in search of young, beautiful wives; many Ukrainian women are also eager to land a green card. (I've heard that this is more prevalent in Kyiv than elsewhere.) The question is, at what price?

Ukraine's brain drain is a problem, but more disturbing still are human watch reports that cite Ukraine as a leader in the female slave trade. An education campaign is under way to protect Ukrainian women from bogus advertisements offering good jobs abroad for dancers and would-be restaurant workers. Documented cases include young girls who found themselves in a new country (Israel and Turkey are not uncommon) where they were beaten and forced into prostitution; some watched helplessly as their Ukrainian passports were burned in front of them.

That said, Ukrainian women do take much better care of themselves than Ukrainian men. Only a small minority of Ukrainian women smoke, in contrast to the majority of Ukrainian men. Most women also strive to dress well and wear makeup. They also wear heels, even in bad weather. This especially impresses me because people walk so much and often on uneven surfaces. They travel great distances from the suburbs, which means that both in the city and on the outskirts they walk to meet the metro, trolleybuses, trams, buses, and minibuses. Or they simply walk. Women also drink less alcohol than men and live significantly longer.

The CIA Factbook estimates life expectancy to be 61 years for males and 72 for females (although I have often read statistics in the mid- to upper 50s for men). While male mortality statistics may somewhat skewed due to the number of World War II deaths, life expectancy has nonetheless dropped by several years since independence, which is a precipitous drop in such a short period. Alcohol is an enormous factor contributing to this decline, aggravated further by malnutrition, unvaried diets, stress, fear, work issues, and unemployment.

Ukrainian society is sexist. (One reader begs, "And whose isn't?") But the old Soviet statistics regarding equal pay for equal jobs were overstated like so many other statistics, and today this is clearly not the case. There are few women in high positions in the government; women are more likely than men to be laid off; and they are excluded from some of the higher-paying jobs because of the physical strength required. Why then is it that so many women work like beasts of burden, for example, hauling wheelbarrows of gravel and stone? Some Ukrainians admit that this embarrasses them, but others accept it as business as usual.

The concept of "sexual harassment" is far removed from the Ukrainian mindset, which is to say it exists but is taken for granted, and sexual favors for bosses are not unheard of. Many newspaper ads are discriminatory, specifying an age range and gender for applicants (such as "female aged 23 to 29"). The age issue, according to some, is necessary because older applicants cannot be trained properly. On the other hand, some foreign men have admitted they like working here because they can hire whom they want and don't have to deal with the strict hiring practices encountered in their own country.

An American man told a Ukrainian friend that Ukrainian women are so pretty but don't smile enough. She replied that Ukrainian women never have any rest. She argued that they work as hard as the men, or harder, and are expected to be the responsible ones. Not only do they drink and smoke less, they also tend to the children, buy the groceries, mend the clothes, prepare all the meals, and clean the house. They carry a far greater burden in family responsibilities, and these divisions of labor don't appear to be changing with the times, as in the West. Wages for women actually dropped after independence, and female unemployment rose. Thus, while the Soviet stigma of not working has changed in the last decade, for many women paid employment still isn't achievable or adequate. Let us hope that the improved economy will open up new opportunities for these women.

FASHION SENSE

Much has changed in recent years on the Ukrainian fashion scene. It used to be that, while Ukrainian women strove to dress well, their business attire was not always appropriate by Western standards. For example, they would wear jeans and a nice sweater to a meeting where a skirt or dress would have been a better choice. You still won't see many local women in suits or tailored pants. On other occasions, someone might select a dress more befitting a cocktail party. Youthful inexperience and limited wardrobes may have attributed to such choices. But especially among younger women, there has always been an appreciation for current fashions. Older women tended to ignore fashion, but they clearly lacked the money even if they had been interested.

Today's fashion scene, among young men as well as young women, is very different from five years ago, and even quite active thanks to some new young designers who are making a name for themselves.

Now, as before, business attire for Ukrainian males ranges from fancy, Western-tailored suits to modest, mouse-colored suits, and from standard, military uniforms to jeans and casual attire. For some, flashy colors are favored, with burgundy blazers especially popular. Shiny, nylon running suits are common, with open collars revealing gold chains and a little chest hair. Men huddle on street corners, in entrances, and at restaurant tables; sometimes hiding behind sunglasses, they dangle cigarettes from their lips, and look dour. You will wonder at times who is an entrepreneur and who is mafia.

Men sporting mustaches, and big bushy ones at that, are documented as a Ukrainian folk type. Hetman Bohdan Khmelnytsky and Taras Shevchenko were both mustachioed. In the old days, spectacles frequently distinguished the wearer as a foreigner, but this is no longer a good rule of thumb. Many people swear they can identify nationality by shoes: for example, the man wearing socks with his sandals is more likely German or Ukrainian than American. And Ukrainians generally take pride in the appearance of their shoes, just as they remove their shoes in their homes to help keep the floors clean. Also, men here rarely wear shorts, whereas foreign men— when the weather warms up—are more likely to.

Gold teeth were once viewed as a sign of status, and gold crosses are increasingly worn by Ukrainians rediscovering religion. Crosses and religious symbols dangling from vehicle rearview mirrors are also common. Although attitudes may be changing, tattoos to most Ukrainians are considered in poor taste and often an indication that the wearer spent time in prison. Their designs certainly look crude. Wearing cologne is rising in popularity with the younger and entrepreneurial set, whereas deodorant is used sparingly. I am reminded of a story about a woman trying to buy bread, Tampax, and deodorant in a hyper-inflationary environment. Deodorant was the first to go.

Far more offensive to me is the combined smell of domestic cigarettes and alcohol. Most Ukrainian smokers prefer imported cigarettes to so-called domestic (i.e., Russian) ones, which are high in tar and produced from Russian or Zimbabwean tobacco. These are decidedly foul-smelling and an unmistakable affront to fresh air.

FAMILIES AND FAMILY PLANNING

One solution for people wanting to move to the cities during the Soviet era, but prohibited because of *propiska* restrictions, was to marry someone living in that city. The *propiska* was the stamp in the Ukrainian's internal passport—a carryover from the Soviet era—

93

that designated where the holder must live. (The draconian *propiska* was abolished in Ukraine in 2001.) This led to marriages contracted on financial arrangements. There was even the occasional, if apocryphal, story of a rural married couple that divorced so they could remarry another and move to the city, whereupon they were divorce again to be reunited with their original spouse. Along similar lines, I know of a medical doctor now living in the United States who wanted out of his marriage but was unable to get a separate apartment. He chose to take on a second job sweeping the streets for two hours each day, in addition to his medical post and lengthy commute. Yet the street-sweeping job entitled him to a separate apartment, and this is how he was finally able to move out.

Stories of birth control in the former Soviet Union are not pretty. Access to reliable and safe birth control has largely been denied to Ukrainian women. Abortions remain a common form of birth control, and I have heard both jokes and actual accounts where Soviet, industrial-strength condoms were rinsed and reused. The bigger issue is that men often refuse to wear condoms, and their partners disturbingly accept.

A Ukrainian now living in London tells the story of visiting her gynecologist who asked how many abortions she had undergone. When the woman said there had been none—that in 20 years she had given birth to only one child—the doctor chastised her for being dishonest with him about her medical history. In fact, there are accounts of women who have had as many as a dozen abortions; the Soviet average according to many sources was seven per woman during her childbearing years!

One cynical view maintains that doctors have unethically perpetuated the practice of numerous abortions despite adverse effects to the woman's health. This was because abortions were technically illegal, and hence a higher fee could be charged. It is true that medical salaries are pitifully low. It is also true that the majority of doctors in Ukraine are female.

Ukraine currently has a negative birth rate, and people express fear of having children in the wake of Chornobyl and other environmental hazards. Friends in Kyiv do report seeing more pregnant women now than several years ago, which would be good news if supported by actual statistics.

An unwed mother is considered a disgrace, whereas a divorced mother raising children is almost expected. As elsewhere, grandmothers play a significant role in raising their grandchildren.

Unmarried couples living together are common and accepted; the woman is often referred to as the *zhena* ("wife" in Russian). In Ukrainian, *zhinka* means both "woman" and "wife." Until recently, marriage ceremonies were performed in "wedding palaces" in light of the Soviet dismissal and disapproval of religion. (Divorces were also easily obtained.) Today's "church weddings" are increasingly popular, and attendance at church services is rising sharply.

An old Russian wedding tradition was that guests shouted *"Gorko!"*—meaning bitter, a reminder that life is hard; so the couple should kiss and make life easier.

One change in independent Ukraine is the difficulty in marrying a non-Ukrainian. One friend nearly abandoned the paperwork process for his Moldovan fiancée; obtaining proof that she was single turned out to be a bureaucratic nightmare. One irony is that the couple met while she was legally working in Ukraine. Now married, the wife is required to stay in Ukraine or the former Soviet Union for five years before she can obtain Ukrainian citizenship.

CITY ANIMALS

Pets are popular with Ukrainians, and you will come across a number of large dogs being walked throughout Kyiv. Kyiv is lovely with lots of green space, including small and large parks. Cats are less visible.

A few years ago a news story described a horrific place on the outskirts of Kyiv where stray dogs were killed for their hides. If you own dogs, take care that they do not stray.

For several years there has been a city tax for owning dogs: on a resident's utilities bill, in addition to heating and water, there is an item called *sobaka*, meaning "dog." This seemed to me yet another attempt to impose unreasonable taxes because the state's coffers are empty, but a Ukrainian friend, who owns a dog, says the tax is very minimal and justified.

HOMOSEXUALITY

In December 1991, homosexuality was legalized in Ukraine. Most argue that it is still not accepted and its legalization was merely an attempt to appear more progressive in the eyes of the West. Ukrainians enjoy making gays the butt of many jokes, although some say attitudes are improving. An American friend, who is gay and Jewish, says in his experience, accounts of Ukrainian prejudice against both these groups are exaggerated.

Nevertheless, the gay movement is only just beginning, and its most vocal spokespersons tend to be very young. In Ukraine's macho culture, most older gay men remain closeted. More likely than not, they describe themselves as bisexual and often indicate that they still intend to marry one day. Russian slang for "gay" is *goluboi* (say **gahlooBOY**), which is derived from the word for "light blue."

A gay and lesbian association called Ganymede was founded in 1991 but has not received adequate support within the gay community; one explanation is that the founder, despite good intentions, is a straight woman. A gay publication *Odyn Z Nas* or *One of Us* has been well received within the gay community since its introduction in 1997. The Internet has helped draw the younger computer-literate generation together on a broad spectrum of issues ranging from gay activism to environmentalist issues. A mainstream radio station now advertises an online dating service for gays with over 500 personal ads. This is a radical departure from a couple years ago.

Kyiv's gay scene, like much of the capital's nightlife and restaurant offerings, is constantly adding new venues. Until recently, gay discos and bars operated on an infrequent basis and were criticized by some as seedy and sometimes unsafe. This has changed and there are gay bars operating on a regular basis. Some openly advertise that they are gay establishments.

Ignoring larger issues of prejudice, the privacy problem for young gay couples is essentially the same as for straight ones. Where can they go to find privacy? A lot of gay sex reportedly goes on in public parks but removed from public view. Most gay sex is unprotected, and recent figures regarding HIV infection are disturbing. In recent years, Ukraine distinguished itself for the fastest growth of HIV in Europe, with 70% of Ukraine's current cases attributed to drug use. The Ukrainian acronym for AIDS is SNID (say *sneed*); in Russian, it's SPID (say *speed*).

Gay friends noted that gay bath-houses do not exist in Ukraine despite the popularity and long tradition of bath-houses in this region. Gay men visiting the *banya* or *sauna* should know that sex does not take place there, and the actions of the man wielding the traditional birch branches should not be interpreted as any sort of sexual advance.

JEWS AND PASSPORTS

Several years ago, I blurted to a recent emigré to America, "I didn't know you were Ukrainian." He had just told me he was raised in Kyiv, not Russia where he was educated. "I am not Ukrainian," he said politely. "I am a Jew."

The internal passport continues to be used in Ukraine, but what changed early on after independence was the infamous fifth line (or fifth point) of the passport, reserved for nationality; in Soviet times Jews were considered a separate nationality. They still are, but not for passport identification. Today the fifth line is for citizenship, and for passport identification—the reference to Jews has been dropped. It's no longer quite as easy to discriminate against Jews, although historically last names often identified a person's nationality.

Photo: Meredith Dalton

The site of the Jewish synagogue in Lviv. It was destroyed in World War II.

Non-Jewish Ukrainian friends have told me that discrimination against Jews is exaggerated or even unfounded. Some report that Jews discriminate against them; you'll notice that Jews work together, and they cite that many of Ukraine's wealthiest men are Jews. So this is proof that there is no discrimination! Jewish friends tell a very different story, and many of them remain interested in emigrating abroad. There is also jealousy on the part of non-Jews because, historically, it has been easier for Jews than non-Jews to emigrate.

RACISM AND DISCRIMINATION

On several occasions, I overheard staff members voice prejudices against Jews without batting an eyelid. Racism against dark-skinned individuals appears equally ingrained. A common claim is that much of the current criminal element hails from Central Asia, where skin color is darker than in Ukraine. Other Asians also tend to be suspect.

Technically speaking, Ukrainians must carry their documents with them at all times. Likewise, foreigners are advised to have their passports on them, although I would suggest a photocopy is safer than the passport itself. The following anecdotes seem to indicate that it is a good idea to carry one or the other with you at all times.

A U.S. Army recruit told me about when he spent three weeks in Kyiv on a training course. Because he is African-American, he was repeatedly stopped by the transit police demanding to see his documents. In a single day, he was stopped three times in precisely the same spot, just as he was entering or leaving a central metro station. A friend had advised him only to show his passport but never to hand it over, or he might be forced to pay a bribe to get it back.

A very close friend, a bronze-skinned Englishman whose father is from Delhi, tells of being harassed by the police. He didn't have his documents on him, so they took him to the station where they detained him for 20 minutes. One officer even hit him in the face for no apparent reason. It is not surprising that he is now skittish around *militsiya*.

Finally, another close friend, a man from Ecuador with a proud Inca heritage, came to study at the University of Kyiv on full scholarship at age 17. I met him after he had finished his bachelor's and master's degree equivalents, but he remained in Ukraine, in part because he had a young son there. The son had asthmatic problems. Also his marriage had failed. Willie's dark skin presented him with challenges, but none was insuperable. There was a brief period when his Ukrainian visa wasn't in order, and he was between student and business visas. His solution during this period was to walk about the streets wearing only business suits; he said he was less likely to be stopped if he dressed professionally. That he is fluent in Russian was a valuable, even necessary, skill for his long-term success. He has also learned to drop the names of powerful allies when necessary— a useful technique in this society where connections truly matter.

I cite the above stories about these expat friends because foreigners need to recognize that some will have a harder time than others. For some it may not be worth the hassle.

ATTITUDES TOWARD WESTERNERS

One overwhelming perception is that all Westerners are rich. Some Ukrainians will try to exploit and overcharge them. But there are also some gracious souls who would never overcharge because they treat Westerners as guests in their homeland. Most Ukrainians lie somewhere in between; some are looking for green cards, some for English tutors and friends, and some simply want Western business contacts. Westerners need to be prepared for those who aim to exploit them and be worthy of those who honor them.

An Englishman in Kyiv ventured provocatively that the British (as well as the Dutch) were probably better suited for living in Ukraine than Americans because of the Empire's colonial traditions. It's a perspective that might easily make Ukrainians champ at the bit, given their recent break from centuries of outside domination.

Americans do have cultural traits that can be exploited as weaknesses, especially in situations abroad. Americans tend to be sociable, and they place high importance on candor and trust. They often exhibit a superior attitude toward others, and their emphasis on money and materialism as a measure of one's success is at variance with those Ukrainians who regard spirituality as the more noble pursuit. The need for professional recognition and ambition is a common American trait. Contrast their individualism with the collective mentality of Ukrainians who never truly appreciated the free thinking encouraged by the Renaissance.

For all foreigners abroad, the absence of friends and family can lead to isolation and loneliness; Americans are especially vulnerable to people offering friendship and flattery, whereas Europeans are considered more reserved.

STEREOTYPES

Old Soviet stereotypes included the Communist Party bosses, the *nomenklatura*, *apparatchiky*, the military, the proletariat, the intelligentsia, dissidents, *babushky,* and pensioners. Newer post-Soviet stereotypes include a significantly expanded bureaucracy, the New Rich, the mafia, entrepreneurs, and an emerging middle class. The *babushky* and pensioners remain, but their disastrous financial straits set them apart from their Soviet counterparts. Lastly, you might count today's expatriate community, including the diaspora, as an additional post-Soviet stereotype, because in Soviet times foreigners were close to negligible (and certainly the goal was that they be invisible) within Soviet society at large.

In simplistic terms, the Soviets could be divided into the haves and have-nots. The *apparatchiky* and *nomenklatura* were in the minority (estimated by some to be roughly 20%), and this group was, on the whole, on the winning side. Only a very small minority belonged to the Communist Party, and only the highest ranking military officials comprised the privileged class. The proletariat (or

101

working class) was a catchall for the rest. These terms are used today most often to refer to these Soviet stereotypes, yet some believe that the primary change after the Soviet Union collapsed was that many former communists became the earliest and strongest advocates for democracy. This is because they were best poised to take advantage of so-called market reforms.

While the West watched eagerly to see if and how reforms were being implemented, the Communist Party bosses managed to line their pockets by breaking up state monopolies and selling off chunks among themselves at fire-sale prices. The consensus today is that the super-rich in both Russia and Ukraine did not add any value when they usurped their present wealth—they merely redistributed their country's mineral resources among a select group of friends. To the have-nots, this talk of democracy does little more than perpetuating the glaring inequities of the totalitarian regime. Pessimistic observers remark that they have only succeeded in rearranging the deck chairs on the *Titanic*.

There are also diehard communists who are attempting to make a comeback. They are playing to the nostalgic sympathies of older voters who have been left behind and whose lives are so diminished. But these communists, like the voters they attract, are mostly older generation, in a country where youth has a decided advantage.

The intelligentsia of yore is largely disillusioned by society's reforms, and their struggles to survive are nearly as acute as for the pensioners. Some have turned to more entrepreneurial, if less palatable, professions by default rather than desire; sadly, others have turned more to the bottle.

Where are the Soviet dissidents? Most dissidents were Jews, and because of Soviet and Ukrainian discriminatory practices, they continued after independence to emigrate in record numbers. The lives of pensioners and *babushky* have been irrevocably altered due to the devaluation of their pensions amidst society's vast changes. Likewise, aging Soviet military heroes sometimes wear their uniforms and medals of honor, their stoic pride now tinged with sadness. The military no longer holds the prestige of the Soviet era, and in fact is racked today with brutal hazing rituals, bad morale, and stories of obsolete (or nonexistent) equipment and insufficient fuel supplies. The Cossack tradition was cited as good training ground for the military and contributed to very high percentages of Ukrainian officers in the Russian Army. Today, sons of career military personnel are choosing career paths different from those of their fathers. This proud Cossack tradition may be soon permanently displaced by nostalgia.

Bureaucracy has expanded greatly since independence, in part because the power base has shifted for Ukrainians from Moscow to Kyiv. However, the younger generations seem much more likely to turn their backs on governmental careers, including military ones, now that so many business opportunities are available to them. However, some still aspire to join the police, while others denounce it as legalized corruption—certainly not all divisions of the police are created equal. Some claim optimistically that the situation in Ukraine will improve once the current wave of bureaucrats retire. Certainly, we have seen enough changes in the last five years, as distinct from the last decade, to know that only time will tell us how Ukrainian society will evolve during the next decade.

The greater concern remains the powerful grip of the mafia in post-Soviet countries. The New Rich, or New Russians, refers to the new breed of moneyed businessmen whose most defining characteristic is ostentatious spending habits. Many will tell you that the New Rich and the mafia are one and the same. You may hear the term *krisha* (say **KREEsha**), meaning "roof," which is slang for mafia protection.

LIAR, LIAR

It is hard for many Westerners to grasp the state of corruption and bribery in Ukraine; it is equally difficult to truly understand Ukrainian attitudes toward democracy and capitalism. For over 70 years, the Soviet system infected most of its citizens with the notion that capitalism is about grabbing, cheating, and wheeling and dealing. Today the actions of the mafia and top government officials support this premise. According to many, these two groups are both the main product and sole beneficiary of capitalism in Ukraine, whereas for the average citizen, democracy is marked primarily by free elections, increasing hardship, and *tufta* (say ***toofTA***) as usual.

Tufta roughly translates as "institutionalized b.s."—inflated harvest figures and tourist-speak of yore, intended not only to sanitize but to paint a rosier picture to Soviet citizens and outside observers. In large measure, *tufta,* which is a Russian word, is an affront to the intelligence of ordinary Ukrainians. (*Tufta* can also mean just "b.s.") Two related Russian words are *vranyo* versus *lozh.* Both essentially refer to lying, but the first resembles a fib or white lie or even blarney, told to avoid offending someone. *Lozh* is a harsh, deliberate lie.

CORRUPTION AS USUAL

Petty corruption and bribery go hand in hand in Ukraine. For some, bribery is merely one cost of doing business, just as reliance upon personal connections (*svyazy* or *blat*) is obligatory.

Visibility in Ukraine attracts unwanted attention. Several years ago foreign investors spoke to me about avoiding types of businesses requiring storefronts, such as restaurants. One prominent European entrepreneur, in the true sense of the word, announced in late 1998 that he was throwing in the towel after seven strong years in Ukraine. Relentless corruption had finally exhausted his patience. Today's entrepreneurs are a slightly modified breed—their paths have been nominally eased by the passage of time and by observing the experiences of those who came before them. But they can only survive here as long as they remain savvy, tenacious, and skeptical, as opposed to cynical. Storefronts are possible, they assure me, but don't be so naive as to think that you can avoid the petty bribes and ever-changing rules.

Visibility does invite the tax inspectorates in search of fabricated fines and bribes. One friend who sells used car parts was fined because the time stamped on his cash register receipts was not adjusted for daylight savings time. The $200 fine was intended to discourage further "defrauding" of his customers. There was a second trumped-up, but less expensive, fine. The irony is that when they dropped the cash register fine, he felt like he was getting away with something, although he still had one bogus fine to pay! Be prepared for this common psychological ploy.

Another ruse is the discovery of new inspection violations during a reinspection of a past violation. This means getting a new fine now and being revisited later to make sure that you have corrected the problem and are now in full compliance. Obviously, more problems may be uncovered during subsequent visits. These violations can be as nonsensical as: you were never given permission to paint the walls this color, or you cannot sell new and used items in the same physical area.

Also common is a an official offering you a lower fine as if he's doing you a favor. For example, when I was stopped for jaywalking in 1998, the policeman said that the fines ranged from two to nine *hryvnia* (then roughly US$1 to $4.50). He gave me the smaller fine, which made sense because there was absolutely no traffic nearby, but I had been at fault. A friend joked that it's harder to understand a range of fines for not wearing your seatbelt; either it's fastened or it's not!

Some foreigners skirt the issue of bribery with talk of finding a "common language" with the different parties. Others will tell you that a necessary trait for survival and sanity in Ukraine is "flexible ethics," which is essentially the same thing. One important point to remember is that Westerners are perceived as wealthy, and thus money should be no object to them. But if Westerners give in too easily, they will assuredly drown.

BUT CUSTOMER SERVICE IMPROVES

Attitudes toward customer service have improved dramatically. Restaurants catering to Western clients first recognized this because they wanted this dollar-denominated business. (Contrast this with the state hotels that wouldn't give you a room without a reservation 24 hours in advance, even when they had the space!) Today all forms of businesses, not just restaurants, can clearly see that Ukrainians have choices. Also, both business owners and their customers have had 10 years of studying Western marketing and advertising strategies. The more successful businesses have adapted to Ukrainian tastes and culture. I used to remark that some of the waitresses in Kyiv's expat hangouts seemed to smile too much, as if that was the focus of their training. But I think it was the arrival and widespread success of McDonald's that ultimately raised the level of customer service in the smaller establishments, including those that cater mostly to local customers.

SNAPSHOTS OF TRANSITION

The following vignettes provide a mere glimpse of the many changes in customer relations and attitudes in general during recent years.

I went with friends to see a movie in the days before all the fancy, Western-styled theaters opened. The projectionist had started the film early, so it would finish early, and he could go home. But he had started the movie without any audience! We made him restart the reel. A couple weeks later, I boarded a plane from Crimea to Kyiv— the plane likewise took off 20 minutes early. I was shocked, as not all the seats were filled.

In a poker game with expatriates and locals playing, a Ukrainian friend turned his cards over and excused himself to go to the rest room. When he returned a few minutes later, his face was ashen; he openly panicked that spending too much time "around foreigners" had made him overly trusting. When he had walked away from the table, he had failed to take his cards with him. He never considered that another player might try to cheat him in his absence. In an unrelated event that evening, the same Ukrainian proposed that he and another player remaining in the hand simply split the kitty. Rules against collusion were alien to him.

An American friend ordered tea in a hotel restaurant. The waiter offered him the standard choice of black tea or one of several imported specialty teas. After hearing the choices, my friend still selected the standard tea. When his colleague requested one of the imported teas, the waiter retracted his offer. The colleague was flustered and then became insistent, but the waiter wouldn't budge and excused himself. A second waiter brought the tea and explained that the original waiter was trying to sell teas from his personal stash, but he had panicked upon thinking that his boss might find out.

One of my favorite stories took place in the dining room of the Hotel Rus nearly five years ago. At the end of the meal, I asked the waiter for separate checks. I explained that I was sorry, but my boss required this for accounting purposes. The waiter cordially smiled and disappeared for a long time. He returned at last with six checks, which he laid out very carefully on the table for the three of us who were dining together. "This is for you; this is for your boss." In each case, the boss's receipt was roughly three times the actual amount of the meal. What the waiter didn't know was that my boss was at the table!

Foreigners should be wary of being overcharged. One friend discovered that his check for dinner trebled one night. When he complained, the waiter said that chicken was sold according to grams and that the menu's price was for 100 grams. My friend argued that this was not the case in the past and demanded to see a manager. The manager then explained that this was a mix-up and apologized Clearly the waiter (or the establishment) had been hoping to overcharge.

Similarly, in Lviv I complained when I was overcharged for my *shashlyk* (meat kebab); however, it turned out the menu price was for 100 grams whereas the serving portion was 150 grams. Along these lines, be aware that menus often show the price of wine, like vodka, in 50-gram or 50-ml measures. A standard wine glass, however, is three to four times this. Without this knowledge, you'll think someone is trying to stiff you when the bill arrives.

THE EXPAT COMMUNITY

Ukraine's expatriate community boasts its share of personalities ranging from the genuine do-gooders to the occasional bottom-feeders. Most people seem to fall somewhere between these poles. The composition of the expat community has changed over time and in response to a changing Ukraine. For example, the consultants working within the donor community have contracted in recent years, just as most of the representatives of multinational corporations (and their families) have returned to their home countries. Today's more prominent members of the expat community include diplomatic personnel, journalists, volunteers, missionaries, and entrepreneurs.

The Ukrainian diaspora stands apart within the larger expat community. This community is unique in that its parents or grandparents fled Ukraine for the United States and Canada. (Often the parents cannot understand how the children could possibly want to return.) The diaspora comes with its own set of issues and agendas; I've heard locals criticize this group for its staunch nationalism (at times) and occasional patronizing tendencies.

The nature of expatriate work attracts singles (and wannabe singles). In Ukraine this includes many men in search of Ukrainian girlfriends or wives. Fortunately for them there are lots of especially attractive Ukrainian women, who genuinely appreciate the way that most foreigners treat them.

The expatriate community, here as elsewhere, also attracts its share of misfits. Some are married but have problems at home with their wives or children. Others come to Ukraine hoping to avoid an alcohol problem or the stigma that accompanies it, but they are choosing the wrong country—alcohol is a key element of Slavic culture and a large factor in expatriate social life. Still others had trouble with work at home; maybe jobs were hard to find (or keep), or maybe life was just too boring. There's a certain "big fish" allure to living and working overseas, even if that means subsisting in a fishbowl.

Many foreigners working in Ukraine chose to come because of their professional background and the search for an intellectual challenge. Some get addicted to the lifestyle and say that the status quo back home is at best stifling. One young consultant described the United States now as high energy and stasis, Ukraine as lethargy and motion.

Finally, a small number of young expatriates come to Ukraine in search of entry-level jobs. They are not part of the backpacker set found in other parts of Europe, Latin America, or Southeast Asia, partly because visa restrictions don't make it easy to enter Ukraine. But Ukraine has its off-the-beaten-track allure—and not just for the Russian majors and students of Ukrainian descent. For a large percentage of Ukraine's working expat community, Ukraine offers a glimpse of the edge without the free fall of Russia.

Lastly, we're seeing a growing crop of short-term visitors to Ukraine. Some come hoping to adopt a Ukrainian child, but with Ukraine's low birth rate, I would advise thorough research before coming. (Check the website http://www.ukremb.com for the Ukrainian Embassy in Washington, D.C., where there is a special section on adoptions, listed under consular information.) Others come to research their Ukrainian or Jewish roots; special travel agencies have arisen to meet this need. But the majority of short-term visitors arriving today appear to be following up on contacts they made via the Internet through one of the numerous dating or marriage agencies that have mushroomed in recent years. I've heard success stories and horror stories, so please proceed with caution.

Holders of the "Diplomatic" Green Card

The donor community is far less visible today in Kyiv than even a few years ago. Members of the donor community today include the employees and contractors of USAID (United States Agency for International Development) and TACIS (Technical Assistance to the CIS, which is the EU's equivalent). Also present are EBRD (European Bank for Reconstruction and Development), the World Bank, the British Know How Fund, Soros in various manifestations, Canadian aid organizations, and others. In overall terms, the EU is Ukraine's largest aid donor, and Ukraine wants EU membership. (It also says that the EU discriminates against it, unlike its neighbors to the west.)

Embassy and foreign aid personnel should probably be differentiated from their contractors and the community at large. For example, most of the direct hires live in truly Western apartments surrounded by modern appliances and the rugs and trinkets accumulated during previous assignments in Africa and Latin America. The fact that their cars display diplomatic plates means that they won't be hassled by the dreaded DAI traffic police. Also, they get to shop in the commissary and have periodic shipments of food from home, even if the value of this last perk has diminished significantly over time, just as check-cashing privileges mean less in this age of ATM cash machines, Western Union, and American Express. Not that I would turn this privilege down.

Aid contractors, unlike aid and embassy employees, don't get commissary or check-cashing privileges. But they do live in nice apartments, even if the furnishings are not their own. And, while they don't get diplomatic plates, many have successfully diverted traffic fines by flashing the green cards issued by their embassy. These cards suggest diplomatic immunity for the holders, but you shouldn't rely on them in a real pinch. These cards are also passed out capriciously and only to foreign contractors hired in their home country to work in Ukraine for a minimum of one year.

Just remember this: capriciousness, or the arbitrary application of policies, is something you will come to accept more in Ukraine, or you just might not make it here. There is real diplomatic immunity for real diplomats; and while these green dip cards (if you hold one—and many contractors do) can be of assistance, my advice is, don't abuse your privilege. There are many arrogant foreigners and probably more Ukrainians who would like to snag them for it. However frustrating aspects of Ukraine's laws, customs, and culture may seem to you, your challenge is to work within that system. It will require creativity, guts, and sometimes tolerance verging on madness. And did I mention patience?

Volunteer Organizations

Volunteer organizations such as the Peace Corps, the MBA Enterprise Corps, together with the missionary community deserve kudos as the altruists within the larger expatriate community. Other volunteer groups such as the International Executive Service Corps (IESC) and Volunteers in Overseas Cooperative Assistance (VOCA) also provide a tremendous service; however, their presence is less visible within the expat community because their assignments are short-term.

In 1998 the Peace Corps's largest mission worldwide was in Ukraine with 170 volunteers. Tragically, one volunteer was murdered that year in his Chernihiv apartment during an apparent robbery. While conceding that violence can occur anywhere, another volunteer remarked that he generally felt safer in Ukraine than at home in Chicago. For the record, Ukraine had had no previous problems. Most Peace Corps deaths worldwide are the result of auto accidents, not violent crime.

Most expatriates in Ukraine still stand out in their community, probably more so outside of Kyiv, and it is important to recognize this. On the other hand, Peace Corps volunteers are dispersed throughout Ukraine and are not necessarily visible in Kyiv's expatriate community. They also tend to live a more local lifestyle, both in terms of income and functional language skills. Specifically, volunteers are expected to speak Russian or Ukrainian depending on the location of the assignment. While the MBA Corps offers larger monthly stipends than the Peace Corps, neither group of volunteers is flush.

Contrast this with VOCA and IESC volunteers who have comfortable, though not luxurious, apartments provided by their host organizations. These apartments are most often near the city center. The farther you venture from downtown Kyiv, the more affordable the rents become and the better your language skills need to be. Because VOCA and IESC assignments are typically for shorter periods, these volunteers can hardly be expected to speak Russian or Ukrainian. Moreover, these volunteers generally provide specialized expertise; often, the high level of their positions at home cannot allow for extended tours abroad.

The Missionary Community

Ukraine's missionary community has been steadily growing, even if its presence tends to be less visible within the expatriate community at large. One reason is that the missionaries, like some of the other volunteers, tend to live farther from the city center where there is more affordable housing. Usually, their housing is not paid for, or there are considerable financial constraints. One missionary wife with children remarked that embassy staff, aid workers, and their contractors, had driven the rents up so high, not that this group care because they don't pay their own rents—their taxpayers do.

Many missionary families are united in their own tightly-knit community, which is separate from the larger expatriate community.

The missionaries started their own school called New Hope Christian School. Non-missionary children may be admitted according to a higher tuition scale; naturally, all students must follow the school's religious instruction. Still, tuition costs significantly less here than in the other private schools available in Kyiv, including the Kyiv International School (KIS), the Pechersk School International, The British International School, a French school, and others.

The missionaries are somewhat isolated from other expats, because they are not part of the bar scene that is so popular, especially among the singles set.

The Private Sector

The Big Five accounting firms arrived in Ukraine soon after independence to implement various aid-funded energy projects. These firms later opened registered offices in Ukraine for their for-profit work. Ukraine's then 50-million strong population (now closer to 49 million) also attracted multinational consumer products companies: Procter & Gamble, Pepsi, Coca-Cola, Cargill, Monsanto, John Deere, and a host of others all had their reasons for coming to Ukraine. And so they came.

Expatriate employees of the large companies lived well, in their Western-style apartments with Western appliances, as opposed to most of the expat population who lived well, but in furnished apartments of the so-called modern local style. Many families were comfortable moving to Kyiv because it offered several established international schools. Also in its favor was that it lacked Moscow's insanity.

Today, however, most of the larger companies have only skeletal expatriate staff, if at all. Ukrainians now hold the jobs that were formerly held by expats and at significantly lower salary costs, to say nothing of the generous overseas packages that were once the norm. Smaller companies with long-term goals don't need a large expatriate staff either, if their goal is to establish a presence for future Ukrainian business activities. A long-term commitment means laying a lot of groundwork over time; personal and business connections are the key, but this doesn't have to mean a large staff.

The smallest companies within the private sector often include what I call the maverick entrepreneur, athough none could survive without a skeletal local staff, including an accountant-type or two. To me all the expat entrepreneurs are mavericks, it's just that some are more reckless than others. Early on there were cautionary, if intriguing, tales about Western businessmen going astray, or at least trying to play by Ukrainian rules and hiring their own mafia security to play hardball and level the playing field. Of course, the field isn't level, whether you're diaspora, a fearless (or feckless) maverick, or even Ukrainian. The Californian bar owner who jumped into bed with the Chechen mafia to avoid some Kyiv thugs was lucky to go home alive. The Pennsylvanian who several years ago opened the luxurious Grand Hotel in Lviv pulled out of that joint venture the way others have before and since: either someone you know gets deep-sixed and you reconsider, or one day you learn that you are no longer part of a joint venture.

In spite of this, there exists a new wave of entrepreneurs in Ukraine. Some are diaspora and have their own reasons for staying, but more are Western entrepreneurs who have been seduced by Ukraine's excitement and opportunities.

In the past, this group was more likely to criticize the donor community, which was then larger and louder. And life was decidedly harder without all the perks, especially when just getting cash was a huge ordeal. Some claimed that their experience was more authentic, because they had to deal with the Ukrainian bureaucracy on a daily basis as Ukrainians do. For example, one friend complained of the arduous paperwork process required for bringing a pet in and out of the country. Like the traffic fines, she stated that simply flashing one of the green "diplomatic" cards could have eliminated the hassle.

Probably those who held the green cards did a disservice to those who didn't. A valid point was that the green cards perpetuated discriminatory pricing practices against foreigners.In Ukraine there used to be separate rates for everything: hotels, trains, and planes, all depending on who you were: Ukrainian ministers, Ukrainian citizens, foreign diplomats, or foreign citizens. The argument then was that the very people in a position to influence standardized pricing did nothing to help those outside of their beloved perks system. It's much like the apartment rent issue; people don't care how much their rent is as long as their paycheck isn't involved.

The situation has improved and there are no longer separate fares for train and air travel. But I could write another book about the bureaucratic hurdles suffered by the expatriate masses. Yet another book could be reserved for tales of woe from my Ukrainian friends. As of early 2002, some of the previous decade's nightmares for expats have been sufficiently resolved, but the day-to-day hassles still defy logic. The entrepreneurs working in Ukraine today seem less likely to point the finger at the big companies or at the aid hires and contractors. Maybe this is simply further proof that the community is more diffuse: there are fewer factions, less infighting and finger-pointing. But the fact is that there wasn't ever much to begin with!

All I can (lamely) say is that every situation is different, which is why those who seek pat answers may not be happy working here for long. With that said, the private sector's occasional whining in the past about its lack of special treatment was generally valid. But authentic, what's that? Authentic is what happens to you.

On Dating and Aging

If you're female, your coat will be removed for you, your cigarette will be lit for you (and you won't be treated as a pariah for this nasty habit), and frequently your bar tab will be paid for you. If you're single, you'll probably date some of the expatriate men and then become bitter if and when they prefer to date the local women. One young man explained, "It's weird, it's like dating your mother or someone from the 1950s, but Ukrainian women are really supportive in what you do." Along these lines, young Ukrainian girls, when asked what they want to be when they grow up, often respond, "I want to be really beautiful so I can marry a rich man."

Ukrainian women are extremely attractive, and many have stolen a Westerner's heart. You rarely see the converse: few expatriate women date local men, although one woman told me of her female friends who came to Ukraine in search of men. A distinguishing feature here was language fluency: she was speaking about her (bilingual) friends in the diaspora community. Clearly, those who speak the language have a very different experience; they also tend to survive longer in Ukraine.

Age is highly appreciated in Slavic cultures. A lot of middle-aged foreign men come to Ukraine and attract younger, beautiful, and devoted wives. A 67-year-old consultant told me that ageism in America was one reason why he now lived in Ukraine. At his age, he couldn't find a challenging job in America, whereas in Ukraine he is appreciated for his age and expertise. He views his graying hair as a positive attribute, even now when there are so many advantages enjoyed by Ukraine's youth. In his case, he worked with Ukrainian bureaucrats who largely preferred to work with someone closer to their own age when possible, as opposed to the 20- and 30-somethings offered especially by the larger consulting firms.

One last remark about age: a former Peace Corps volunteer once said the corps heavily scrutinizes recruits in their 30s and 40s, because often they are running away from something, whereas younger or older volunteers have other motivations. This echoes some of the revious remarks about misfits within the larger expat community, but this is hardly a phenomenon unique to Ukraine.

THE EXPATRIATE EXPERIENCE

Living abroad expands your way of looking at the world. Living in Ukraine encouraged me to examine how different cultures approach negotiations and problem solving and how they view and treat diversity and conformity. Individuals continually reshaped my cultural stereotypes, not just of Ukrainians but of the North Americans and Europeans whose paths I also crossed. Living in Ukraine also made me treasure the bounties I had left behind. Overall, Ukraine's expatriate community is just that—a community that encourages and supports friendships drawn from many ages, nationalities, and professions.

What bothers me most within this community are basic concerns about arrogance and limited cultural sensitivity. An "us versus them" mentality arises, and is even natural, because of cultural differences and economic considerations.

Expatriates clearly need to make greater efforts to improve their foreign language skills. One expat said that foreigners who don't learn the local language will spend their time abroad essentially trapped behind a glass wall. Homesickness or loneliness is also more likely. So study, take classes with a tutor, and by all means learn the alphabet before you arrive! Buy a pocket phrasebook now so that you can begin to learn the basic pleasantries. If you can speak a little Ukrainian or Russian, be proud of your foreign language skills and use them.

It's really presumptuous to blurt out English in a restaurant, although you won't believe how common it is. Unfortunately, more often than you would like, if you try to order something and butcher the Russian or Ukrainian language, the server will respond in English. But give it a whirl first. You need to keep practicing for all those other daily encounters where possibly no English is spoken. This might include buying vegetables at the *rynok* (market), hailing a cab across town, or negotiating a better price for tourist items on Andriyivsky Uzviz (okay, most vendors speak some English). Still, if you leave the confines of the major cities, the rest of Ukraine speaks only pidgin English at best.

Refrain from criticizing Ukraine in English in front of Ukrainians, who in most cases will understand English far better than the average foreigner will understand Russian or Ukrainian.

UKRAINIANS ON EXPAT EXPERTS

Many Ukrainians were skeptical early on about the many foreign consultants who came to advise them, often in areas that, even without advice, Ukrainians would eventually come to decide for themselves. A Ukrainian-born colleague proved unwilling or unable to handle revisiting Ukraine after 17 years in America. I recall an occasion when he tried to give a waiter a lesson on proper service. After making the waiter sit in his own chair, he draped his napkin over his forearm. His air was condescending. The fact is that this man felt all Ukrainians who hadn't emigrated from Ukraine, as he had done, were cowards. (It is relevant that he was Jewish and never felt fully Ukrainian.) It is no wonder Ukrainians tire of outsiders telling them how to live their lives differently. What surprises me is that more Ukrainians don't tell their "foreign advisors" off!

These same Ukrainians watch how foreigners spend money, on projects and in restaurants, and you'd be amazed at what they know about our salaries. (If they don't, they are likely to ask.) Ukrainians have openly observed that the expatriate community holds more than its share of marital, extramarital, and alcohol problems; they recognize those people who are running away from home, often because they'd like to themselves.

At times I have found myself among the harsher critics of the donor community; the way it spends money and the work that its contractors sometimes do. Yet I also recognize that some of the loftier projects—which are also among the most challenging and interesting—would not receive any support at all if it weren't for foreign aid. There are still so few foreign businesses ready for the plunge, and Ukrainian firms and the state itself lack the financial resources for many of the improvements to infrastructure still needed.

My hope for all Ukraine's expatriates is that they will add value and encourage greater understanding of Ukraine and dialogue with Ukrainians.

— *Chapter Three* —

HUMOR AND LANGUAGE

HUMOR

Bohdan, Ihor, and Vasily went fishing one cold winter day. Alongside its banks the Dnipro was starting to freeze, but it was still possible to navigate the small boat through the water. The three men were clearly more interested in drinking vodka than in fishing, and all three became drunk quite quickly.

"Pass the bottle, Bohdan," said Ihor. Bohdan thrust the bottle toward his friend, but his abrupt movement threw the boat off balance. In an effort to steady himself and the boat, Bohdan stood up. In his woozy state he toppled into the ice-cold water.

Ihor and Vasily panicked as they watched their friend sink below the water's surface. Each hoped the other would make the first move, but neither did. At last Ihor exclaimed, "Well, we have to do something." So he dipped his arms into the icy water and shrieked from the cold. He flailed around hoping to catch his friend's arm or leg. At last, he yelled with great relief, "I've got his jacket! Help me drag him aboard!" The men hoisted the body into the boat and immediately saw that the man was not breathing. Ihor knew that Vasily would not take any initiative, so he started to perform mouth-to-mouth resuscitation.

"Good God," Ihor announced, "I never knew what bad breath he had."

Vasily looked at the man's feet and said, "Yeah, and I never knew he was wearing skates."

Some contend that the best test of a foreigner's fluency in a given language is the ability to understand jokes and local humor. Few foreigners spending time in Ukraine will achieve the fluency or language skills necessary to comprehend fully or communicate via humor. Foreigners coming to Ukraine are mostly businesspeople who may or may not have the time or interest to devote to language studies. This may change now with fewer expat development types coming over for one or two years, and the presence of more entrepreneurs who intend to do business in Ukraine and see returns on their investment. These will require a combination of language skills, time, and patience. To a certain degree, hiring qualified locals can help in the areas of language and patience. But to genuinely succeed, these entrepreneurs need to focus on the long haul. With that said, what better time is there to learn the language than the present?

Recent college graduates, many of who majored in Russian, and Ukrainian diaspora from Canada and the United States are also coming to Ukraine to use their skills. Entry-level jobs, for those lucky enough to find them, typically don't pay well, but language skills can partially make up for this. Those who studied Slavic languages in college, or learned them in the home as children, have a decided advantage.

For most expatriates moving to a foreign country, taking language lessons upon arrival in a good idea. However, for many of us, to achieve fluency might well take several years. You will have to weigh the practicality of studying Ukrainian or Russian depending on your personal circumstances. You should start with the basic niceties in both languages, then concentrate on learning one language better. Whichever language you decide to learn, exposure to local humor is always a good means toward understanding some of the subtleties of a different culture.

COMMON THEMES

Regional humor often reinforces, even perpetuates, cultural stereotypes. Jokes pertaining to excessive alcohol intake, bureaucratic inefficiencies and corruption, the New Rich/New Russians, and the increasing role of the mafia in post-communist life are among the most popular themes in Ukraine. One of the remarkable features of humor in this post-communist era is, of course, the relaxed climate for jokes. Some argue that the characteristic biting sarcasm of the dissident era is no longer possible in the present (democratic-leaning) situation.

1. Vodka

Jokes about vodka are legion and certainly not unique to Ukraine and Russia. (It also follows that Ukrainians often tell these jokes about Russians and vice versa, rather than simply about themselves.) Within the former Soviet Union, many countries share strong vodka traditions, although customs may be influenced regionally by Muslim abstinence traditions, for example, in Kyrgyzstan and Uzbekistan, or by the celebrated viniculture of Georgia and Moldova. Crimea is also celebrated for its wines, and its Tatar population is Muslim.

Outside the former Soviet Union, Scandinavia and Poland are leading vodka producers, sharing many of the Slavic traditions and, consequently, many of the jokes about overindulgence. Certainly, none of these places can claim exclusive rights on jokes about vodka—or alcohol in general. The following, for example, has been told as an Irish joke, substituting whiskey as the drink of choice:

A man was staggering home with a bottle of vodka in his pocket. He slipped and fell to the ground with a hard thud. Struggling to his feet, he felt something wet running down his leg. "Please, God," he begged, "let it be blood!"

In contrast to the deep sarcasm of the dissident jokes treated separately below, a host of silly, sometimes slapstick, jokes abound pertaining to excessive alcohol intake:

—*Excuse me, what time is it?*
—*You know, I could use a drink too.*

Alcohol often masks other issues or problems; below, we see the strained relationship between a (nagging) wife and her husband:

Wife: You promised me you'd become a different man.
Husband: I know, but he drinks too.

This contemporary (post-communist) joke evinces the bittersweet realities of inflation and hardships incurred as a result:

—*With the rising cost of vodka, Daddy, it looks like you'll have less to drink.*
—*No, sonny, that's where you're wrong. You're going to have less to eat.*

A final joke in this category assumes knowledge of the reference to 50 grams as a standard measurement for vodka.

—*They say that life begins at 50.*
—*Yeah, but it's even better after a 100 or more.*

2. Marriage, Infidelity, and In-laws

Common joke themes revolve around marriage difficulties and infidelity. While neither is uniquely Ukrainian or Soviet, the popularity of these themes is telling. Below is a sampling of these jokes:

—Honey, when we get married, I'll be there to share all your troubles and sorrows.
—But I don't have any, my love.
—I said, when we get married....

—Masha! I didn't know you smoked. When did you start?
—That night my husband came home early and found a cigarette butt in the ashtray.

A woman is admiring a fur coat in front of the mirror.
"Mother, did Daddy buy that new coat for you?" asked her son.
"No, my dear, if I relied on your father, I wouldn't have you, let alone this nice fur coat."

The rest of the world has its in-law jokes, but in the former Soviet Union these jokes are especially popular. Similar in many respects to the jokes about strained marriages, in-law jokes are often attributed to many years of severely cramped living quarters, often shared by multiple generations and extended family members.

—Mr. Gorsky, do you have any children?
—Yes, I have three daughters.
—Do they live at home?
—No, they aren't married yet.

A mother tells her daughter, "Your boyfriend is such a jerk, I would be delighted to be his mother-in-law!"

Or another joke is the mother-in-law who liked to talk so much that, while on holiday, her tongue got sunburned. Contrast this with the traditional Christmas toast to a man's mother-in-law: that her throat never becomes dry.

A young woman tells her husband the bad news—that her once rich father is now bankrupt.

The young man exclaims, "I knew that old miser would find some way to separate us!"

Here's an example of a standard mother-in-law joke, but updated by the addition of the New Russian who is able to throw his money around.

A New Russian took his family to a nearby lake to go swimming. The New Russian panicked suddenly and called out to a nearby fisherman. "Please help me. My wife is drowning, and I can't swim! I'll give you $100 to help me save her!"

Within moments, the fisherman had dragged the lady to the shore. "Sir, you said there's a reward?"

"You know," said the New Russian, "everybody was flailing around in the water. The one I thought was my wife, well, I was mistaken. It was my mother-in-law."

"Oh, dear," grimaced the fisherman. "How much do I owe you?"

A man watching a funeral procession was struck by what he saw. Behind the hearse was a man leading a goat on a rope. And behind them trailed a line of young men.

The bystander approached the man leading the goat. "Excuse me, sir. Can you tell me who died, and why this strange following?"

"The woman in the hearse was my mother-in-law. A couple days ago, while picking vegetables in our garden, she was struck from behind by this goat. She was killed instantly,"

"Really!" exclaimed the bystander. "Any chance I might borrow him for a day or two?"

"Sure," responded the man, "but you'll have to get in line like everyone else."

3. Everyday Life and Minor Hassles

While the previous jokes about vodka, strained relationships, and in-laws are not unique to the former Soviet Union, the following jokes address aspects of everyday life as lived and handled in Ukraine. Although the division is somewhat arbitrary, I am separating minor hassles here as distinct from major hassles and the dissident jokes.

Lada

Like the jokes about the Aeroflot national airline (which seem equally popular outside of the former Soviet Union), Lada (a.k.a. the Soviet Fiat) jokes remain quite popular:

—*Why does the Lada Samara have a heated rear window?*

—*So that your hands won't freeze when you push it.*

Shopping

Since independence, shopping has taken on a new dimension, and there are many jokes now about the outrageous spending habits of the New Rich. One real frustration for the average Ukrainian is that he is visually assaulted by what he cannot afford.

The following joke makes sense when you understand that most Ukrainians carry their own plastic bags whenever they go grocery shopping.

Soviet dementia: A man stands in front of a grocery store with an empty bag and cannot remember if he was going into the store or coming out.

Another joke claims that the destruction of the Berlin Wall paved the way for the collapse of the Soviet Union.

Specifically, the fall of the Berlin Wall marked history's first feminine revolution: there was no violence, and when it ended everybody went shopping.

SHE SUDDENLY
BECAME NOSTALGIC
FOR THE QUEUES

Queuing

One of the many negative images of the Soviet era was the notorious shopping queue. For former Soviet citizens, it remains a pervasive memory that is occasionally revived. These jokes are examples:

The plural of man: "queue"

—*Grandma, what was the biggest road catastrophe of all time?*
—*My dear, it was when the Kyiv queue crashed with the Moscow queue.*

—*What is 150 yards long and eats potatoes?*
—*The meat queue in Moscow.*

Mushroom collecting (and related jokes)

This joke plays on the popularity of mushroom collecting—and the occasional tales of poisonous mushrooms:

—*Doctor! Which mushrooms can you eat?*
—*All of them. There are just some that you can only eat once.*

And here is a vehicular take on the "only once" theme:
—*Is it true that a Moskvich can get up to 120 kilometers?*
—*Yes. But only once.*

Taxes

Given the prohibitive tax structure, there is rampant tax evasion.
A doctor says to his patient, "You say that you're happy to pay your taxes. And when exactly did this start?"

Changing borders

Lviv, the so-called capital of western Ukraine, is often cited for its changing political borders. Lviv entered the 20th century as part of the Austro-Hungarian Empire, until the Hapsburg Empire collapsed at the end of World War I. Following the Russian Revolution, Lviv was very briefly the seat of an independent government but was quickly restored to Polish rule. It remained under Poland (except for a brief period in 1920 under Soviet rule) until 1939, when Moscow seized control. From 1941 to 1944, Lviv was occupied by German forces and subsequently liberated by the Red Army (although few of Lviv's citizens regarded this as particularly better). In 1991, when Ukraine declared independence, Lviv was at the forefront of the nationalist movement. This staunchly Ukrainian-speaking region never fully succumbed to the dominance of repressive Moscow.

This is a long-winded history lesson as lead-up to a one-liner joke, but it demonstrates how complicated shifting borders can be:
An old lady upon hearing that her home is now in Ukraine, not Poland, responded: "Thank God, I don't think I could have handled another of those cold Polish winters."

Poking fun at other former Soviet nationalities

Ukrainians enjoy poking fun at other nationalities, just as Americans have a penchant for Polish, Irish, and Aggie jokes. For example, after being introduced to a neighbor from Moldova, the jocular Ukrainian response is, "I'll speak slowly then." Of course, Ukrainians tell lots of jokes about Russians and vice versa. Another ethnic group that was a primary target of many Soviet-era jokes is the Chukchi. These jokes have been described as "Russian Eskimo jokes" because the Chukchi live in easternmost Siberia, in the frozen tundra of Chukotka. While these jokes seem innocuous enough, they are probably not to the Chukchi, because the jokes poke fun not only at their clime but also at their native intelligence.

Georgians were another nationality especially targeted in Soviet times. They were frequently the butt of jokes because of their entrepreneurial habits and desire to make money. While the term "Georgian speculator" had derogatory implications (because speculating, or profiteering, was illegal), these jokes portrayed Georgians as crafty as opposed to unintelligent.

A man wielding a loaded gun hijacked a plane flying to Moscow. "Take me to London!" he demanded. A second hijacker burst into the cockpit with two guns, demanding, "No, fly this plane to Paris!" A Georgian entered the cockpit and announced, "I have a bomb, and this plane is going to land in Moscow as scheduled."

After the plane landed, the first two hijackers were carted off to jail. The Georgian was honored in a special ceremony: "We present to you today this medal and the esteemed title of state hero. But what made you so bold as to demand that the plane fly to Moscow?"

The Georgian replied, "What was I going to do with 5000 carnations in Paris?"

4. Dissident Wit

Jokes describing minor hassles of everyday life provided for good humor, yet they lacked the creative edge and biting sarcasm of the dissident jokes. Dissident jokes are poignant for their treatment of the harsher realities of Soviet life.

Dissident wit reached its pinnacle during the twilight years of the Brezhnev era, reflecting a growing cynicism in the USSR. Corruption was on the rise, and the propaganda machine was weakening. The

Young Pioneer camps, whose goal was communist indoctrination, were losing their once-powerful grip upon Soviet youth. However, to trivialize the danger inherent in dissident jokes is to naively simplify a tense, political environment. A carefully selected audience was paramount, but there was still an element of Russian roulette in the telling. That a person could be sent to the gulag for an improper joke redefined the art of joke telling; the very nature of dissident humor was always improper by Soviet canon. Still, the themes of these jokes were a fair yardstick of the concerns of Soviet citizens.

Among these themes were the difficulties of Jewish and Soviet emigration, communist propaganda and the exaggerated claims of the Soviet leaders, political repression, chronic shortages, corruption, the KGB, the neutron bomb, Chornobyl, and Brezhnev, who was quite senile at the end of his life.

Visas

The term Soviet dissident conjures up several images for me. Familiar names included Aleksandr Solzhenitsyn and Andrei Sakharov, as well as a host of Soviet athletes who defected from the Soviet Union. Another group of dissidents included Soviet citizens seeking against odds to emigrate from the USSR.

Most dissidents were Jews, reports Rabbi Telushkin in his book, *Jewish Humor: What the Best Jewish Jokes Say about the Jews,* further noting that Robert Toth, former *Los Angeles Times* Moscow correspondent, is certain that Jews created the majority of dissident jokes. Telushkin's book is insightful as he presents jokes as a form of instruction. Some of the more popular ones are repeated here.

The following joke reflects the anti-Semitism felt both during the Soviet era and today. OVIR is the Office of Registration and Immigration, where people seeking to emigrate filed their applications. This office also issued internal passports, in which the nationality of the passport holder was recorded: Jews were identified as a nationality distinct from Ukrainian or Russian.

A Ukrainian Jew paid a visit to OVIR. The OVIR official sat at his desk shuffling papers without bothering to look up at his visitor. The bureaucrat began with the usual questions: "Why, specifically, would you like to emigrate from the Soviet Union?" The Jew began, "There are two reasons, really. The first is that, every time my neighbor gets drunk, he bangs on the wall and shouts, 'When the Soviet Union falls, we're going to expel all you Jews!'" At this point, the official looked up at his visitor and interrupted, "Well, I don't think you should worry about that. I'm quite confident that the Soviet Union will be around for many years to come." The Jew replied, "That's the second reason."

This joke has a bittersweet aftertaste in that both Jews and non-Jews wanted to emigrate from the Soviet Union. Soviet Jews recognized that the end of communism would not solve the problem of anti-Semitism. Given the statistics on Jewish emigration since independence, this joke was somewhat prophetic.

Soviet leadership and propaganda

Rabinowich is a common Jewish character in Soviet jokes.

"Rabinowich," a friend asked, "do you read communist newspapers?"

"Yes, of course!" he responded. "How else could I know what a happy life I lead?"

A similar joke recounts that Soviets know the future; it's the past they're not sure of. This is, of course, poking fun at communism with all its promises for the future and its revision of the past. The phrase "Shining Future" referred to a standard piece of communist rhetoric designed to win popular support.

— What was the nationality of Adam and Eve?

— Russian, of course. Why else would they think they were in paradise when they were homeless, naked, and just had one apple for the both of them?

The next two jokes were circulating during Brezhnev's leadership. Variants on the first one were later updated to accommodate more recent Soviet leaders:

All the Soviet premiers were assembled on a train. The train stopped in the middle of Siberia. The locomotive driver announced, "This is how far the tracks have been built."

Stalin shouted, "Kill the driver!"

Khrushchev said, "Let's disassemble the track behind us and use the supplies to build the track ahead of us." (Alternatively, "Let's pardon the crew and bring in a new one.")

Brezhnev said, "Let's close the curtains and imagine the train is moving."

Andropov was asleep and didn't notice anything.

Gorbachev ran out and started shouting, "This train isn't moving! This train isn't moving!"

Jimmy Carter and Leonid Brezhnev died and were preserved in ice. In 1995 they were revived.

Brezhnev opened the Pravda *newspaper and laughed: "Top U.S. communist leaders meeting tomorrow."*

Carter opened The Washington Post *and laughed: "Border dispute between Finland and China."*

This one I have heard told of Western politicians as well:

A famous politician decided to throw a dollar bill out of his private plane.

"Why are you doing that?" his aide asked.

"I wanted to make the person who catches this happy today."

The politician drifted into reverie, then interrupted himself.

"But now I have a better idea," said the politician excitedly. "Why not throw out a stack of bills and please lots of people?"

"Actually," the pilot interjected from the cockpit, "you could please everyone in the country if you threw yourself out."

A placard near the coat check inside the Rada, the Ukrainian Parliament building, reads: Hooks are intended for the express use of members of parliament (or their coats).

Here are examples of the intentionally misunderstood:
A young man is asked, "Why didn't you attend the last communist meeting?"
"Surely, I would have come if I had known it would be the last!"

Three Young Pioneers were asked what good things they had done to help their fellow citizens.
The first boy, Oleh, replied, "I helped an old lady cross the street this morning."
The second boy, Andrey, replied, "I helped Oleh help her across."
The third child answered, "And I helped Andrey and Oleh."
The teacher smiled approvingly but felt obliged to ask, "Now why did it take three strong boys to help one old lady cross the street?"
"Oh," replied the third child, "she didn't want to cross."

Outrageous promises, exaggerated claims
The communists were known for their exaggerated claims, ranging from overstated production figures to outright denial of poverty. Here's an example:
In an effort to bolster his popularity, Mikhail Gorbachev decided to visit an important agricultural community in Ukraine.
"Well, Comrade," Gorby asked one of the farmers, "how did the potatoes do this year?"
"Very well, Comrade President," the farmer replied. "If we piled them high, they would reach God."
"But God does not exist, Comrade Farmer."
"No, Comrade President. Neither do our potatoes."

133

Some of the wittiest jokes stem from the outrageous promises made by the Soviet leaders themselves. One of the better-known jokes about Brezhnev's absurd and grandiose claims is worth repeating here:

At a press conference Brezhnev boldly announced, "By the year 2000, every Soviet citizen will have his own airplane."

A heckler in the crowd interrupted, "What do we all need airplanes for?"

Visibly irritated, the Soviet premier replied, "Idiot! Suppose you are in Moscow and you hear that in Kyiv they have potatoes!"

Rabbi Telushkin offered a variant of the above joke:

Brezhnev was boasting about the Soviet Union's supremacy in space, going so far as to propose that one day every Soviet citizen would receive a ticket to Mars. A heckler in the audience exclaimed, "But I just want one to Vienna."

Finally, a third variant poked fun at Brezhnev's dim wit when the premier announced that the Soviets would outdistance America's space program—the Politburo had voted to send a team to the sun:

"But we will be burned alive," pleaded one cosmonaut.

"And you think we know nothing?" barked Brezhnev. "We are arranging the details so that you will land at night."

Ultimately, it was the deliberate fabrication of history that was one of the distinguishing features of the Soviet Union:

Lenin was planning his first trip to Poland. In the final weeks before departure, the Communist Party Central Committee decided that the greatest gift to the Polish hosts would be a painting of Lenin in Poland. Immediate concern was raised about locating the best artist. The Artists' Union was called upon to hold an emergency meeting. The artist selected for the assignment was visibly concerned. He told the central committee chairman that, while he was appreciative of the honor, he had inadequate time to do the subject justice. The chairman disagreed and said that, if necessary, the artist should forgo sleep until this important assignment was completed.

Three weeks passed. Twenty-four hours before Lenin's departure, the central committee summoned the artist to deliver his masterpiece to party headquarters. The artist arrived, carrying a large, covered canvas. When the painting was unveiled, the committee members were aghast to see a nude man and woman in a compromising position.

"Who is this woman?" the chairman thundered.

"Why, Comrade, that is Mrs. Lenin," the artist replied.

"And who is this man?" demanded the chairman.

"That is Trotsky," the artist replied.

"And where is Lenin?" the chairman roared.

"Lenin is in Poland."

This is a great joke on two levels. Trotsky, of course, was the revolutionary leader later vilified as traitor, and Lenin never visited Poland. This joke makes fun of the communist manipulation of history to continually support its agenda.

Environment
One occasionally hears jokes about irradiated Chicken Kiev or Chornobyl. These are tasteless at best (no pun intended). The actual extent of environmental damage, fostered through years of the catch phrase "production at all costs," is far from known.

The following joke is poignant for its black humor:

—Why did Stalin wear knee boots whereas Lenin's were much shorter?

—Because during Lenin's time, Russia was polluted only up to the ankle.

135

Medical care

An American physician asked his Ukrainian colleague:

—Is it true that there are cases in your country where a patient was treated for one disease, only to have the autopsy reveal another cause of death?

—Absolutely not. All our patients die from the diseases we treat them for.

Internal security

The Hermitage Museum was hosting a grand exhibition. One of the prize Egyptian mummies from the museum's permanent collection was to be included. Unfortunately, this mummy had never been properly dated. The curators met with a team of art historians and archeologists in an effort to decide how best to label this fine specimen. An unannounced visitor arrived late and said that he could ascertain the age. He asked for no interruptions for 30 minutes or so. The team of scholars was perplexed but followed instructions; once the stranger disappeared into the vault, they began asking one another in hushed tones who knew anything about this visitor. There was silence.

Two hours passed, and the man finally emerged; he appeared tired and cross. "This mummy is 3200 years old."

"How did you determine that?" the curators asked in unison.

"Let's just say that, initially, he was not very forthcoming." announced the KGB officer. "But I made him confess."

Chronic shortages and absurd inefficiencies

For years, Westerners heard the tales of long queues, chronic shortages, and absurd inefficiencies of the Soviet system. Here is one of my favorite jokes:

A man is at last able to order a refrigerator, and the clerk tells him that it will be delivered to his apartment in 10 years.

"Will that be in the morning or afternoon?" he asked politely.

"How could it possibly matter? This is 10 years from now!" bellowed the clerk.

"Well, it's just that I have the plumber scheduled for that morning."

Here are a couple more jokes about the frustrations (and absurdities) of the communist era:

Conversation overheard in a Soviet department store:

—Don't you have any shoes here?"

—No, we don't have any furniture here. No shoes is one floor down."

—Is it true that under communism people could order food by phone?

—Yes, but the delivery was by TV.

Corruption and theft

Tales of corruption and crime have soared in the post-independence era, but the Soviet era had its share. Here's a well-known joke:

A man leaves the factory one day slowly pushing a wheelbarrow covered with a piece of cloth. The guard stops him at the gate, lifts up the piece of cloth and, seeing nothing, shrugs and lets the worker pass. The following day the same worker is stopped, but again the guard waves him through. On the third day that this happens, the guard can no longer contain his curiosity. "I don't get it, Comrade. Every day you leave and I know you are stealing something. What is it?"

"Wheelbarrows," replies the worker.

5. Current Jokes: The New Russians

A new category of jokes has emerged since independence. The New Rich/New Russians, are the wealthy citizens prevalent in Russia and Ukraine who have scads of money and revel in flaunting it. The New

Rich and the mafia are considered one and the same by most, and their money is considered tainted in origin.

Two New Russians were strolling down the street. The first one turned to his friend and said, "What good taste you have; your lovely designer tie is just like mine— and how much did you pay for yours?"

The friend coolly boasted, "$1200."

The first man gloated, "Why, you fool, you can buy that same tie down the street for $2000!"

A New Russian walked into a restaurant.
—Can anyone tell me, was I here last night?
—Yes, you were.
—And did I really spend $5000 on drinks?
—Yes, that's true too.
—Thank God! I thought I lost it.

Jennifer Gould, in her 1996 book *Vodka, Tears and Lenin's Angel*, recounts the joke of two New Russians who travel to Spain to locate a birthday gift for another friend back home:

Outside the Prado Museum, the two encountered a huge line. They knew that this queue meant something of great importance was available. An exhibition of Salvador Dali, including some works for sale, was the source of the queue and excitement. Once inside, the New Russians happily located a Dali painting for which they paid $1 million. As they left, one turned to the other and said, "Now we've got the card, let's find the present."

I've heard lots of New Russians and Mercedes jokes.

A New Russian walked into a car dealership and said he wanted to buy a silver Mercedes 600 SEL.

"Excuse me, sir," the salesman asked, "but didn't you buy that same car three days ago?"

"I did," replied the New Russian, "But the ashtray is full."

138

A New Russian was caught weaving down the road at breakneck speed. He was pulled over by a traffic cop.

"Sir, your driver's license, please. You were driving recklessly and speeding. You are clearly intoxicated."

"Not at all. I am sober."

"Let's see if you can pass a breathalyzer test. I'll need you to breathe into this tube."

The New Russian did as instructed. "That's odd," said the policeman. The New Russian had shown no visible reaction to the test. "Let's have you take another test. I want you to close your eyes and stretch out your arms. When I say so, I want you to touch your nose with both index fingers."

Again, the New Russian passed the test.

The puzzled cop had one last test. He drew a line on the pavement with a piece of chalk. "Do you know what to do?"

"Not a problem," said the New Russian. He knelt on the ground, pressed his left index finger against his left nostril, and quickly inhaled the whole chalk line.

A New Russian stumbled around in a daze after smashing up his new Mercedes. He was missing his left arm below the elbow.

"Oh, my Mercedes!" he moaned.

A passerby examining the wreckage responded: "What do you mean, your Mercedes? What about your arm?"

The New Russian looked down at his bloody stump and wailed, "Oh, my Rolex!"

The following is perhaps my favorite New Russian joke these days because it's not especially New Russian at all. Ukrainian (as well as Indonesian) friends have observed the following as expat behavior, which some of them clearly found offensive. But I'll stick with the easy target of New Russians:

A New Russian visited a journalist in his office. The journalist watched in silence as the New Russian propped his feet on the journalist's desk.

"Does this bother you?" asked the New Russian.

"No," said the journalist. "Feel free to put all four of your legs on my desk, if you want."

My little sister heard this one in St. Petersburg. It says a lot about how ordinary people view the New Rich:

A New Russian asked his friend about new places to take a vacation. The friend suggested that an African safari might be a good idea.

"That doesn't sound all that relaxing to me, but maybe I don't know enough about it. What exactly do you do on a safari?"

The friend responded: "Well, first you get to buy a new wardrobe. Then you buy a new jeep. As you drive around, you'll look out the windows on your left side and shoot; then you'll look to the right and shoot."

The first one said, "No, I want to relax on my vacation. You just described my job."

New Russian jokes poke fun not only at the lack of good taste and intelligence of the nouveaux riches, but also at their defamation of sacred things:

A New Russian rushed into a jewelry shop and said, "Look here, brother, I need a cross— a good gold cross, about a kilo in weight— on a heavy gold chain. And I need it quick!"

The shopkeeper was alarmed by the man's behavior, fearing that the New Russian might be carrying a loaded gun. The shopkeeper excused himself to check his vault for an appropriate cross.

The shopkeeper returned quickly: "Let me show you this lovely cross, sir. It is gold, with diamond and emerald inlay, from the 16th century, weighing 650 grams. It belonged to Archbishop..."

The New Russian looked at the cross with disgust and said, "Damn, couldn't you find one without a gymnast on it?"

Themes of corruption accompanied the dissident jokes about bureaucratic inefficiencies. These problems persist today, and so do the jokes, albeit with modern twists:

A Russian businessman met a genie who promised to grant his three wishes.

—I want five million dollars, U.S., in cash.

—You've got it.

—And the top-of-the-line Mercedes sedan, royal blue, tan leather interior...

—Easily done.

—And rid me of the Solntsev mob "protection."

—Are you crazy? I pay the Solntsevs myself!

"Pasha, what do you want to be, when you grow up?"

"A policeman."

"And you, Dima?"

"I want to be a gangster, so I can still play with Pasha."

—Are you aware of what will happen if you present false evidence in court?

—Sure. I'll be driving a fancy new car.

LANGUAGE

Just a few years ago, it was said only peasants and intellectuals spoke Ukrainian. This is clearly changing, and Ukrainian is now the official language of Ukraine. However, the business language of Ukraine remains Russian, and in Ukraine's eastern and more populous half, Russian is more commonly spoken in homes.

The Ukrainian language is not a dialect of the Russian language as Soviets wanted the outside world to believe. Rather, each language penetrated and interacted with the other's syntax and vocabulary. The similarities between Ukrainian and Russian have been compared to those between German and Dutch, although there are different dialects within the Ukrainian language, especially around Galicia (called Halychyna in Ukrainian, the capital of which is Lviv) and Volhyn. These dialects are almost incomprehensible to heartland Russians. In Ukraine's western oblasts ethnic Russians are truly a minority: in Galicia, Volhyn, Rivne, and Transcarpathia, there are fewer than 350,000 ethnic Russians.

Compare this with Left-Bank Ukraine, where the majority of Crimea's population is Russian, as are one million of Kharkiv's 1.6 million residents. Another 4.5 million in Dnipropetrovsk, Donetsk, and Luhansk are Russian, with an additional one million Russians in Odesa and Mykolayiv. Consequently, you will find that Ukrainian and Russian speakers from Left-Bank Ukraine understand each other. A mixed idiom (known as "*surzhyk*" in Ukrainian) is not uncommon in many areas.

Ukrainian is the more lyrical language of the two; it is softer and less guttural than Russian. You'll notice that *tak* means "yes" in Ukrainian, while *da* is Russian; "no" is pronounced *nee* in Ukrainian in contrast to the world-familiar, and often emphatic, *nyet*. Even the untrained ear might reasonably distinguish Ukrainian and Russian. Ukrainian also shares more similarities with Polish, a West Slavic language, than Russian does. The months in Ukrainian (as well as Polish and other Western Slavic languages) are especially poetic: my favorite example is *lystopad*, for November (literally, "leaves are falling"), although October might seem more appropriate. Regardless, Ukrainian months are named after flowers, grasses, ice, and other seasonal features. Russian names for months are much closer to our Latin equivalents (*Yanvar, Fevral, Mart*).

The Eastern Slavic languages (Russian, Ukrainian, and Belorusian) are written in Cyrillic script in contrast to the Western Slavic tongues (Polish, Czech, Slovak, and Serbian), which are written in Latin script. The Southern Slavic languages are split, reflecting the historic differences between Eastern Orthodoxy and Catholicism. Thus, Croatian and Slovenian are in Latin, whereas Serbian, Bulgarian, and Macedonian are in Cyrillic, as is Old Church Slavonic.

English speakers notice that several Russian or Ukrainian block letters resemble English ones, while some in script form resemble others; for example, *d* and *t* in script resemble Latin *g* and *m* (generally drawn with a line over it). The River Prut is one such example. In Cyrillic, it looks like Прут and in cursive, it is closer to *прym*. While students are expected to exhibit good penmanship, there is little appreciation or tolerance for adding unconventional flourishes.

Ukrainians also don't tend to use block letters much; cursive script is the norm.

Especially in Russian, one can see influences from French, which was at one point the preference of the Imperial family and other nobles. Here's a sampling of these influences: *bagazh* (luggage or baggage); *bilet* (ticket); *buro* (bureau or office); *dush* (shower); *passazh* (passageway); *magazin* (store); *pliazh* (beach); *etazh* (floor, level, or story). In *biznes* (say **BEEZnes**), you will recognize a lot of terms derived from their English equivalents. From German, there are fewer words. *Buterbrod*, meaning sandwich (or simply *sandvich*), is one of the more common ones.

Basic Grammar

The articles "the" and "a" do not exist in Ukrainian or Russian. It is therefore necessary, and not difficult, to determine out of context whether someone is referring to "a" table, for example, or "the" table. (This partially helps to explain why native Russian and Ukrainian speakers speaking English often delete and misuse articles.)

In both languages words have gender: masculine, feminine, and neuter. Fortunately, it is almost always possible to identify the gender by the word's ending. It is nonetheless necessary to ensure

YOU'RE SUFFERING FROM
UNFAMILIAR CONSONANT
CLUSTERS AND PALATALIZED
CONSONANTS...

that adjectives agree in gender and case with the noun they are modifying. In Russian and Ukrainian, there are six cases, and the case ending of a particular word will indicate whether it is the subject, the direct object, or indirect object of a particular sentence. In this sense, word order is not as important as it is in English, for example. (Think of, "I threw John the ball." You can't replace "I" with "John" or "the ball" without altering the verb or changing the meaning of the sentence.)

To foreigners, verbs of motion are difficult to grasp, because these verbs differentiate between foot and vehicular travel and whether the action of the verb is uni- or bi-directional. Another characteristic feature of Slavic grammar is the division of verbs according to aspects: perfective forms (often with a prefix) indicate a completed action whereas imperfective indicates an incomplete one.

Finally, Slavic languages have been portrayed unfairly as being difficult to pronounce. Because the Cyrillic alphabet is easily mastered, the main source of this frustration may be the unfamiliar consonant clusters as well as the soft and palatalized consonants, marked by raising the tongue to the roof of the mouth. What is nice about Ukrainian and Russian is that the rules of pronunciation are quite simple (much like Spanish). In Russian, unstressed vowels are short whereas in Ukrainian they are not. Thus, take the word for "beer," which is written the same in both languages. To confuse matters, however, it transliterates as *pyvo* from the Ukrainian and as *pivo* from Russian. In both cases, the first syllable is stressed, making it sound like ***PEEvo*** in Ukrainian and ***PEEva*** in Russian.

Learning any foreign language is a noble, time-consuming goal, and certainly not everyone is capable of doing it well. On the other hand, learning the basics is often not as complicated as some people fear. In Ukraine, it's a matter of practical necessity, and your painstaking efforts to speak the local language will be greatly appreciated, especially because many foreigners fail to go beyond the bare minimum.

Basic Greetings

I recommend that all visitors bring with them Russian and Ukrainian phrasebooks. For Russian, there are many options—I like *Barron's Russian at a Glance*. For Ukrainian, both Lonely Planet and the Rough Guide have good phrasebooks. All are inexpensive, fit easily into a pocket, and handy to have with you wherever you go.

The following list of greetings is essentially provided as an introduction to the basics and to show similarities and differences in the two languages.

Ukrainian	Pronunciation	Russian	Pronunciation	English
Так	*tak*	Да	*da*	Yes
Hi	*nee*	Нет	*nyet*	No
Ъудь ласка	*BoodLASka*	Пожалуйста	*paZHALoosta*	Please

Дякую	*DYAkooyoo*	Спаснбо	*spaSEEba*	Thank you	
Доброго ранку	*DOBroho RANkoo*	Добрый утро	*DObree OOtra*	Good morning	
Добрий день	*DOBriy den*	Добрый день	*DObree dyen*	Good afternoon	
Добрий вечір	*DOBriy VEcheer*	Добрый вечер	*DObree VYEchir*	Good evening	
Добридень	*doBRIden*	Здравствуйте	*ZDRASTvuytye*	Hello	
До побачення	*dopoBAchennya*	Досвндания	*dasveeDAneeya*	Goodbye	
Привіт	*pryVEET*	Привет	*preeVYET*	Hi	
Як справи?	*yak SPRAviy*	Как поживаете	*KAK pazhiVAyete*	How are you?	
Добре	*DOBre*	Хорошо	*kharaSHO*	Fine; good	
Я знаю	*YA ZNAyoo*	Я знаю	*YA ZNAyoo*	I know	
Я не знаю	*YA NE ZNAyoo*	Я не знаю	*YA NEE ZNAyoo*	I don't know	
Я розумію	*YA rozooMEEyoo*	Я понимаю	*YA paneeMAyoo*	I understand	
Я не розумію	*YA NE rozooMEEyoo*	Я не понимаю	*YA NEE paneeMYoo*	I don't understand	
Скільки коштуɛ?	*SKEELkyKOSHtooye*	Сколко стоит?	*SKOLka STOeet*	How much does it cost?	

The familiar Russian *do svidaniya* (say ***dasveeDANeeya***) and the Ukrainian *do zustrychy* (say ***doZOOstreechee***) and *do pobachennya* all mean "until we meet again." *Pryvit* or *privyet*, meaning "Hi," is reserved for friends, not strangers.

General Advice on Language

Learn the Cyrillic alphabet, and this means before you go. You can learn it on the plane if you like. It is really not as hard as you think. Most people learn Russian first, then Ukrainian.

There are a few hitches, so start with the ones you already know:
A is A
K is K
M is M
E is E or Ye
Ë is Yo (and is always the stressed syllable)

O is O
T is T

These are a bit tricky:
В is V
И is ee as in *meet*
Й is y as in *yes*
Р is R (and it's rolled—rumor has it that Stalin couldn't trill his
very well)
С is S as in *Siberia*
Н is N as in *no* or *nyet*
У is oo as in *boot*

These are the easy weird ones; some have Greek influences:
Б is B as in *borshch*
Г is G as in *girl* (H in Ukrainian)
Д is D as in *doctor*
Л is L as in *lamp*
П is P as in *Paul* or *Pavel*
Ф is F as in *football*
Я is Ya

At last, the weird ones:
Х is kh, like the ch in Scottish *loch* or German *ich bin* …
Ц is ts as in *tsar*
Ч is ch
Ш is sh
Щ is shch as in *cash check*, *fresh cheese*
Ы is y as in *Daddy* (this letter does not appear in Ukrainian)
Э is e, used only as the initial letter in words
Ю is Yoo

In Russian there are two silent signs; Ukrainian has only the soft
sign:

Ъ is the hard sign
Ь is the soft sign

Then, put them in order:

А Б В Г Д Е Ё Ж З И Й К Л М Н О П Р С Т У Ф Х Ц Ч Ш Щ Ъ Ы Ь Э Ю Я
(The highlighted letters don't appear in the Ukrainian alphabet.)

Finally, Ukrainian variants:

А Б В Г Ґ Д Е Є Ж З И І Ї Й К Л М Н О П Р С Т У Ф Х Ц Ч Ш Щ Ю Я Ь
(The highlighted letters aren't in the Russian alphabet.)

A Few Notes on Ukrainian Variants

The difference between the Ukrainian Г and Ґ is that the former is more like an h, the latter (which is far less common) like a g.

И, І, Ї and Й are pronounced as follows:

И is like i in *bit*
І is like ee in *beet*
Ї is like yea in *yeast*
Й is like y in *yet* (and always pronounced strongly, even at the end of a word).

In Е and Є, the former is like e in *yes*, the latter like ye in *yes*.

Common Signs

Once in Ukraine, you will find that even a basic ability to read the alphabet will help you with common signs. You will frequently encounter these basic words:

мет о

This is the metro. Once inside, you'll notice that the entrances have signs designating вхід (or вход in Russian); the exits will be designated by ыхід (or ыход in Russian).

ресторан
Restoran (the famous Pectopah to non-Cyrillic readers).

ремонт

Remont (say *rayMONT*) is a general word for repair or renovation that you will frequently encounter. If you ask why something is closed, this is the likely answer. Like *rynok* below, this word is used by many foreigners in English conversation to discuss the ongoing reconstruction of roads and apartments.

рінок (or рынок in Russian)

The *rynok* (say *RYnok*) is the farmer's market. Discussions on food and shopping in latter chapters will describe the *rynok* in better detail.

Learning to read only a few basic words will make your life easier from the start. You'll recognize these words in the signs around town designating a particular establishment. One thing many foreigners new to these Slavic languages appreciate is that, in Ukraine, you won't be overwhelmed by signs such as "Try our fresh loaves, baked daily." If you can read the word for "bread," you're in good shape. Other useful words to learn early on include: coffee, milk, juice, vegetables, fruit, flowers, shoe or watch repair, key (as in "Keys made here"), university, institute, hospital, hotel, and church. (Some of these listed are similar to their English equivalents, which makes them easier to recognize if you are just starting out.)

A Digression: Anthony Burgess

Did you ever wonder where Anthony Burgess got his *Clockwork Orange* slang? He adapted it from Russian, so that the slang wouldn't date or localize the book to a particular era or region. Maybe you recall the words droog, bog (say *boag*), moloko, kravvy, horrorshow, or grazny. They are from Russian words for friend, God, milk, blood, good, and dirty. "Good," however, isn't *horrorshow*. It's more like *KHARashow*, the initial *kh* pronounced like *ch* in the Scots *loch*.

A Handful of Useful Words

можна/можно (say *MOzhna*)

Mozhna means "possible," as in "Is it possible?" This word is used a lot for "Please" as in "*Mozhna sche pyvo?*" (May I have another beer?) The division of what is allowable versus what is forbidden is an important cultural distinction. For example, Westerners often believe that anything not forbidden is allowed—the proverbial glass is half full. For Ukrainians anything not explicitly allowed is probably forbidden. *Nemozhna* should be learned alongside *mozhna*. This means "it is forbidden or impossible."

Pyvo is "beer." It's Піво (say *PEEvo* with a long "o") in Ukrainian, and Пиво (say *PEEva*) in Russian.

Similarly, вода, meaning "water" in both languages, is pronounced *voDA* in Ukrainian and *vaDA* in Russian.

Сік (say *seek* in Ukrainian) and сок (*sok* in Russian) mean "juice".

Хліб (say *khleeb* in Ukrainian) and Хлеб (*khleb* in Russian) mean "bread".

A mixture of Russian and Ukrainian words or phrases you are likely to hear include пашли (say *pashLEE*) or поэкали (say *paYEKalee*), both used for "Let's go." The first is on foot, the second by vehicle.

Пока (say *paKA*) is slang for "See you later."

Ладно (say *LADna*) is slang for "Okay."

Нормално (say *NORmalna*) or ничего (say *neecheVO*, literally meaning "nothing") is also common.

Иди суда or идите суда (say *eeDEE suDA* or *eeDEEtye suDA* for the plural form) means "Come here."

Понятно (*PaNYATna*) means "(It is) understood." Male speakers may say понял (*PONyel*) for "I understood," while female speakers will say поняла (*panyaLA*). The "a" at the end of a verb indicates both past tense and that the subject is female.

In Ukrainian, Що це (say *Shcho tse?*) means "What's this (or that)?"—and is often said while pointing. In Russian, for Что это?, say *Shto eta?* These are always handy to know in any language. In both Ukrainian and Russian, there is no present tense of the verb "to be." Since there are no articles, the response you get will begin with *Tse* or *Eta* meaning "This is ..." and followed by the noun, for example *telefon*. You also might hear the more emphatic Что это такое? (with *takoye* at the end). It is translated as "What the heck is this?"

In Ukrainian, the words for "black" and "red" may be confusing at first; чорний (say *CHORnee*) is black; червоний (*cherVOnee*) is red. In Russian, чёрный (*CHORny*) is black and красный (*KRASny*) is red. Thus, Red Army Street is Chervonoarmyiska vulytsia in Ukrainian and Krasnoarmeiskaya ulitsa in Russian.

Finally, there may be days when you have to deal with a кошмар (say *koshMAR*). This means "nightmare." But don't dwell on it.

ADDRESSING PEOPLE

The old days of *tovarish* (say *taVARish*) meaning "Comrade" are over. Don't revert to it; it's considered rude now.

Gospidin and *Gospozha* are Russian for Mr and Ms; *Pan* is Ukrainian for Mr; *Pani* is for Mrs. (Rarely will you hear *Pana* used for Miss.) *Pani ta Panove* is the plural form used for Ladies and Gentlemen. In written correspondence, "Dear Mr Chomiak" is not used. You will instead write "Respected Mr Chomiak."

The Use of Patronymics

Tradition has been to use the first name and patronymic in work situations to show respect, but without the formality of saying, for example, Ms Marchuk. At the same time, this practice wasn't as informal as simply calling her by her first name.

Ukrainians are quick to correct outsiders who make reference to patronymics as middle names. The patronymic is derived from their father's first name; it is placed behind their own first name.

The -*ovich* or -evich (or -*ivich* in Ukrainian) in a man's patronymic is loosely translated as "son of," whereas -*evna* or -*ovna* (or -*ivna* in Ukrainian) for women indicates "daughter of."

In this way, my friend Pavel, the son of Valentin, becomes Pavel Valentinovich Ustimenko; his sister is Olga Valentinivna Ustimenko. (If their grandfather's first name was Konstantin, their father would be named Valentin Konstantinovich Ustimenko.) Ustimenko is the family name or surname.

Patronymics are tricky for foreigners, who don't tend to use them much. Ukrainians know that we have no equivalent form, but it's a gesture that will be appreciated if you use it.

Ukrainian and Russian Name Equivalents

The following list includes a selection of common first names in Ukrainian, followed by their Russian variants. Be aware, however, that there are different transliteration systems in English. Because both the Russian and Ukrainian alphabets have more letters than English, there isn't a one-to-one correlation, despite certain Cyrillic letters that translate as two letters and Щ which is transliterated as *shch* (or, in another transliteration scheme, as *sch*). (Throughout this text I have omitted soft signs, whereas some sources transliterate them with the symbol '.)

For the name Andrew, you will find many transliterations such as Andriy, Andrii, Andrei, Andrey, and even Andrij in English. The real difference between the two languages in this case is in pronunciation, not transliteration. For example, Ukrainian approximates *AhnDREE*, whereas Russian is *AhnDRAY*.

Some i's in Russian (but not all) are transliterated as y's from the Ukrainian, for example, Borys, Iosyf, Maksym, Nykyta, and Osyp are Ukrainian variants for the names Boris, Iosif, Maksim, Nikita, and Osip. The Russian variants are far more common to English readers. Similarly, g's in Russian are h's in Ukrainian. Thus you will see Bohdan/Bogdan, Ihor/Igor, Oleh/Oleg, and Olha/ Olga.

The "o" appears more often in Ukrainian names than in Russian:

Oleksiy, Aleksei
Oleksandr, Aleksandr
Oleksandra, Aleksandra
Olena, Elena
Dmytro, Dmitry
Evhen, Evgeny (pronounced and sometimes transliterated as
Yevgeny or **Yevgenii**.)
Hryhoriy, Georgy
Mykhailo, Mikhail
Mykola, Nikolai
Pavlo, Pavel
Petro, Petr (pronounced **Pyotr**)
Serhiy, Sergei
Vasyl, Vasily
Volodymyr, Vladimir

Refrain from addressing Ukrainians by their English equivalents, for example, Petro as Peter, or Olena as Helen or Elaine, and so on, unless they prefer it and tell you so.

Ukrainian and Russian Surnames
Traditionally, the ending of one's surname indicated one's nationality. For example, many Georgian names end in -vili, Armenian in -ian, and Russian in -ov (transliterated as -off or -ow in French and German spellings). Surnames ending in -sky or -y (with their various alternates such as -ski) often indicate Russian or Polish nationalities. An -a at the end of a name designates the person is female, for example, Goncharova or Gorskaya. But not all names change to the feminine form, for example, those ending in –enko, which is a common ending for many Ukrainian surnames. Think of the Ukraine's most celebrated poet and artist, Taras Shevchenko. Another common ending for Ukrainian surnames is –ko, as in the famous Klichko boxing brothers.

Other common endings for Ukrainian surnames are -*uk* or -*iuk*, such as Kravchuk, the surname of independent Ukraine's first president, and the Burliuk brothers, who were famous Ukrainian artists around World War I.

you and You

Both Ukrainian and Russian (like other European languages) have two forms for "you." The familiar *ti* or *ty* is always singular, and *vi* or *vy* is both the formal and the plural form.

Foreigners need to be aware of these distinctions; to be on the safe side, use the formal "you" for all business dealings unless instructed otherwise. When you slip up, don't worry. Ukrainians will understand, but they also appreciate sensitivity to their cultural and linguistic traditions.

Diminutives as a Form of Affection

Pick up a copy of a Russian literary classic like *Anna Karenina,* and you will see that diminutives are exceedingly common for family and friends. Aleksandr or Aleksandra becomes Sasha; Alla, Allochka; Evgeny, Zhenia; Olena, Olenka; and Pavel, Pasha. But this is just a start. I've seen as many as 20 variants for the name Maria. Masha is just the first of them.

Ukrainians don't seem to object to foreigners calling them by their diminutives, because after all these are an indication of affection. My sisters Catherine and Elizabeth have never had English nicknames, but Ukrainian friends have no qualms about calling them Cathy and Betsy. Ukrainians don't view calling friends by their nicknames or diminutives as presumptuous, as long as the form is used in their native language. In addition to first names, diminutives for some nouns often designate a smaller version; *stol,* or table, becomes *stolik. Dochka,* derived from *doch,* means "little daughter," but in a particularly affectionate way. The Spanish language has similar diminutives for degrees of size and affection: for example "very small," and "very, very small," are endearing forms of "small." The word for "water" in both Ukrainian and Russian is *voda*; the diminutive becomes *vodka*. But *vodichka*, not *vodka*, is the term commonly used to indicate "a little water" as in "I'll have a little water."

Chapter Four

SOCIALIZING,
FOOD, AND DRINK

UKRAINIAN HOSPITALITY

Ukrainians are generous people and gracious hosts. It is a real treat
to be invited into a Ukrainian home where guests are treated like
royalty, and an even greater compliment to be invited to sit around
the kitchen table. Be prepared to remove your shoes upon entering
a friend's home. To keep their apartments clean, most hosts will
provide you with a pair of slippers called *tapochky*.

When invited to dinner in someone's home, casual attire is
generally accepted. For your part, bringing a small gift is customary
and, in my opinion, mandatory. Acceptable gifts include alcohol,
juice, chocolates, cake, or a bouquet of flowers. If you bring flowers,

make sure that the number is odd; even numbers are reserved for funerals. It is also entirely appropriate to give flowers to other men's wives, just don't get carried away. Perfumed hand creams or a bar of fancy soap are a welcome treat for your Ukrainian hostess. If there is a child, it is customary to bring a small gift as well. Gum or candy is generally appropriate; by all means if you have a souvenir from your own country, this will be well received.

On certain occasions, you may want to give a small gift other than food, drink, or flowers. This small token of friendship doesn't have to be expensive, and probably should not be. In the old days foreign cigarettes were welcome, now Western brands are available everywhere and outsell domestic tar. Instead of giving something that is available in Ukraine, souvenirs from your home state or country, such as postcards, pins, and key chains are a good idea. Likewise, in business settings, a pen or other trinket with your company's insignia is always appreciated. I carried with me a stash of lapel pins displaying American and Ukrainian flags, which I doubt were worn much but were well received. Indian arrowheads were always a hit and especially appropriate because my home state was Indian Territory until 1907.

One thing I've always enjoyed about Ukraine is that you won't find many homes, or even some parts of homes, that you might call unliveable. Homes that I've visited, and by this I mean apartments and occasionally *dachas*, are eminently liveable, lived-in, comfortable, and sometimes a bit disorderly. Furnishings vary; the luckier homes may have a piano, and bookshelves are generally prominent and well stocked. I've encountered several homes with a wall-sized photograph resembling the backdrop of a late-night talk show that never changes regardless of the season. Rugs hanging on walls are both decorative and serve as insulation. I especially love that the furniture and space have multiple purposes: the living room or den becomes an extra bedroom, thanks to all those amazing chairs—to say nothing of the couches—that convert into beds; the writing table is also the dining table, and so on.

Ukrainian homes reflect the personalities of their owners, which is to say that they are unpretentious, practical, and adaptive. Your hosts, or more likely hostesses, are generally unapologetic if their floors are less than well-scrubbed. The constraints of limited space and the need for adaptable uses means that the homes are generally neat and ready for the next transition.

In the Ukrainian kitchen, guests are treated like family—or at the very least as intimate friends. This point should not be taken lightly: in a culture accustomed to communal living, privacy and trust are at a premium. In the Soviet era, one learned to be very selective in choosing friends; only with your most trusted friends could you sit in the kitchen and speak a little more openly if you dared.

When visiting friends, you should be prepared to accept all food and drink that is offered. Flatly turning down food may be considered rude. Ukrainians don't seem to understand vegetarians, dieters, or alcoholics, so if any of these applies to you, you will need to proceed gingerly. Sometimes people get around this by saying that they have an allergic reaction. Ukrainians do understand the concept of *vranyo*, or white lie. They are known to fib under certain circumstances so as not to offend their guests.

At the dinner table take small helpings, as you will be encouraged to take more later. Also, be careful when complimenting your hosts' belongings, as you might be offered the admired object.

When you are invited into someone's home, amateur entertainment is sometimes part of the evening's festivities. Occasionally your hosts will ask you to sing something, but it is more likely that your female hostesses will perform for you.

DRINKING CHOICES

Water Safety

I recommend drinking bottled water, but this can be expensive and heavy to carry; if you live in a multistory walk-up and try hauling a box of bottles once a week, you may start to consider boiling water or filtering systems. There are various purification systems available, including hand-held pumps, some of which can remove the parasite giardia, as well as other impurities.

If you drink or cook with tap water, it is recommended that you boil it for at least 10 minutes. It is highly improbable that you can fully avoid tap water, because your friends will offer you tea, or you will have food and drink from a restaurant. One reason cited, as far back as the 15th century, for the growing consumption of beer is that people were worried about water quality in Kyiv.

People often ask about present levels of radiation and residual safety issues related to Chornobyl's tragedy. For most of the country, the larger concern now is that the Dnipro and other water sources were contaminated by the wanton disregard for environmental pollution during the Soviet era. Many radioactive pollutants have leached out of the soil and have contaminated water sources. Obviously, growing crops in some regions is extremely hazardous. Foreign embassies monitor changes in radioactive levels and regularly perform tests for their foreign personnel living in Ukraine. Air quality continues to test within acceptable ranges.

If you are dining out, you may wish to order water. Specify *mineralna voda bez gazu*, meaning "mineral water without gas," if you mean "still," like Evian. Or say *mineralna voda gazovana*, meaning "with gas," if you want fizzy water like Perrier. You might ask for Evian or Perrier by name, and the waiter can recommend an equivalent European substitute that is not local or of former Soviet Union origin.

If you are attending a Ukrainian dinner, more than likely the water placed on the table will be one of the mineral waters produced in the former Soviet Union. These are gassy, and some have a decidedly salty taste. Georgia is reputed to have the best mineral water, and it has many spas. (*Gruzia* is the name for Georgia.) Within Ukraine, the Carpathian spas also produce sulfurized mineral water. Among the best waters are Lavtusa, Morshenka, and Hutsulschina.

People frequently warn against accepting drinks with ice cubes because the water used to make the ice is suspect. Although iced drinks still aren't common; the few cubes floating in a McDonald's drink are fine because purified water is used. You should ask for drinks without ice if you think the cubes are frozen tap water. Also watch for unwashed fruit and vegetables; only eat them if you are confident that they were properly cleaned.

When in doubt, remember the saying, "Boil it, cook it, peel it, or forget it."

Milk or Moloko: Local or UHT

When I lived in Moscow in 1992 and bought local pasteurized milk, it always soured within 48 hours or so. I later learned that when you buy milk, even so-called pasteurized milk, you must boil it first. In Ukraine you can buy milk from a *hastronom* or from a milk store. *Hastronom* (*gastronom* in Russian) means a state grocery store, which differentiates it from a Western-styled grocery store. A milk store is really a dairy store because they also sell farmer's cheese, hard cheese, eggs, and *kefir* (a tasty yogurt drink). One drawback is that milk stores smell like soured milk upon entering. You might also occasionally find milk for sale from stands set up in the streets. It is sold in plastic bags, and I know of no foreigner who buys it. If you choose to, I would recommend boiling it immediately.

Not surprisingly, some advise viewing all dairy products as suspect. I usually purchased the ultra-pasteurized milk because it was widely available and had a long shelf life (about six months if unopened), but I bought my eggs, cheese, and sour cream at the *rynok,* which also carries a wide selection of fruits, vegetables, meats, honey, and cut flowers.

UHT milk (ultra-pasteurized at high temperatures) is common throughout Europe and in the larger Ukrainian cities. It is great to keep on hand for cooking, cereal, or coffee, as it tastes so much better than powdered milk. Parmalat is a Dutch-Ukrainian joint venture that also produces many of the fruit juices in cartons, but many brands are now available. It is also easy now to find both whole and low-fat milk.

Smetana is a lightly soured cream. It is commonly used in sweet and savory soups, in sauces, dressings, marinades, and desserts. It is used as a filling in both soft dough dumplings and fritters.

When you buy eggs, you will typically say *desyatok yaiyets,* which is asking for 10 eggs.

If you want to buy cheese (*sir*), ask for a kilo or a *polkilo* (say *polkilO* in Russian) or *piv kila* (in Ukrainian) if you want half. You can also ask for several hundred grams. This also applies to buying sausages at the *rynok*.

In the *rynok*, you can sample items before you buy. Simply ask, *Chy mozhna sprobuvatu*? (Is it possible for me to sample?)

Tea

Chai appears to be a universal term for tea in much of the world, and tea is quite popular in Ukraine, especially Georgian tea. The Carpathians are known for their *chornika* tea made from bilberries or huckleberries grown in the mountains.

The samovar (literally, self-boiler) has Russian origins, and while they seem most common today on trains, you will see them available for sale. Do be aware that any items produced before 1945 are not permitted to leave the country. One friend who left several years ago still has two samovars in Ukraine!

The electric samovar speaks for itself, but otherwise the samovar is filled with coals. Very strong tea is steeped, then diluted with water. The teapot is placed on top and kept warm, and hot water is dispensed through the spigot. The metal tea-glass holder, called a *pidstakannyk* (*podstakannik* in Russian), meaning "under the glass," is generally made of silver and holds a simple glass, a *stakan*, filled with tea. You will still find these in use on the trains and at the stations.

161

Tea with lemon and lots of sugar is most common, but preserves are also a popular sweetener. Tea is never served with milk. Also, tea is served not during but after a meal. If you want it served during a meal, you must specify: *seichas i potom*. This is Russian for "now (literally, right away) and later."

Kofe and Kava

These are the Russian (say *KOFyeh*) and Ukrainian (say *KAva*) terms for coffee. Much coffee in this country is Nescafé or some similar powder. If you buy instant coffee for home or your office, be forewarned: not all instant coffees are created equal. Coffee is typically served very sweet (and without milk) in demitasse cups.

In almost all business meetings, you will be served instant coffee; sometimes you will be asked to choose between coffee and tea. Cookies or chocolates will very likely be served; other occasions may call for open-faced sandwiches of cheese, sausage (*kovbasa* in Ukrainian or *kolbasa* in Russian), or salmon roe. Vodka or *konyak* (which is brandy) are frequently paired with these sandwiches.

For your part, it's a sign of good hospitality to offer at least a few cookies when serving coffee or tea. When serving alcohol, it's mandatory.

Soft Drink Competition and Boxes of Juice

Coca-Cola and Pepsi have battled it out in Ukraine as elsewhere, and many outdoor umbrellas seem to advertise one or the other. Pepsi came to Russia early and arranged a business deal with Stolichnaya Vodka, but Coca-Cola is stronger in Ukraine today. The soft-drink company built a large bottling plant outside Kyiv, and Coca-Cola, Sprite, Fanta, Coke Lite are all widely available.

Many companies now produce a variety of juices in paper cartons (or Tetrapak). They are pricey but very good. Apple, orange, peach, pear, cherry, banana, pineapple, strawberry-kiwi, passionfruit, mango, and blackberry are among the flavors available. In restaurants or

SOCIALIZING, FOOD, AND DRINK

bars, you will ask for *sik* (or *sok* in Russian), meaning juice. Are you ready for the choices? Learn your favorites and the most common choices:

apelsinoviy is orange, not apple!

yablochniy is apple.

ananasoviy is pineapple (like *ananas* in French).

tomatniy is tomato, even though the word for "tomato" is *pomidor*.

vinogradniy is grape.

Zero Tolerance

Whatever you may have heard about excessive drinking and alcoholism in Ukraine, don't even think about drinking and driving. There is zero tolerance, meaning that just one drink before driving is too much. As in other parts of Europe, this credo is taken very seriously in Ukraine. Professional drivers will not touch a drop of liquor during work hours, and foreigners must designate a driver if drinking is to be part of their evening entertainment. Locals and expatriates alike use drivers, official and gypsy cabs, and public transport after they have indulged in any drinking.

A deputy's son once remarked, after being arrested for drinking and driving, that the arresting police were less easy to bribe than in the old days. He got off easily nonetheless; he was only detained for three hours. As we had earlier attended the same party, every one of us recalled that he had drunk very little. But that isn't the point: Zero Tolerance is Zero Tolerance.

The traffic police in Ukraine do not need a reason to pull you over. Don't risk getting randomly stopped after drinking even a small amount of alcohol.

A rare thing happened when some friends hailed a gypsy cab in Odesa late one night and discovered very quickly that the cab driver was drunk. Luckily the cab ran out of gas whereupon my friends escaped on foot! (More on gypsy cabs and other transport in the chapter *Settling Down*.)

Vodka and Horilka Origins

No cultural assessment of Ukraine can be complete without an examination of the role that vodka has played throughout history. Both Polish and Russian historians have asserted that their respective homeland was the birthplace of vodka; their argument is essentially academic.

In Russia the origins of vodka date back to the Middle Ages, and by 1478 an official monopoly on the production of grain spirits had been established. While there were numerous names for alcoholic beverages, the term "vodka" was not in usage until significantly later. In its earliest usage, vodka as a generic term referred to medicinal remedies and fragrances; this is one of the reasons cited for drinking vodka neat and in small gulps. One would never sip medicine or dilute it with water. The term "vodka" in the sense of drink presumably did not appear in Russia until the late 19th century, and then it was the lower classes who popularized its usage. Vodka (in this word the *d* is pronounced more like a *t* and the *o* is long) is actually a diminutive for *voda*, meaning "water." *Vodka*, then, is "a little water," and the diminutive form implies an improved version of one of life's staples.

Wine and mead were well documented early on, and wine in many cases was a catchall for both traditional wine and grain spirits. Both grain wine and burning wine, among others, referred to vodka. The adjective "burning" refers to the distillation process and to the fact that the alcohol could be set alight. The Ukrainian word for "vodka" is *horilka* (say *horEELka* or *gorEELka* in Russian), meaning "flaming." In Ukraine you will hear both *horilka* and vodka.

Vodka in Russia was primarily distilled from rye. Pokhlebkin and other apologists for Russian vodka maintain that anything else is inferior and can lead to drunkenness, alcoholism, and hangovers. Nevertheless, the starch used need not be grain; hence in Poland and Ukraine, depending on local availability, we find vodkas also made from wheat, sugar beet, or potatoes.

A (Marxist) Snapshot of Vodka

Gorbachev's well-publicized attempts to reduce Soviet alcoholism failed. His error was in attacking vodka as the source of alcoholism, when it was merely a scapegoat. The difficulty, of course, is that the causes for excess alcohol consumption were many—and far more elusive than vodka. Rampant alcohol abuse reflected deep-rooted ills of society: mass disillusionment and demoralization, the Communist Party's diminished focus on education, and a contradictory, even hypocritical, stance toward alcohol usage. A popular joke around this time described the plight of a man who had finally lost all patience with Gorbachev. He announced to his friends that he was off to kill Gorby. His friends applauded the boldness of his gesture, but he quickly returned to them with a very sad face. Alas, the queue had been too long.

By attacking drunkenness in standard top-down, Communist Party fashion, the social and economic roots of alcoholism were essentially driven underground during this period. The production of *samohon* (moonshine), *samagon* in Russian, increased; this was dangerous because improper distillation always contributes substantially to alcohol-related deaths. In the wake of Gorbachev's campaign, there was a run on sugar, which is used in many home brews. The only good news from this campaign was that violent crime dropped; it quickly rose after the campaign was abandoned.

Evidence suggests that proper alcohol distilling in Russia started in the monasteries, as it had in Catholic Europe. The Church probably wanted the vodka monopoly, just as in Kyivan Rus the salt monopoly was held by the Church, specifically by Kyiv's Monastery of the Caves. By the late 15th century, however, vodka distilling quickly became concentrated in the hands of a secular state monopoly. This no doubt contributed to the Church's negative attitudes toward the "devil's poison."

In the 16th century, "tsar's taverns" were introduced. Innkeepers were responsible for both the production and sale of vodka. Essentially,

165

they rented the monopoly. Annual receipts were handed over to the government, but the innkeepers were otherwise free of controls. Large-scale corruption, bribery, theft, and drunkenness arose from the unholy union of production and sale. Historians argue that these traits—often considered "Russian"—were not characteristic before the advent of vodka distilling. Selling vodka on credit also led people into debt and semi-enslavement. At the same time, this system drove up prices without improving quality. "Tavern revolts" erupted in the mid-17th century, and this system was soon abolished.

In 1705, Peter the Great decided that the state's priority during the Northern War was to obtain the highest possible profit from vodka sales. His solution was to reintroduce the earlier system despite its ruinous consequences. He also required that innkeepers pay in advance, thus obtaining money to fund his fleet regardless of revenues, which he anticipated would rise. The system only lasted 10 years because Peter feared the people couldn't tolerate more.

Peter the Great was also known for the drinking punishments he enforced wherein the offender had to publicly drink more than a liter of vodka—vomiting, alcohol poisoning, and public mockery were the desired results. Peter waged a war against the Old Believers in the Orthodox Church who espoused sobriety; he also handed out free vodka to soldiers, sailors, shipyard and road workers, and builders. His rule serves as an example of the ways in which the government's manipulation of vodka policy and reliance upon vodka sales effected significant social change.

By the late 19th century, vodka consumption distinguished Russia's social classes. For the Russian peasant, who often received free vodka, little had improved since the Middle Ages. The problem then as now involved the manner of consumption (cups of vodka gulped while standing and without food) and inferior quality.

After the October Revolution of 1917, the new regime banned alcohol. This was in response to the frightening degree of drunkenness witnessed during the revolution and in the preceeding years.

After 1924, a new state monopoly limited the alcoholic strength of vodka to 20% (by volume). During World War II, Stalin issued vodka as part of the troops' regular rations. He had observed that vodka appeared to diminish the sensitivities of his terrified subjects during the Great Terror; now he hoped to bolster confidence during wartime. After the war, massive alcoholism surfaced, primarily among the working class. Stalin continued to maintain very low vodka prices as a bribe to his workers. A delicate balance was needed to deaden their consciousness without destroying their ability to work. (It's especially desirable to have sober armed forces.) Further, vodka sales then as now were a critical source of state revenues.

Between 1917 and 1937, disapproval of drunkenness marked a true communist. After World War II, official opposition to drunkenness was maintained; yet the government was attacking the consequences of the nation's moral decay and never its underlying causes.

In the wake of Gorbachev's failed anti-alcoholism campaign, critics argue that what is needed today is comprehensive alcohol education. Drinking without eating and drinking adulterated products, especially *samohon*, is deleterious and potentially suicidal. Genuine help must be available for those who need or request it, and product quality must be maintained as high as possible—by the state. If it does not, the populace is at risk. Further, if prices are too high, people will make their own illicit home brews, which is even more dangerous. Without these measures, the prophetic wisdom of the popular saying, "More people are drowned in a glass than in the ocean," is inescapable.

Vodka Traditions and Toasts

Vodka traditions are an irrefutable part of Slavic culture. Vodka serves as the ideal complement to the salty, spicy, and fatty cuisines of northern and eastern Europe. Nevertheless, Russia and Ukraine share mixed attitudes toward vodka: there is both pride in their drinking traditions and embarrassment due to excess consumption.

Ukrainian and Russian vodkas are widely available throughout Ukraine; prices are quite cheap by world standards and quality varies. New, high-quality vodkas have been appearing to compete with the best foreign labels. Some vodkas have fancy designs etched on the back of the bottle that are visible through the glass (and clear liquid). Others are bottled in ceramic figurines wearing traditional Ukrainian costumes.

Be aware that bottles may be sealed with a foil cap, a standard bottle cap, or screw top. Some people say not to touch any but the screw tops. In all cases, pay especial attention if you buy vodka from kiosks—I've heard of cases where bottles were tampered with and refilled with alcohol of inferior quality. Lower grades of Soviet grain alcohol contain trace amounts of ether; in cases of excess consumption, this impurity can lead to blindness. Given the above hazards, some people prefer to buy, at higher prices, imported vodkas from Finland, Sweden, and Poland, widely available in Ukraine. When you are invited to Ukrainian banquets, however, you will more likely be drinking Ukrainian *horilka* (or Russian vodka).

In Ukraine, *horilka* (and sometimes *konyak*) is typically served throughout the duration of the meal. A Cossack tradition was to sometimes serve warm brandies and vodkas. Nowadays, vodka is chilled and drunk neat in small clear glasses.

Flavored vodkas are also popular in Ukraine. *Nalivka* is alcohol infused with fruit; because it's so sweet, its potency can creep up on you. Some say that these first appeared to mask the impurities. Regardless, Ukraine's specialty is *horilka z pertsem* (pepper-flavored vodka).

There are many traditions associated with vodka drinking, some of which approximate superstitions. Some say you must leave your glass resting on the table while another person refills it. To lift the glass then or before all glasses are poured is considered bad luck. Others say it's less bad luck than bad manners, when I thought bringing the glass closer to the server was the polite thing to do!

Filling the glass more than two-thirds full is the mark of boorishness. You should not refill your own glass, and never pour from a bottle backhanded—this is very insulting. It is also mandatory to serve at least a bite of food when serving alcohol. Serving only drinks without a bite is a serious breach of etiquette.

When toasts are being made, you cannot piggyback a second toast on someone else's. Two toasts means two separate shots of vodka, not one. Along these lines, guests are often asked (or expected) to give toasts at dinner, so you should be prepared in advance to do so. This applies to both business and personal situations.

Many foreigners know that *na zdorovya* means "to health," but this is really more appropriate for food. *Za vashe zdorovya* (Ukrainian) or *Za vashe zdarovye* (Russian) literally means "to your health," and this is considered the better toast where alcohol is involved.

A smattering of common toasts:
Smachnoho—Bon appetit! Very Ukrainian!
Za druziv—To friends.
Za vas—To you.
Remember *dyakuyu* and *spasibo* mean "Thanks" in Ukrainian and Russian, respectively.

Never drink before the first toast is made. Typically, after any toast, guests clink their glasses together, then drink their shot at the same time. Don't clink your glass if your drink is non-alcoholic. The first shot is usually drunk all in one gulp, although women can get by with nursing their glass from the very start. A whistling sound, a loud breath, or even the smelling of one's sleeve are common immediate reactions followed by the salty bite of pickle, herring, or other appetizer. Subsequent shots are not necessarily downed in one gulp, which is good news if there are many toasts.

If you intend to stop drinking early, you shouldn't start. This is a courtesy issue. With that said, people who don't drink are suspect.

Frankly, despite the problems associated with alcohol abuse, alcoholism (like vegetarianism and dieting) is little understood in Ukraine. The key to drinking vodka is to follow the example of Ukrainians. This means eating between every toast. There will be plenty of food to sample. Traditionally, the third toast is to the women present, and the men will stand up during this toast.

Aside from banquets and dinners, you should recall the tradition of drinking in groups of at least three people. Also, the tradition is to finish the bottle, and empty bottles must not be left on the table. Also, when drinking bottled beer with Ukrainians (or bottled water or soft drinks), it is not uncommon to share one bottle before pouring the next.

Breaking a glass intentionally is considered good luck according to some; to others, it's a waste of a valuable commodity. If you do break a glass, expect to pay for it. Many view drinking directly out of the bottle (or flask) as utterly uncouth and not open for consideration. Only the basest of alcoholics could do this. I heard of a group of friends who, during Gorbachev's temperance campaign, drove an hour into the woods to drink vodka privately. When the men stopped their car in the woods, they discovered they had forgotten to bring glasses, whereupon they returned home, sober and without speaking.

Samohon

Samohon, or homemade spirits, is illegal, tastes evil, and is commonly unsafe. On a farm near Cherkasy, I tasted what our hosts proudly boasted was made the day before our arrival; I tried a second taste with tomato juice, and then I vowed never to touch it again.

In late 1998 the Russian government decided to increase vodka production. The recent increase in imported vodkas and bootleg production, including *samohon*, had been cutting into state revenues. The precipitous rise in the production of *samohon* in the post-Soviet era bodes poorly for both Ukraine and Russia for health and political reasons.

Photo: Meredith Dalton

Taking a breather outside a wine shop in Crimea.

Wine, Champagne, Brandy, Beer, and Kvas

Ukraine today produces one-third of the wine (*vyno* in Ukrainian) in the former Soviet Union. Its principal wine-producing regions include Transcarpathia and Crimea. Its wines typically compete with those from Moldova and Georgia, the former Soviet Union's other primary wine producers, or with wines from Romania, Bulgaria, and Hungary. Other imported wines are increasingly available in Ukraine.

Ukraine is the largest producer of sparkling wines in the former Soviet Union and has fine dessert wines. The Sauterne-like sweet wines of Crimea's Massandra cellars are especially notable; this

171

esteemed winery dates back to 1785. Ukraine also produces brandy, locally called *konyak,* the best in the former Soviet Union presumably comes from Armenia. Like vodka, Crimea's ruby and Madeira wines, as well as Ukrainian *konyak,* are often downed in one gulp. *Konyak* is served neat.

Under the Soviet system, farmers were paid based on the sugar content of the grape. Hence, grapes were frequently picked too late or even after they had rotted. The machines were not cleaned often enough either, and this imparted off-flavors, or the wine was simply allowed to stand too long. These problems need to be rectified if Ukrainian winegrowers intend to compete in world markets.

Like Moldova, Crimea produces a distinctive ruby-red champagne in addition to its traditional sparkling wines. Soviet champagne is widely available and has kept its Soviet name, Sovyetskoe Shampanskoe Vino; other brands widely available include Ukrainsky brand and Krim (meaning Crimea). There are five levels of increasing sweetness, but even the driest is quite sweet by Western tastes.

This sweetness makes for nice mimosas, the traditional combination of orange juice and champagne. In fact, sweet champagne works better in mimosas than dry champagne, which should ideally be drunk on its own. The tang of passionfruit juice (*maracuya*) mixed with champagne is an excellent variation.

Pyvo means beer, although in the Middle Ages it had a generic meaning of drink. Kyiv's ubiquitous Obolon beer has improved its selections and quality over the years. It is cheap and unpasteurized, so doesn't keep long. Many cities including Odesa, Lviv, and Vynnytsa have produced their own beers but apparently without Obolon's recent marketing success. Obolon's competition for the time being is Slavutych, but so far Obolon has stayed ahead by test-marketing new products. In addition to its high and low alcohol beers, Obolon also bottles its own rum and cola drink, a gin and tonic drink, and hard cider. These all have a high alcohol content and are sold in many kiosks.

In the outdoor cafés and in bars, Carlsberg, Tuborg, Guinness, and Kilkenny are often available. Bitburger and Corona are in Ukraine, as is the occasional American Budweiser. More often, Budweiser is the Czech pilsner like Budvar. Expect to pay Western prices for all but local beers. There are two standard sizes: literally, small (*malenkiy*) and large (*bolshoi*, like the theater, or *velykiy* in Ukrainian), which translates into half-pints (or glasses) and pints.

Kvas is a murky, mildly alcoholic drink made from fermented brown bread. Sometimes it is flavored with currants. *Kvas* is sold only in the warmer months and is dispensed from large tanks. You should bring your own empty bottle. You can also buy a glass on the spot, but, like the old machines that dispensed water for kopeks, there is usually only one glass, and chances are good that it won't be well cleaned between patrons.

UKRAINIAN FOOD

Two of Ukraine's staples are wheat and sugar beet. It is no wonder that vodkas in Ukraine are produced using these crops. Regional food specialties naturally take advantage of the "breadbasket's" bounty.

Bread (*khlib* in Ukrainian; *khleb* in Russian) is considered the mainstay of the Ukrainian diet, and there are endless varieties available. White and brown bread are standard fare. They are chewy, sometimes tangy, and quite tasty when fresh; like milk they lose their freshness within a day or two of purchase. *Baton* (say **bahTONE**) is a popular white loaf; *bulka* (say **BOOLka**) is a roll; *bulochka* (say **BOOlochka**) is a small roll; and *bublyk* (say **BOObleak**) resembles a bagel with its chewy texture and hole in the middle. Pita and Georgian flat bread, *lavash,* are also available. There are also wonderful decorated breads created for special celebrations.

The combination of bread and salt is a traditional symbol of hospitality. The idea is that, even if the host has little to offer, there will always be bread and salt to share with guests. The guest should

173

dip the bread into the pile of salt and enjoy. There was also a tradition that a guest bringing bread could not be refused entertainment.

Sweet breads are popular in Ukraine, and they retain their freshness a bit longer, thanks to the honey or molasses in the dough. One of the more popular sweet loaves is poppy bread.

Mak (say **mahk**) means "poppy," and *khlib z makom* or *makivnyk* are among the names you might hear. *Medivnyk* is a honey cake; *med* in Ukrainian (in Russian, *myod*—rhymes with "toad") means "honey" which is always available at the *rynok*. Fried pies filled with fruit and jam are also tasty.

Babka is a type of sweet bread known for the abundance of eggs in its batter. Traditional recipes called for as many as 70 eggs! *Kalach* is a traditional braided bread, also rich in eggs. Ukrainian sweet breads generally have a much lower sugar to flour ratio than American breads. But some of the Austrian-influenced sweets and many Ukrainian cakes more than make up for this sugar deficit.

In Ukraine, there are certain breads associated with one particular holiday. *Paskha*, meaning Easter, is the traditional Easter loaf, although there are many regional variations. In the east it is typically tall and iced, more like a cake; in western Ukraine, it is more bread-like and decorated with dough shapes. *Korovai* is the traditional tall wedding bread decorated with fantastic forms of flowers, animals, and sheaves of grain.

Typical Ukrainian Fare

To Western tastes, much of Ukrainian food may appear heavy and fatty. Regional cuisines reflect local climate and growing conditions. To the average Westerner, much of Ukrainian cuisine also resembles Russian, although regional variations share similarities with Polish and Hungarian cuisine. Some of the sweet breads, strudels, cheesecakes, and tortes were influenced by Viennese cuisine. To essentially lump Ukrainian and Russian cuisines is an oversimplification; it is more accurate to recognize elements adopted from the other's cuisine. For example, Ukrainians borrowed *shchi* and *solyanka*, two kinds of soups, while Russians adopted from Ukrainian cuisine *borshch*, *varynyky* (filled dumplings), and cheese pastries, among other things. A Polish cookbook from circa 1900 included French and Austrian recipes, some of which were subsequently assimilated by Ukrainian households. Thirty years later, a Ukrainian cookbook included some of the same recipes.

Holubtsy (literally, little pigeons) are stuffed cabbage leaves, which originated in Turkey. Today, the Black Sea cuisine exhibits a Mediterranean influence, with eggplant especially popular, as well as many seafood dishes. In the Carpathians, beef and dairy cattle are raised; sheep were especially popular in the 19th century. This region is noted for its *bryndzia*, made from ewe's milk and similar to Greek feta cheese.

Varynyky, another Ukrainian Staple

One of the most common national dishes is *varynyky* (say *vahRENyky*), or boiled dumplings akin to ravioli. They are often doughy and may be filled with meat, mushrooms, cottage cheese, potatoes, cabbage, or sweet cherries. Potato-filled *varynyky* smothered with mushrooms and onion sauce make a good combination. *Varynyky* are sometimes confused with *pelmeni*, which are Siberian dumplings.

Dumplings and pancakes are also common. Pancakes, called *bliny* (say *bleeNY*), are thick and doughy like American pancakes and quite small (or thin like French crepes), rolled and filled with caviar (*ikra*, say *eeKRAH*), berries, mushrooms, sour cream, or a sweet cheese pastry filling. *Mlintsy* are the thicker ones; *nalysnyky* are the thinner ones, filled with cheese, for example. *Pirohy* or *piroshky* are pies or turnovers, with sweet or savory fillings; meat-filled *pirohy* are reminiscent of Britain's meat pies.

A Penchant for Meat

Both fat and garlic are essential Ukrainian ingredients, and pork is as highly prized for its fat as it for its meat. Ukraine's diet tends to include more meat than Russia's, because raising livestock was always an important feature of Ukrainian agriculture. When meat supplies are limited, meat may be distributed at the table according to age or rank.

Typically, Ukrainian *borshch* includes more meat, and also more vegetables, than Russian *borshch*. Also, Ukrainians have a reputation for making better and more varied kinds of sausages than the Russians. Ukrainians visiting America are often appalled by the lack of good sausages and the limited varieties. Larded meats and meats in aspic are also typical Ukrainian fare.

In general, simply prepared meats are not a feature of Ukrainian cuisine. Chicken Kiev was presumably an early 20th-century invention to upgrade provincial food. The food in the cities is rarely considered as good as that found in the provinces. Certainly many Ukrainian home-style dishes are not ideally suited for restaurants.

The Orthodox calendar is marked by periods of fasting or restrictions followed by religious feasts. During Lent and Advent, for example, only meatless dishes are served.

Kotleta Po-Kyivsky and Other Meat Dishes

You've heard of it as Chicken Kiev, but *Kotleta po-Kyivsky* is not a national dish by any stretch. It's easiest to find in the old Soviet Intourist hotel dining rooms; it's tasty, but it's plenty greasy. After all, the sign of good Chicken Kiev (I have yet to see it spelled Kyiv!) is butter spurting out when you first cut into it. That's because it's made from boneless chicken stuffed with or wrapped around butter, then seasoned, floured, and deep-fried.

A more common menu item is fried or baked chicken leg and thigh; the leg is often adorned with a miniature white-paper chef's hat.

Pork cutlets are common menu items; these include Wiener schnitzel equivalents or breaded cutlets stuffed with mushrooms. Like Chicken Kiev, these are served with potatoes, or you might instead request a side dish of *rys* (rice).

Stroganoff, made from meat and mushrooms in a rich sour cream sauce, is traditionally Russian. In Ukraine it is not served on a bed of noodles, so you might request rice.

Shashlyk (say **shashLEEK**) is marinated shish kebab, typically made from pork. It is served with a sauce similar to ketchup or barbecue sauce. The grilling process is best suited for open-air restaurants. The easiest place to find *shashlyk* in Kyiv is at Hidropark; you can also find it in Lviv just off Prospekt Svobody (Freedom Avenue), near the outdoor beer places. I also highly recommend stopping at one of the many *shashlyk* stands, some hidden among the trees, en route to Yalta, Crimea.

"Ukrainian chocolate"

Ever tasted raw pork fat? It's better if it's marinated in garlic. Then you smear it on a piece of bread, and you're practically Ukrainian. Actually, the tradition is to have *salo* when you're drinking vodka. Ukrainians say that *salo* and vodka go together because the fat helps to absorb alcohol or maybe to break it down in your system. I've even heard *salo* affectionately called "Ukrainian chocolate."

Some time ago, I heard that Ukrainian visitors to the United States sometimes consume raw bacon as a substitute for *salo*. I didn't believe it until I witnessed it firsthand. I did not, however, participate. Indeed, I discouraged it, but my health warnings were ignored.

Ukraine's National Soup

Russia and other Soviet republics, as well as traditional Jewish cuisine, have adopted *borshch*, but the soup whose base is a broth of beets and other vegetables originated in Ukraine. A Ukrainian woman's cooking is often judged by her *borshch*.

There are endless regional variations on *borshch*: the broth may be clear before the customary dollop of sour cream is added and muddies it; or the soup may be thick like stew and overflowing with ruby-red beets, onions, cabbage, carrots, beans, and potatoes, each depending on local availability and tastes. Some *borshch* has a hunk of meat tossed in for flavoring. There are hot and cold varieties of *borshch*, as well as green *borshch*. Garlic and dill are especially popular seasonings in Ukraine and are used to flavor its national soup. Parsley is often added. Vegetable-based *kvas* is used extensively as stock for soups, stews, and sauces; and *kvas* from beets lends a delicious tangy flavor to *borshch*.

Borshch is a first course in Ukraine, not an entree. It may follow appetizers or be served in place of them. *Pampushky* (say **pamPOOSHkee**) are often served with *borshch*; these are fresh rolls, sometimes resting soggily in a saucer of crushed garlic and oil. It is especially delicious when the garlic mixture is served on the side in a gravy boat. A *pampushka* can also be a jam- or fruit-filled roll.

Like beet *kvas*, fermented cabbage is another staple in Ukrainian kitchens because of its tartness, texture, and storage capability. *Kapusta* (say **kaPOOsta**) means "cabbage," and *kapusniak* is a cabbage soup with many variations. Made from fresh or brined cabbage, it might be thin like broth or thick like stew.

Wheat is concentrated in the central steppes of Ukraine, but buckwheat is especially popular in the north. *Kasha* is porridge made from buckwheat. Buckwheat is actually a fruit, but it is generally prepared like grain. In the higher-altitude Hutsul and Boiko regions, corn and barley are harvested, and they influence regional diets. Potatoes are commonly associated with Ukrainian cooking, but before the 19th century the potato was scarcely used.

Adopted from Russia, another popular soup is *solyanka*, which is typically thick and mildly spiced. *Myasna* and *ribna* (meaning "meat" and "fish," respectively) are typical *solyanky*. *Shchi* is a cabbage soup very popular in Russia. *Zharkoe* (say **zharKOYye**, which means "roast") is a tasty meat and potato stew.

Mushrooms

Mushroom collecting is a national hobby shared by the peoples of Ukraine, Russia, and Belarus. Wild mushrooms can be found in the forests bordering northern Ukraine and Belarus, including the Chornobyl region, which were historically famous for hiding runaways from the law or foreign oppressors. Early September is reputedly the best time for mushroom collecting.

It is best to enter the forest on a dry morning after several days of rain. There is a longstanding tradition of silence when collecting mushrooms. The mushrooms are twisted at their base or cut with a paring knife; they are not yanked from the ground. They then are laid carefully in a flat-bottomed basket.

Wild mushrooms are very perishable, and, of course, not all mushrooms are edible. They are only abundant for short periods—old ones are dangerous to eat. Some mushrooms are not worth preserving, while others reconstitute well and can keep for several years if properly treated. Preserving methods include salting and layering in crocks; cooking and layering in pork fat, melted butter, or oil; pickling in vinegar; blanching and freezing; or sautéing and freezing.

In Ukraine mushrooms are cooked and served in a variety of dishes, but they are not eaten raw. One of my favorite dishes is called *zhulien*. The mushrooms are cooked in a very rich sauce of cream and cheese—this is an excellent first course. The word for "mushrooms" is *hryby* (say **hryBY**, or **greeBEE** in Russian).

Caviar

Caviar is imported from the Caspian Sea region. It is available in some of the better markets (take along a knowledgeable Ukrainian

Photo: Meredith Dalton

Buying caviar with friends in Kharkiv.

friend who can help you) or at higher cost in the Western-styled grocery stores. The large salmon roe is tasty and quite salty; the smaller black caviar comes in different grades, ranging from so-so to magnificent. Expect prices to continue to rise as quantities become increasingly scarce.

Zakusky

Zakuska (literally, "little taste") means hors d'oeuvre or appetizer; usually you will hear it in its plural form, *zakusky,* because the variety is often extensive. No self-respecting Ukrainian will drink vodka without *zakusky* on his table. These might be slices of brown bread, or bread with cheese, sausages, or even caviar. The large salmon roe—pink and salty and less expensive than black caviar—is often served on buttered bread. Smoked salmon, much of it Norwegian, is a wonderful treat and widely available in the Western grocery stores.

Other *zakusky* are pickles, including remarkably crisp dills, and pickled lemon slices soaked in sugar—excellent with vodka.

There are also congealed salads and lots of fish dishes; in fact the Ukrainian love of salted herring has been attributed to the influence of the Varangians, the Swedish Vikings who settled in Kyiv and along the Dnipro over 1,000 years ago. Most *zakusky* are salty, fatty, and spicy—considered an ideal accompaniment to vodka. *Zakusky* were traditionally served upon arrival to guests who had traveled long distances.

Fruit, Vegetables, Salads, and Pickles

The days of post-independence banana queues are long over. Today, you'll find sidewalk vendors selling domestic fruits and vegetables. (Sometimes their scales are weighted in the seller's favor.) But you can also find imported kiwis for sale in the underground passageways. Pumpkins and eggplants are grown in Ukraine's warm south, and Crimea is noted for its delicious red onion unavailable elsewhere.

For convenience's sake, you may purchase most of your fruits and vegetables in Western grocery stores or at the new, large supermarkets. You should note that any piece priced individually is probably very overpriced but may be worth it. Haggling is not acceptable in stores, only at the *rynok*.

Shopping for fruits and vegetables at the *rynok* will test your language and haggling abilities, but I always found it a lot more interesting. Check around to find out who really wants your business, and taste the samples that they offer you. Bessarabskiy Rynok is not the only market, and its prices are higher than the others, but it's more convenient for people who live or work near Kreshchatyk. Find out which market is closest to you. At all of them, expect to pay higher prices than your Ukrainian friends, or ask one to come along and advise you.

You'll also want to take along plastic bags for shopping. For buying eggs, plastic egg crates are far more reliable than the seller's thin plastic baggie (unless you're walking only a few blocks). *Smetana*, honey, and caviar will be sold to you in glass receptacles. You might choose to bring your own jars when buying sour cream, cottage cheese, etc. At the *rynok*, you can also buy cheese and all sorts of sausages and meats. For the adventurous, there are the salty, sun-dried fish that Ukrainians enjoy as snacks, and few Westerners would deign to try. Why is it that they will taste *salo*, which you can also buy here in thick slabs?

Ukrainians have mastered the fine art of pickling vegetables to preserve their bounties long after the harvest has ended. Homemade jams and fruit preserves are also very popular.

Ukrainian salads are varied, but traditional salad greens are less popular, except in some of the newest restaurants. In private homes, you will more likely be served salads made from chopped vegetables in a mayonnaise-based dressing. Spiced carrots are juicy and crunchy, although they, and some of the other salads served in the hotel buffets, initially struck me as odd breakfast offerings. In the state hotels, soggy or greasy potatoes also used to be the norm, but this is changing over time. Elsewhere they should be prepared properly.

When dining out, you might order a simple salad of cucumber and tomato slices; I advise requesting this without oil, *bez masla*, as sometimes rancid salad oil is drizzled on top. If not rancid, it tastes like vegetable oil without vinegar. Foreigners are advised to avoid lettuce (called *salat*, as are salads, to throw us off), which may not have been washed properly, except in the nicer restaurants, including those catering to Westerners.

Garlic and Other Seasonings

Garlic (Ukrainian *chasnyk*; Russian *chesnok*) is ubiquitous in Ukrainian cooking. Garlic is known for its medicinal as well as magical powers. As an appetizer, it may be eaten raw or dipped into salt first. Like many other vegetables, it is frequently pickled—do try the tasty, pickled garlic cloves sold at the *rynok*.

Ukrainian cuisine is not especially spicy. There is a definite preference for dill weed. Fresh dill is especially tasty in creamed dishes. Dill is also available in salted, dried, or frozen form. Other popular spices or seasonings include horseradish, caraway seeds, cilantro, celery root, and parsley.

Desserts

The standard dessert in restaurants is ice cream (*morozyvo* in Ukrainian; *morozhenoe* in Russian). Ukrainians, like Russians, love their ice cream even when it's freezing outdoors. There are vendors selling Italian ices, Belgian chocolate-covered ice-cream bars, and many local treats. However, Ukrainians complain that the local products have declined in quality.

Bon Bon in Passazh is famous for its ice cream, but you'll have to pay a deposit for the plastic bowl if you want to eat it outdoors.

Cakes are generally reserved for special occasions. People take them home for parties or serve them at banquets.

Sweet cream-filled pastries (and sometimes fried pies) are sold in busy street locations or just inside the entrance to TSUM, the state department store on Kyiv's Kreshchatyk. These treats were traditionally served on a strip of coarse paper, intended to serve as a napkin and to catch any excess grease. Good pastries are often found where the best coffee is served, with delectable pastries filled with custard, (such as napoleons and glazed tarts), more widely available than a couple years ago.

DINING OUT

Ukrainians mostly reserve dining out for special occasions, as restaurant dinners are expensive. A Ukrainian banquet always entails a full meal with alcohol, appetizers, and a main course. Often the menu is set, and you won't be making selections. A variety of alcoholic and nonalcoholic drinks will be laid out—you won't have to order a thing. These banquets are always seated affairs, sometimes with dancing to follow.

Before you are seated, sometimes you'll notice that the dinner chairs are placed at 45-degree angles to the tables. You won't need to pull your seat out; you'll just have to straighten it as you sit down. It's a clever oddity.

When dining out today in Kyiv's restaurants, it is possible to find all sorts of ethnic food. Besides Ukrainian and Russian, you can find Chinese, Vietnamese, Thai, Japanese, Indian, Mexican, Italian, Lebanese, American, Tex-Mex, Caribbean, French, Swiss, German, Austrian, and kosher. Expect to pay for such variety. Increasingly menus will include Ukrainian dishes alongside other non-Ukrainian menu items. I used to advise against ordering something non-Ukrainian from a Ukrainian menu; however, the days of "Italian" pasta dishes smothered in ketchup seem sufficiently over!

A *kafeteria* typically serves coffee, alcohol, and light food and can be found in universities, for example. A *kafe* is found in the city and used to carry similar fare. Today the arrival of more European-styled cafès has expanded the traditional meaning of *kafe*. A *yidalnya* (*stolovaya* in Russian) is a company cafeteria or private dining hall. All the old factories, institutes, and government offices had one for their employees; essentially mess halls subsidized by their (state) employer, where hot meals were served daily. Today the *yidalnya* is still an important perk for many Ukrainians, but few receive high kudos for their fine cuisine.

Fast-food Fare
Ukrainian fast-food restaurants, such as Stop or Boston Burger in Kyiv, typically serve hamburgers and fried chicken. My personal favorite, now closed, was Kentucky Beirut Chicken on Shevchenko just up from Bessarabskiy Rynok; Kyiv's first five-star hotel, the Premier Palace, has now taken its place, and its restaurants are definitely not fast-food fare.

McDonald's golden arches arrived in 1997 with aggressive plans to expand in Ukraine. There are a number of drive-through locations. Be prepared to pay extra for ketchup but otherwise prices are quite reasonable, even if everyone is complaining that they're higher than they used to be.

Another popular fast-food chain in Mister Snak, which serves hot sandwiches and nice desserts and has various locations throughout the capital city.

Pizza is popular and inexpensive in Ukraine. New places are always cropping up, and delivery service has been available since the mid-1990s. Eric Aigner is a name you might hear in Kyiv's expat community. This German entrepreneur has opened a series of restaurants, bars, and nightclubs. He was one of the early pizza makers, but his place was takeout only. Now look for the American Pizza Company, founded by three American brothers.

Photo: Meredith Dalton

Potatoes, on Kyiv's Independence Square, is one of the new fast-food enterprises to appear in Ukraine's capital.

IT'S MY PARTY...

If it is your birthday, you will be expected to pay for the party. Traditionally, name days were celebrated, and, to some, were more important than the actual birthday. However, Soviet attitudes altered this practice. Formerly, a child at baptism was given the name of a saint, often one whose saint's day was closest to the child's birthday. It was hoped that the child would emulate the best qualities of the particular patron saint.

Birthday cards were traditionally reserved for people who were far away and with whom you could not celebrate the event. (Hallmark Cards might find resistance here, but I'm guessing not for long.) Wrapping gifts was also not an important tradition.

At birthday celebrations, the first toast is always to the honoree; the second should be to the parents. And it is never good form to congratulate someone early, and this includes bestowing birthday wishes in advance. You will be congratulated on the various holidays, including your own country's (such as American Independence Day for me), but only on or after the day has passed. Along these lines, never ask expectant parents if they have a name selected for the baby.

TIPPING

The word for "tip" (in Ukrainian and Russian) comes from *chai,* meaning "tea." In the past a tip was nominal, the idea was that it covered the price of a cup of tea for the waiter. Today tipping is expected, especially of foreigners. People tend to tip better in the expat hangouts, although the servers in the local places might benefit even more from your generosity.

Always check first to see if a service charge was included in your bill. (Useful words for receipt, bill, or check include *kvitansiya, schot, rakhunok,* or *chek.*) A standard tip is 10% and sometimes up to 15%. Remember to check to see that you weren't overcharged. Note that the cost of bread is often added to your bill, even if you didn't eat the bread that you didn't order that was brought to you. If

187

you don't want it, refuse it when they bring it to you, not when the bill arrives.

In the Soviet era, people had to request a *chisty stol* (literally, "clean table") when they dined out, otherwise an assortment of *zakusky* were brought to the table—and naturally added to the bill.

If you pay by credit card, leave the tip on the table in cash, or your server will never see it.

DINING ETIQUETTE

It's patently obvious, but wait to eat with your host. On the other hand, in restaurants, sometimes it's best for people to eat when their dish arrives, because not all dishes will arrive at the same time. You should not leave before the guest of honor does, and if you are lucky enough to be that guest, don't linger too long. The oldest or the honored guest may be seated at the head of the table. Ukrainians strive hard to live up to the tradition of gracious hospitality as expressed in the Ukrainian saying, "Guest in the home, God in the home."

In serving yourself, take moderate portions. Obvious? Yes, but there is also the tradition that the hostess will offer you more helpings several times during the meal. It is your duty to praise the food and its variety and to compliment your hosts on their graciousness, as stinginess or carelessness convey a disregard for hospitality. The hostess will nonetheless humbly apologize for the meager presentation. Some Ukrainians have told me that you may honor your hostess by leaving a small portion of food on your plate, indicating that your hunger was satisfied; others have said that this is insulting. Food is expensive and precious, and many Ukrainians would probably eat what the rich Westerner would leave behind.

It's not considered polite at a formal dinner to pick over an assorted platter to get only the items you want. It is acceptable to reach across in front of others.

Eating is continental style: this means, hold your fork in your left hand and your knife in your right. When you have finished, place your knife and fork—tines up and utensils side by side—on your plate at a clock position of 5:25. Sweets are eaten with a spoon.

A FEW MORE USEFUL WORDS

Vkusny (say *fKOOsnee*) means "tasty" in Russian. *Ochen vkusny* means "very tasty." In Ukrainian, you will say *smachniy*. It's always polite to compliment your hostess on a *vkusny* or *smachniy* meal.

Pyaniy means "drunk." Don't compliment your hostess this way.

Sche in Ukrainian and *yeshcho* in Russian mean "again," "still," or "more." For example, in Ukrainian, you'll hear "*Sche pyvo, bud laska,*" which means "Another beer, please." In Russian the same phrase is "*Yeshcho pivo, pozhalusta.*" Or you'll simply hear *Yeshcho raz*, meaning "one more time."

Dyevushka (say *DYEvooshka*) means "young woman" in Russian and is also used to get the attention of a waitress or shop assistant. It is not considered rude to use this word to attract attention. The diminutive is *dyevochka*—"little girl." In Ukrainian, *divchyna* and *divchynka* mean "young woman" and "little girl," respectively, but they are not used for attracting attention. To get a man's attention, you will say *mushchina*, meaning "man" in Russian. *Malchik* is "little boy."

189

Finally, *charka* is a shot, generally of vodka or *samohon*, which may lead to a *hopak*, a traditional Ukrainian dance.

UKRAINIAN CELEBRATIONS

Because of Soviet attitudes toward religion, Ukraine's centuries-long tradition of religious feasts was ignored or forbidden for many years. Instead, Labor Day (May 1) and October Revolution Day (November 7) were celebrated in place of church holidays. Ukrainian folk rites were also suppressed because they presumably encouraged nationalism and separatism. Some traditions were therefore better preserved in Ukrainian emigré communities.

Pagan rites were observed before the arrival of Christianity more than a thousand years ago. Later these were often adopted or incorporated into Christian celebrations and folk traditions. Ukrainians traditionally celebrated Christmas with *kutia*, a pudding made from whole-wheat kernels, poppy seeds, and honey, a custom that dated to ancient times. Christmas was the only time of year that this dish was served. Easter was marked by the tradition of *pysanky*: the intricately decorated eggs. *Krashanky* are dyed cooked eggs, and these predated Christianity in Ukraine. Along the Black Sea coast, ancient Ukraine was exposed to Roman and Hellenic culture, and the traditional singing of *koliady*, or carols, may be traced to the Roman calendar.

For centuries the Church had called for fasting and abstinence at times, and both Advent and Lent limited meat and dairy intake. On Christmas Eve, an elaborate holy supper broke the fast from the previous day. Usually, 12 dishes were served as this number symbolized Christ's disciples. On other feast occasions, the numbers nine and seven were chosen for their magical properties. Underneath the white tablecloth lay hidden hay, preferably the first hay from the summer's harvest, symbolizing the manger. Garlic cloves were also included to bring good health to the family in the coming year. There was no Christmas tree, although wheat or rye sheaves were placed under the icon of the Virgin and Child. A church service beginning at midnight ended around 2 am. Men would wear their traditional embroidered shirts. The Ukrainian Christmas symbol of *Deed Moroz* (Grandfather Frost) is a carryover from the pre-Christian era. In Soviet times, Grandfather Frost brought his gifts on New Year's Eve in the anti-religious holiday spirit.

Easter Day was likewise a huge celebration including meats and sausages that were restricted until the last week of Lent, called Masliana. A folk proverb wished for seven Sundays of Masliana and one of Lent, instead of the reverse. During this last week, all work outside the home ceased. Exchanging Easter eggs was also the tradition. People attend the all-night Easter service carrying baskets of foods to be blessed for the celebratory meal.

Opportunities were made for young village people to meet in proper social settings after the hard work of the harvests. There were rituals and divining practices to help reveal the future.

For the Feast of Saint Catherine (around December 7), girls would cut boughs from fruit trees to place in water. If they sprouted by New Year's, the girl would be blessed with a bright future and much happiness. And if they dried up, you know the rest.

There was also a tradition of listening for the direction of a rooster's first crow of the day or the sounds of dogs barking. These were believed to herald the direction from which a future husband would arrive.

The marriage ritual was intricate and also used as a guide against uneven matches. A boy who wanted to marry would tell his parents, who invited two respected older males to act as emissaries on the family's behalf. The emissaries (or *starosty,* from *starist,* meaning old age) would visit the girl's parents to propose the idea. They brought bread and vodka, which would be offered if the contract was sealed. It was considered rude to be forward so they expressed humble surprise and joy if the parents agreed to the union. If the parents weren't interested they would tell the *starosty* that the girl was too young. This was *vranyo* intended to avoid insult. An old joke still heard today makes reference to the consolation prize: if a man was refused, all he got was a lousy pumpkin.

If the parents agreed, the *starosty* shared bread and vodka with the girl's family, and embroidered ritual cloths (*rushnyky*) were exchanged to symbolize the agreement. The *starosty* were also responsible for negotiating the dowry. Both sets of parents gave equally to help the couple's new start. A formal dinner was held, wherein the wedding date was set. A special bread, baked with two eggs symbolizing fertility, was served. The fiancée received a beautiful scarf and the man an embroidered shirt.

Many customs are associated with the wedding process, including the exchange of ritual gifts, blessings, and breads. On the day before the marriage, a special evening for maidens was held where advice was dispensed and games were played. The groom arrived late and gave gifts to all the guests. The following day, the parents blessed their children before the wedding ceremony but did not attend the service. Rather, the couple gave themselves away. They dined with the groom's parents, then went to the bride's house for the reception. At both houses, they were greeted with bread and salt.

At the reception, the table was decorated with the *korovai*, the traditional wedding bread, two *rushnyky,* and a large pine bough, a fertility symbol. More ritual cloths and gifts were exchanged, and toasts made by every male adult relative. The newlyweds did not eat their own cake. Today, a miniature *korovai* is made for the couple to keep. It is common for close women friends to contribute tortes, and, instead of the groom, it is the guests who now give the gifts.

In addition to religious and folk celebrations, the most important life events were celebrated; these included births, christenings, betrothals, weddings, and burials.

Traditionally, mirrors were covered for nine days or turned around after a death in the family. Death anniversaries were commemorated, and twice a year special grave site services were held. Both food and *pysanky* were shared with the dead. A third ceremony for the dead was held in the home.

Ukrainians believed that the souls of dead ancestors sometimes returned to earth in the form of unfortunates, such as orphans, beggars, the homeless, or infirm. They also believed that the souls of the departed would help to preserve the family's fortunes. This partially explains the tradition of setting an extra place at the Christmas table or inviting a guest in from the street. It was also a tradition to leave a bowl of food in the window sill.

Deference to dead ancestors was one of the primary tenets of Ukrainian belief. The other important tenets were reverence to God and supplication to the elements of nature. For example, the Feast of the Epiphany or the Feast of Jordan, which commemorated Christ's baptism on or around January 19, or 12 days after Christmas, was also a time for appeasing the forces of nature. Specifically, river water was blessed in an effort to protect the villages from floods.

It is sad yet understandable that so many colorful folk traditions are dying or have disappeared altogether.

Chapter Five

SETTLING DOWN

GET YOUR VISA BEFORE YOU ARRIVE

It sounds obvious, doesn't it? But tourist visas are available upon arrival at the airport—with one caveat. I've seen the airport visa office both open and closed. If it's open, you will need to pay a fee and provide passport photos. But if the counter is closed, you've surely made a long trip, and who knows how long you will have to stand in line? I've heard of people who were stranded at the airport for more than four hours because the visa office was closed. There have also been periods of several days or weeks when the practice of granting visas in-country was suspended. In short, unless you're headed to Kyiv on a brief, last-minute trip, I strongly recommend that you obtain your visa in advance of arrival.

Another warning: don't enter the country with a tourist visa if you really need a business visa. I entered with a tourist visa, expecting to be in Kyiv for one month only. Plans changed quickly and I assumed (that dangerous word) that changing my tourist visa to a business one could be easily handled in Ukraine. I was twice declined; both times I was told that it was categorically impossible to make such a change in class of visa. In the end, I prevailed—and most things are possible in Ukraine if you have the money to pay. Yet having had the business visa in the first place would have saved me undue aggravation. I was especially ticked off that I might have to leave the country at the last minute because of an avoidable error. Renewing an expired visa is fairly common and far less complicated. Also, most people traveling on business visas will want multiple-entry.

The good news regarding visas is that invitations are no longer required for citizens of the United States, Canada, Japan, or the EU. Check for further information, including visa fees and processing time, at http://www.ukremb.com

IMMIGRATION AND HEALTH INSURANCE

Before landing, you will fill out your immigration card, which is the same thing as a landing card in some countries. In the old days, you were give a receipt, printed on a slick piece of paper that looked more like an advertisement than an official document; lots of people threw this away, assuming it was trash. Now your receipt—more like a ticket stub—is clearly marked, so you shouldn't make this mistake. It even notes at the bottom that this card must be kept for the whole period of stay in Ukraine. It also "must be presented together with the passport to Ukrainian border authorities when crossing the border." In other words, you'll need to hand this over when you leave the country, so keep it in a safe location with your passport.

None of this is particularly surprising, but you will also read on this immigration card that mandatory emergency medical insurance is required for all foreign citizens visiting Ukraine. The 1997 law requiring insurance is irregularly enforced. I've had to buy insurance at the airport and show proof at passport control, along with my passport, visa, and immigration card. Then, as recently as late November 2001, I visited Ukraine when the insurance counter at the airport was closed, and the passport officer didn't request or mention any insurance certificate. More than one long-term expatriate residing in Ukraine told me this was all a scam. They have simply refused to pay it, telling passport control that they pay for their own private health insurance and do not need Ukrainian emergency medical insurance. Should you want more information about the obligatory emergency medical insurance, you might contact the state-owned insurance company DASK "Ukrinmedstrakh" head office at 65 Oles Honchar Street, tel. (044) 216–6755; email: office@ukrinmed.com.ua fax (044) 216–9692. The immigration card also notes that there are branch offices in Kyiv selling insurance policies or certificates at: 8 Pushkinska Street, tel. (044) 229–3927, 229–4028; or at 34 Lesya Ukrayinka Ave., tel. (044) 295–4869. Contact the head office for the telephone numbers and addresses of branch and regional offices that you might require.

I always recommend traveling with photocopies of your passport's front page and your Ukrainian visa, which is pasted directly into your passport, but keep these separate from the originals—the point is to have a copy in the event that the originals are lost or stolen. Don't bother with copying your immigration card, which you can only do, for obvious reasons, once you are in-country. There are cases when you might consider copying your customs declaration.

CUSTOMS AND CURRENCY EXCHANGE

After passing through passport control, you will need to fill in a customs declaration form before you can proceed through the clearly-marked red or green customs channels. I recommend filling in the customs declaration while waiting for your checked luggage. At the very least, this will save you a few minutes and might possibly place you ahead of other passengers who are still filling out their forms.

The questions are self-explanatory—that is, if you picked up the English version of the customs declaration. You must note how many pieces of checked and hand luggage you have with you and include a description of all valuables. This means when you enter the country for the first time, be sure to record on your declaration form your furs and any expensive gold or other jewelry (although I wouldn't recommend carrying these with you in the first place), computers, cameras, video equipment, etc.

Hold on to your customs declaration during your stay as you will need to hand it over when you depart. You'll actually have to fill in the same form a second time. The customs officer will compare the two versions: the one you filled out when you arrived and your departure version.

A friend recommends photocopying your incoming declarations after you arrive because, if you travel in and out of Ukraine, you won't be carrying all of your valuables with you on every trip. Consider someone who traveled recently to Cyprus but didn't take his laptop computer. Now he needs to take it with him to Vienna, but his latest entry declaration doesn't show that he owns a computer. Simply photocopying your declaration forms and carrying copies with you might prove unnecessary, but it's easy enough to do and it could save you time and energy at the airport. My personal experience, coming in and out of Ukraine during the past seven years, is that customs is generally becoming easier for expatriates. But I'm also not trying to bring art and other valuables in either direction. Also, one of my theories is that I was less hassled because I am female. This could change in the future, but I hope not!

HOW MUCH IS TOO MUCH?

I only had trouble with customs on one occasion. I was trying to leave the country with more money than I had carried on me when I entered previously. This is one of the carryovers of the Soviet bureaucracy, and I am sorry to say that this is a hassle that has not improved in the 10 years following Ukraine's independence.

I was somewhat lucky in that logic (I think) prevailed that day. I was leading a Ukrainian delegation to the United States for three weeks. My interpreter recorded on his declaration that he had $200 in his wallet. At the time, he had closer to $800 as I recall. I had close to $1,000 on me, yet on my previous incoming declaration I had entered the country with $800. I therefore broke the $1,000 down on my outgoing customs declaration, indicating one-half of the cash as belonging to me (which was true), and one-half as company money intended to cover unexpected expenses in the United States. The interpreter was waved through, and I was detained. Standing for a long time in front of the curt customs officer, I feared that my honesty could cost me my airline seat that day. Finally, this customs officer exclaimed dramatically and with evident irritation: "This is not enough money to worry about!" and waved me through. One has to remember that Ukraine has archaic and sometimes surreal rules, and the customs officer really was trying to do her job. And I've found that getting mad or crying—even if the circumstance warrants—is rarely worthwhile. Be patient, polite, and stand your ground.

For the record, $1,000 is the maximum amount you can bring into Ukraine if you are going through the green customs channel. Many expats have told me that they prefer to lie if they are carrying more money than this, either when entering or departing Ukraine, but I prefer to tell the truth.

You also need to know your own country's rule about how much money you can carry on you without formally declaring it. A Canadian friend was removed from a plane before departing Canada, but he didn't yet know why. In the United States, you may leave the country with any amount of dollars, but you must declare the amount if it is over $10,000.

You can bring as much cash as you desire into Ukraine, but Customs will demand to see and count it, if it is above $1,000. I first arrived in Ukraine with entirely TOO much money, and the sad truth is that it belonged to my company and not to me. The customs official asked me to go into a separate room where I could count out my money in front of an official. I was relieved to be able to do this in a private office and away from the public chaos of the airport. To my surprise, the private office included about 10 officials sitting around wooden tables and smoking dispassionately. My entrance and my company's money aroused them from their reverie. I felt for certain I would be mugged as soon as I exited the airport. I wasn't, but I didn't forget the lesson either. To restate the obvious: foreigners with a large amount of cash are always a great target for robbery. Foreigners without cash are often suspected of having lots of money, although most will tell you they feel safer in Ukraine than in most places. And times are also different now. Lots of Ukrainians have a lot more money than some of us foreigners!

I decided long ago that I wouldn't carry this much money again. It was far too risky, yet at the time we needed immediate cash for hiring staff and drivers, renting office space, and procuring office equipment before we could establish a business bank account (a six-month experience that turned out to be Kafkaesque). Today, the money situation is wildly different from when I first arrived in Kyiv in 1995. The widespread acceptance of credit cards at hotels and restaurants, the arrival of ATMs in 1998, the presence of Western Union, and now an American Express representative office extend the options for expats doing business and traveling in Ukraine, even before they have set up their dollar-denominated bank accounts to allow for overseas wire transfers. In any event, I encourage everyone to consider in advance all their alternatives, in the event that getting cash proves difficult at some point.

It is certainly possible to have more money when leaving the country than when arriving. But you still don't want to do it or report it, if you can avoid doing so.

Another important point: bring only crisp, clean dollar bills to Ukraine. (I say dollars here, because in Ukraine the American dollar is still king.) This means no bills that are worn, torn, or crumpled. I've had bills rejected because of very slight ink markings. Eventually you should be able to exchange your crumpled notes for better ones, but it's best to start with crisp, new bills.

FOREIGN TRANSACTIONS

Luckily, the days of recording your foreign currency transactions in Ukraine are long over. It is therefore unnecessary to keep receipts from these transactions, although you should still get a receipt every time you exchange foreign currency. These receipts will indicate how much money was exchanged, the exchange rate, the date, and the total amount in local currency received at this rate. Lastly, let's not forget the official stamp.

While it is no longer possible to use dollars when you pay for most goods or services, all the larger stores will have their own currency exchange facilities. Obviously, for some purchases it pays to shop around for the best exchange rate. Also, it is possible to exchange euros or Russian rubles at many currency exchange bureaux (called *obmin valut*).

AIRPORT TRANSPORTATION

The airport will permit you to exchange dollars at bad rates; upon arrival you don't have much choice. Just exchange enough to get you to your hotel or where you are going. You can always exchange more money later on.

Chances are good that you can pay for your taxi in dollars, but in case you can't use dollars, you should have enough local currency. For years, I heard that the cab drivers at Kyiv's Boryspil International

Airport (about 20 miles or 32 km from the airport to the city center) were overrun by the mafia. Today there are official metered cabs parked in front, and there is even a regular bus service to the city center. I still highly recommend that first-time visitors arriving in Ukraine try to arrange to have a driver meet them upon arrival. Also, if the weather is bad, expect to pay more. From 1995 through the end of 2001, I have never paid more than $20 for a one-way trip

One more point before leaving the airport: luggage carts are available and free. They were available before but for a rental fee. However, there are still no porters to help you with your luggage.

LOST LUGGAGE

There were many times when our luggage to Kyiv was delayed by a day or two, and it once took Frankfurt Airport a full week to send several bags to the United States. I received a nylon suitcase one day late that had been sewn shut in Frankfurt, but at least nothing was stolen! Fortunately, we always received our late luggage and without anything missing, but this meant returning to the airport and a lot of hassles to deal with. I used to say to avoid Frankfurt connections if you can, but perhaps the truth is that more luggage was lost here because statistically more planes flew through this airport. Some Irish airline consultants once confirmed my anti-Frankfurt bias, explaining that the airport's layout made it more difficult than other airports to transport luggage between planes.

With that said, only on a domestic flight was I aware of tampered luggage: a close friend had a pair of shoes and other personal items filched from his suitcase in transit.

WHEN WE WERE ALL MILLIONAIRES

The Ukrainian currency called *hryvnia* (say *HRYvnya*) was introduced in 1996. There are Ukrainian kopek coins, not to be confused with Russian kopeks (or Soviet kopeks), and one *hryvnia* is composed of 100 kopeks. In the Middle Ages, the *hryvnia* existed in the form of silver ingots. Indeed, war erupted in Novgorod in 1462 when these were replaced by smaller, thinner coins.

The Russian ruble was the currency in all the Soviet republics. In 1992, Ukraine's interim currency called the *karbovanets*, or simply the *kupon*, was introduced, and all coins were abolished.

Karbovanets (krb.) is difficult to pronounce (a friend jokingly called them "car payments") but easier than *hryvnia* (pronounced *GREEvniya* in Russian), which followed it. In 1996, before the *hryvnia* was introduced, the largest bill in circulation was the million-*kupon* note, worth roughly $5.25. Around that time, the USAID recommended that its contractors pay local staff in local currency. I thought of the stories of German wheelbarrows filled with worthless money during the 1920s and declined the suggestion, which eventually USAID did not follow either.

The Ukrainian government was unwilling to introduce the new *hryvnia* currency until it believed that inflation had more or less stabilized. The earliest *hryvnia* bills in fact show dates of 1992 and were locked in vaults until 1996. There were two variants of the one-*hryvnia* note, one produced in Canada and the other in Ukraine. The *hryvnia* was introduced at roughly 1.80 *hryvnia* (or 180,000 Krb) to the U.S. dollar. I felt certain math scores in Ukraine would soar once the five zeros were lopped off! As of early 2002, the hryvnia is trading at roughly 5.3 UAH, which is the official abbreviation for the *hryvnia*: UA comes from the first and last letters of *Ukraina*, the Ukrainian name for Ukraine, and H from *Hryvnia*. You'll also often see hrv. in print.

In the not-so-distant past, small, Western-styled grocery shops made a common practice of giving gum or candy to customers when exact change was not available. With the reintroduction of coins, this should be an infrequent occurrence. I had a friend who once returned a stick of gum to a shopkeeper when she found herself a few kupons short. The shopkeeper was perplexed to find the tables turned!

OPENING A BANK ACCOUNT

If you want to open a personal bank account, it's quite easy to do. There are a number of banks, many of which I wouldn't trust, but there are good ones. Clearly, the banking scenario has improved.

It used to be that the banks took your money and charged you every time you wanted to withdraw any of it. To top it off, you had to deal with the bank's exasperating procedures whenever you arrived to do business. In short, banks generally treated their customers like convicts from the moment they entered the bank's premises. After passing armed guards, you handed over your passport to a bank officer, who entered your information into a computer and also held your passport while you were there. Guards continued to monitor every step you took and you weren't allowed into the room with the tellers until it was your turn. This meant you stood with other patrons in the bank's hallways and even in the stairwells as you waited your turn. Indeed, sometimes you weren't quite certain whether the tellers were working behind the closed doors or if they were taking a break to celebrate someone's birthday.

This anti-service attitude has improved, but I still always advise people to have a car and driver waiting whenever they visit their bank, i.e., don't just have a cab drop you off, as shady types hang around outside the banks. I've also noticed lots of ATMs in recent years but never a lot of activity. My advice about this and a few other things: Be discreet. Err on the side of paranoia.

If possible, bring a friend or driver/bodyguard into the bank with you. My firm opted to put a vault in the office to minimize the time wasted at the bank. Compare the value of a vault against the risks of not having one in your particular case. However, for firms taking in cash receipts, there are endless rules and regulations about how much cash you can have on hand. Still other rules apply to how much money you can have in your bank accounts at month's end.

Even as the formerly unfriendly attitudes within banks are improving, the average Ukrainian on the street does not trust banks, based on disastrous past experiences. Those who entrusted their savings to the bank got burned, and they see no benefit to opening bank accounts now. The tax situation is tricky enough that I'm never certain who would want to have a bank account anyway.

Obviously, if you're doing business in Ukraine, you won't have a lot of choice. But the banking laws are complex and, like the tax laws, subject to constant change. Some advice that doesn't change: You will need to hire both a Ukrainian lawyer and an accountant—regardless of the size of your business—and preferably in advance of your arrival, if possible (See more about this in the chapter *Doing Business and Surviving Ukraine.*)

Opening a business account is much more difficult than opening a personal account. For this reason, my firm wanted me to open a personal account for our company's use. While other Americans whom I knew did this for their company, I was privately advised not to do so. Americans are required to report all foreign accounts to the Internal Revenue Service—the U.S. tax authority. Just as I'd now not recommend carrying a lot of company money when you enter the country, I'd also advise against opening a personal account for business purposes. But I also know that imperfect decisions are made as temporary solutions to seemingly overwhelming obstacles. We can only hope that some of these systemic inefficiencies inherited from the former Soviet Union will die a natural death—and sooner rather than later.

For business accounts, you will need endless documents, including articles of incorporation and bylaws, translated into Ukrainian and notarized. Everything will take far more time than anticipated. Stamps and seals are still regarded as very important in Ukraine, and we nearly had our bank account frozen two months after we opened it, because someone realized we had no official company stamp. You can get around some requirements if your work falls under the umbrella of international humanitarian aid.

HOTELS

Before you settle into an apartment, you will probably spend some time in a Ukrainian hotel. Or you might travel to other Ukrainian cities on business. Ukrainian hotels are surely part of the expatriate experience. Interestingly, these were one of the few businesses that had contact with foreigners during the Soviet period, but they were of course all state-owned. Their post-independence successors seemed mostly stuck in their old Intourist ways, which is to say, quite Soviet and far from service-oriented. Intourist is the name of the agency though which foreigners were obliged to make all hotel and travel plans during Soviet times. But the hotel situation, certainly in the larger cities, has greatly improved in recent years, thanks to the arrival of private hotels and a new service mentality.

Those Ukrainian hotels that are still Intourist-run are outrageously expensive. In the mid-1990s, the Grand Hotel in Lviv stood out among Ukrainian hotels as Ukraine's first truly Western-style hotel—and was considered one of the best in Central Europe—but there was an ugly story behind it. A U.S. heiress purportedly helped to restore the hotel to its former glory based on tales her grandmother had told her as a child. Once renovated, the American investor who needed a Ukrainian partner hired a Ukrainian relative to oversee her interests. The relative was murdered, and the investor quietly withdrew from the picture.

Ukraine's first five-star hotels appeared in 2001. Expats have told me that the absence of international hotel chains in Kyiv sends mixed signals throughout the foreign community about Ukraine's improved economic status. However, a Kempinski overlooking the Black Sea did open in Odesa during 2001, and there have been fitful plans during the past couple years to open an Intercontinental in Kyiv. The Premier Palace in Kyiv also opened in 2001. Although not part of an international hotel chain, this is a European-styled, five-star hotel. Dnipropetrovsk now has its own Grand Hotel, which is not related to the hotel of the same name in Lviv, but it is grand indeed.

You will surely encounter some of the former Intourist hotels if you stray from the beaten track. Some of these have undergone substantial renovation projects, but most are now quite ragged around the edges. You can still sometimes tell how nice the hotel once was; especially true for the hotels reserved for Communist Party deputies. Still, their Soviet architecture is generally gray and depressing. Inside, dark murals adorn the halls, and large, smoke-filled banquet halls still favor stodgy, greasy meals amidst a background of loud, scratchy speakers blaring sentimental music. Small groups of men down vodka in greedy gulps while occasional couples glide across the dance floor.

Doormen guard entry into the larger hotels and supposedly keep out the riffraff. There used to be a female attendant on each floor who would keep your key (*kliuch*) while you were away. The "floor mom" (*dezhurnaya* in Russian; *cherhoviy* in Ukrainian) is still present, but her role is less apparent. She cleans the rooms and provides hot water for tea, while she monitors the comings and goings of hotel guests on her floor. In those hotels and on floors frequented by prostitutes, the *dezhurnaya* gets a cut for permitting the prostitutes access. The doormen do too.

Hotels in Ukraine are expensive and foreigners have always been charged higher rates than Ukrainians. However, this practice may go the way of train tickets did several years ago and, more recently, domestic airfares.

Opting for Short-Term Apartments Over Hotels

I prefer leasing short-term apartments if I am staying in Ukraine for any reasonable length of time. I like the conveniences of hotels, but most apartments offer a lot more space and include a kitchen. Plus you can save a lot of money. However, there are times when you may prefer the security of a hotel, the social aspects of interacting with other hotel guests, or you may need the services of a hotel business center. I would advise that newcomers plan to stay in a hotel upon arrival. You can later speak to real estate agents if you decide to look at short-term or long-term rentals, depending on your needs and your budget.

If you do rent an apartment, you will have a telephone and, depending on where you are staying, you may have access to cable television. Often you will have to pay cash upfront, although some companies now accept credit cards. You might also need to negotiate in advance that you need a receipt or a signed contract. This is also the time to discuss any cleaning services that you require.

The one sticky problem that I've encountered time and again over the past seven years is how to deal with long-distance telephone charges. In most cases, you are leasing a residential apartment that is not set up for commercial calls.

Long-distance calls within Ukraine are very cheap, and it's easy enough to note your calls and estimate costs. International calls are very expensive, and, in my case, I always promised to use my MCI or AT&T calling cards. But you can see why this is a source of great concern for the apartment owner. If they wish to rent their apartment, they have no doubt encountered this topic before you arrived on the scene. One word of caution to those who choose to go this route: I was never able to use a domestic telephone in Ukraine to access my U.S. voice mail. I could place the call and get into my system, but my access code could not be recognized using tone or pulse dialing.

You might also consider renting a mobile phone when you are in Ukraine. This may solve some of your telephone needs. Cellular rates have continued to drop.

Hotel Dining

In the Soviet days, you often wondered why the waiter didn't begin by telling you what food was unavailable. Then you could decide more easily what to order; it would have saved both you and the waiter a lot of time. Today the food listed on the menu is generally available, or there won't be a price next to the item.

If you are staying in one of the larger cities, more than likely you won't have so many meals at the hotel, given the dramatic increase in the number of restaurants. But eating out is expensive, whereas hotel dining rooms are not. The most common entrées in the state-run hotels these days include pork cutlets or (often greasy) chicken. Both are served with fried potatoes that are often limp.

Hotel Services

The service mentality found in hotels has changed radically during the past five years. New hotels have opened up, encouraging the state hotels to improve the quality of their customer service. Some of the problems earlier encountered in the state hotels were beyond the staff's control, but friendliness was nonetheless in short supply.

In the mid-1990s, only a few hotels accepted credit cards, and they were often limited to transactions of $500 or less, which still had to be cleared through Moscow. They also wouldn't let you have a room, even when they had the space, if you had not made reservations at least 24 hours in advance. Once I was asked to check out of the Hotel Rus because the letter on file, which I had written, said I would be leaving at the end of the month. I went to my office and typed a new letter on office letterhead, and my stay was immediately extended.

One of the carryovers from the Soviet era was that each hotel room had a direct telephone line. This was because these were easier to tap. The mid-1990s advantage was that your international callers didn't have to be connected through an unhelpful or misunderstanding switchboard operator. Then as now, placing calls from overseas to Ukraine is cheaper than the other way around. It's still a good idea if you can to ask family and colleagues to initiate international calls from their end.

One disadvantage then was that the hotels used to block these telephone lines, making it impossible for you to place an international call using AT&T or another long distance carrier. This means you were obliged to dial directly at exorbitant rates, and you had to pay the hotel directly for these calls. They would slip the bill under your door the very next day, and you were expected to pay it immediately and in cash. These charges would not be added to your room charges. On several occasions the hotel staff stopped me as I was leaving the hotel for a meeting, asking me to pay yesterday's bill now.

On a silly note, when accounting firm Price Waterhouse had a temporary office in the Hotel Rus, one consultant was given a whopping phone bill after three months but without a breakdown of any calls. She requested more details, whereupon she received the phone log of every call made from the hotel during that period, not just calls from her office.

Hotel shops today stock basic toiletries, such as shampoo, razors, ballpoint pens, city maps, alcohol, and juices, as well as overpriced souvenirs, including amber and the ubiquitous nesting dolls called *matrioshky*. It's always better to buy your tourist items elsewhere. Also, buy some bottled water before you need it. If the shops are closed, buy it directly from the hotel's dining room.

The hotel business centers can assist you in many ways. Their employees can help you send faxes or advise you about local businesses or services that you might need. You might ask where to find an Internet café instead of accessing the Internet from the hotel. Early on, my hotel's business center staff earned genuine kudos for friendliness and helpfulness, in marked contrast to the hotel's other departments. I was once forced to pay a couple of dollars for a hand towel that hotel staff insisted I had swiped; the housekeepers stole my tampons, then told me it had been an accident when I complained to them; waiters would occasionally try to overcharge us for a meal; etc. My personal lesson learned: be kind to the business center staff. There were clearly times when, without their unflagging persistence, I would never have gotten an urgent, or a not-so-urgent, fax to go through.

APARTMENTS

Urban Ukrainians live in apartments rather than detached houses. Houses traditionally tended to be out in the rural areas. The exception today is a large and growing number of homes that have been built for the New Rich. Many of these are not just houses but mansions, but I've also heard a lot of these are really shells too.

The following sections apply to friends' and my experiences in Kyiv, but the basic considerations regarding accommodation would probably be the same for other cities.

Based on your needs and preferences, you'll have to decide if you want to pay for Western-styled conveniences in renovated apartments; good local standard but centrally located; or flats that are off the beaten track, where you may well save lots of money, but your language skills and patience had better be up to standard.

Many Ukrainians are eager to let their apartments to foreigners for a high rent. They move in with relatives or move out to the *dacha*, weather permitting, and make do. This is especially true for older Ukrainians who cannot survive on their meager pensions. A single month's rent will be worth several months of wages for an average Ukrainian on salary, to say nothing of a typical pension.

I've heard that you should not rent an apartment on the top floor because deteriorating roofs cause problems. I never had this problem, but I know of one friend whose roof caught on fire, and his apartment on the top floor sustained significant damage. His personal art collection was spared, but the walls were badly damaged by water from the fire hoses, creating an environment for the uncontrolled growth of unsightly mold.

On the other hand, I've heard of worse cases where the fire department could not properly respond to an emergency because the city's charming, turn-of-the-century archways were designed for horse and carriage access, not for modern-day fire trucks. It is a good idea to bring with you or buy a portable smoke alarm. You can increase your chances of survival in the event of fire, and you might even help save a neighbor's life in the process.

If you want to live in the city center, you might first get advice and ideas from friends. There are also many real estate agents eager to help. Ask what their fee is: most common is 10% of the first year's rent or half of one month's rent. If you're staying under one year the 10% is based on the annual rent. Deposit requirements can be huge, but I've always found these negotiable. And rents are more reasonable since most of the expat community packed its bags and went home after the 1998 financial collapse. Those who lease apartments know that foreigners have a lot of options with fewer expats in town. They will look elsewhere if rents are too high or anti-competitive.

If you can, try to have the cost of utilities included in your rent. It's not that they will be high—your landlord may disagree—but payment is another hassle for you to deal with. If it is your responsibility to pay for your utilities, understand that you will receive a monthly bill, and you will have to pay this in person, standing in line at the post office. Your landlord may insist you pay him so he'll be sure that you paid. The bill is still in his family's name, after all.

Photo: Meredith Dalton

Beautiful archways adorn Kyiv's residential streets.

Contracts—How Useless Are They?

Contracts in Ukraine have traditionally been unenforceable, and clauses like "the landlord will give 72 hours notice before entering the premises" may well be disregarded. Your employer should insist that you have a signed contract if your rent in included as part of your compensation package.

In most cases, there will be two apartment contracts, one in Ukrainian, and the other in English. The former will include a ridiculously low rental fee. This is the one that will be registered with the local housing authorities, and taxes will be based on this rental agreement. For my company's records, our English-language contract stipulated that this version superseded all others. I also suggest an appendix to the contract that lists apartment furniture, just to be on the safe side. Because of the need for two contracts, the tenant may have some bargaining power on issues such as deposits or the installation of a satellite dish. If you choose not to sign two contracts, finding apartments may prove more difficult.

As an aside, I have heard of scams where someone contacts you claiming to be a friend of the landlord, who needs to pick up one of the owner's books. Many apartments boast at least one central bookcase with some of the owner's book collection. Because you will have no idea where the (fictitious) book is, you may think to let the stranger in to look around. The person is not a friend of the landlord, but someone who wants to rob you. If you get a similar request, tell the person to come back after you check with the landlord.

Logistics Companies

Logistics companies can offer short-term solutions for your immediate needs upon arrival in Ukraine. Fees vary, but the logistics people exist to get you rolling. They will help you find interpreters and drivers on a short-term basis, and you can have one of their staff meet you at the airport the first time you arrive. You shouldn't have to pay too much for this service. You should clarify in advance that you want an English-speaker to meet you, if you care. The logistics folks can also help you locate apartments and office space, although I would probably go directly to leasing agents for this. Why pay the extra fees?

Remont and New Construction

Remont is the Russian and Ukrainian term for reconstruction, renovation, or repair. *Remont* is one of those terms every expatriate knows and uses. I guess this is because it's more succinct than "renovation" or "reconstruction." Also, it seems to have a particular

213

application: if repairs end up taking longer than expected, it isn't all that surprising. It's *remont*, no?

Whereas *remont* has always been part of the Ukrainian landscape, this has not necessarily been the case for new construction, which is today booming, to say the very least, in the capital city. This includes residential and commercial construction, as well as projects by the state. Here as elsewhere, construction attracts all types, from the scrupulous, reliable and professional contractors to the sleazy, unsafe, and fly-by-night operators. A preponderance of corruption in the construction business is well noted, and everyone recognizes that this is one of the better vehicles for laundering money.

Centralized Heating, Hot Water, and Other Utilities

Many Soviet-style homes display rugs on their walls, providing decorative flourishes and some insulation. The latter can come in handy, because most apartments suffer at times from too little or too much heat. You get it when it's turned on, often about November 1. Check to see if your apartment windows can be opened, in the event too much heat gives you a headache. Regardless, expect to buy a space heater or two, and be wary of blowing fuses when you use the heater and run, for example, the television at the same time. Know where the fuse box is and what to do with it. All in all I was quite comfortable at home with my space heater, even during what was called "the coldest winter in more than 50 years."

A duvet helps. In Ukraine, bedcovers are often duvets made from two decorated sheets sewn together; a large diamond shape is cut out of the top sheet. Inside the duvet is typically a scratchy wool blanket.

In the summer months, you may need to buy fans for your apartment. The absence of screens can be a problem. My little sister brought from home a couple of 99-cent fly-swatters from the U.S., but you can also buy these at TSUM. I decided against installing screens, although I once had a bat fly into my apartment in the middle of the night. My first thought was "intruder," and then I thought "bird." When I realized it was a bat, I thought about rabies!

Hot water, assuming you have it, comes from a central boiler house. Due to age and the shortage of parts, there will be frequent repairs, often for days at a time. In the summer, there is generally a period of about three weeks when designated parts of the city will have no hot water. It is then that most of the annual repairs are made to the system. If you don't have a separate hot water heater, expect to take cold showers.

For your sinks and bathroom tub, you might need to purchase stoppers/plugs. My sister also brought me a small oven thermometer so I could bake with greater accuracy.

Laundry Services and Dry Cleaners

Many apartments will have a small washing machine, and in many cases your landlady or housekeeper will do your laundry and ironing (and think you have entirely too much—no matter how much or little it actually is). My landlady didn't want me using her machine, so she paid a housekeeper—out of my rent money—to assist me with my laundry and ironing, as well as cooking and shopping if I desired.

If your apartment does not have a machine, it may well be worth the investment. I really don't know how Ukrainian women survive without washing machines, with all the cooking, shopping, cleaning, and other work that they do. I vaguely recall a public launderette, but it was not convenient to downtown Kyiv. I'm somewhat surprised that launderettes have not gained popularity. Your best bet for your laundry might be to hire someone who wants to earn a little cash on the side. Ask at your office or other friends for suggestions.

The number of Western-styled dry cleaners is increasing with good locations throughout the city. As economic principles would have it, their formerly outrageous prices have now come down.

Housekeepers and Domestic Help

Many apartments come with a maid service; that is to say, the housekeeper is often included as part of the rent. Frequently, people rent out their apartments fully furnished to foreigners and therefore want someone to watch over their possessions. How better to do this than to build into the rental price the services of a maid? In many cases, the housekeeper will be the landlady. In my case, I had my apartment cleaned, my clothes washed and ironed, and *borshch* prepared if I requested it. My housekeeper also made the best dill pickles I ever tasted. Obviously, contract terms, like landlords and housekeepers, will vary.

It is often hard to communicate the concept of privacy or a lease to landlords. I insisted that the landlord inform me, the tenant, in advance of periodic visits. While this should be written into your lease agreement, remember that contracts aren't enforceable. I've heard of bad landlord situations, but most are manageable with some diplomacy and a cup of hot tea. One friend settled his housing dispute with several glasses of vodka.

ON TELEPHONES

Cell Phone Junkies

The joke in an earlier chapter about having a refrigerator delivered in 10 years time (on precisely the same day that the plumber was coming) didn't make reference to Soviet phones, I think, because it would be more painful than funny. The Soviet stories about waiting for phones—and then no phone books or city maps to assist in locating people—are numerous. Even today, waiting for a phone is still a huge problem and exorbitantly expensive.

The attractiveness of apartments often relates to the number of phone lines available, especially if the apartment is to be used as office space. Apartments used as offices are generally rented without furniture. Also, the various telephone exchanges throughout any

given city differ in quality. In Kyiv, they are generally best in the areas close to embassies. The 1998 renovation of Kreshchatyk promised, among other things, better communication lines. But in many areas of the city, the quality of the phone lines has not improved in recent years.

It is now possible to buy new telephone lines from UTEL, a Ukrainian-Dutch joint venture. These lines are expensive, when available, but they solve the problem of waiting for new or clear telephone lines from Ukraine's state telephone company. So far, this company receives especially low marks for its customer service—described by some as customer abuse. For international telephone calls, Western companies like Sprint and AT&T are in Ukraine. Still, the network in place is not always able to cope with current demands. As a result, many Ukrainian and foreign businessmen in Kyiv and other cities were forced early on to purchase mobile phones. The number of persons with mobile phones is mushrooming now, as prices have become more affordable. You can also lease mobile phones on a short-term basis. Check the *Kyiv Business Directory* — usually available for free in Kyiv, but also check its business listings online at http://www.ukrbiz.net

Although I highly recommend cell phones in this day and age, and sometimes they seem absolutely necessary to conduct business in Ukraine, you should note that business is never conducted solely by phone. The phone is used to set up (and confirm) appointments and to let someone know if, for example, you are stuck in traffic. Business etiquette still requires that the parties meet face to face.

Telephone Etiquette

The old practice of hanging up the phone if the call wasn't for you is not entirely a thing of the past. More likely today they are hanging up because they don't understand you. Still, I do recall business meetings where five or more rotary phones were lined up on a desk. One of the phones rang, and a silent hand reached discreetly for it, raised it a inch or so, and quietly dropped it back on the hook. Almost imperceptibly. Except first I heard a phone ring, and then the hand scurried across the desk. The face in front of me never acknowledged a thing.

When you place a call, you normally hear one of three responses: *Allo* is used much like the French use it. It is never used as a greeting in the street per se. It is reserved for telephone usage. Often it's repeated, especially if there is a pause in conversation. Irritating in any language, this is a carry-over from the days when calls were frequently cut off (and also wire taps were more prevalent). You might as well hang up if you are disconnected.

Da, which simply means "yes," is also common.

Ya slukhayu translates as "I'm listening."

As in many parts of the world, Ukrainians divide telephone numbers into thirds, thus 229-3841 becomes 229-38-41. You may well have to repeat and/or record telephone numbers a lot, so it's good to practice your numbers in Ukrainian or Russian early on. This means you need to understand how to say double- and triple-digit numbers, because people (in this example) wouldn't say "two, two, nine, etc." Rather, they would say, "two hundred and twenty-nine, thirty-eight, forty-one."

A Digression: Free phones

My favorite story about Ukrainian telephones stems from Lenin's dream of a day when all phones would be free in the new world he envisioned. During the years of the interim currency after independence, there were no coins in Ukraine. By contrast, Russia retained kopek coins during this period; the two-kopek coin was the most sought after in Moscow in 1992, because it was used in public phones. A few enterprising types would stand by public phones and sell them at a premium—often pretending to have no other change. By the mid-1990s, half of Ukraine's pay phones weren't working; the others were free of charge due to the absence of coins. All this began changing in late 1996; phone cards appeared around the same time that kopek coins made a comeback. But for that one short period in Ukrainian history, Lenin's dream of free phones had become a reality in coin-free Ukraine.

Local and International Telephone Calls

Local calls from pay phones now require phone cards that are sold at the post office and other locations.

Note the emergency access numbers from all Ukrainian phones:

01—fire

02—police

03—ambulance

04—natural gas emergency

When placing long-distance calls, dial 8 and wait for another dial tone. When calling within Ukraine, dial the following city codes followed by the local number. Always include the initial zero with the city codes: for example Kharkiv is 0472, Kyiv is 044, Lviv is 0322, Odesa is 0482, Sevastapol is 0692, and Yalta is 060 or 0654.

International callers have several options. They may dial directly or use AT&T, Sprint, or one of several other services now available in Ukraine. It is no longer necessary to book in advance international calls to Asia. Expatriates from the United States and Europe should investigate call-back services for international calls where you place a call directly to the United States, enter a personal code, and hang up. Immediately you will receive a call back, whereupon you will enter the telephone number of the person whom you wish to call. When signing up for this service you will pay for calls in advance, but the savings will be substantial.

To place an international call directly from an apartment, dial 8, then pause for the second dial tone. For the United States, dial 101, followed by the area code and number. For Europe, dial 8, pause, then dial 100, followed by the specific country code, city code, and number.

To access your AT&T operator, dial 8, wait for a new tone, then dial 10011. You can then speak with an operator in English. The English code for a Sprint operator is 10015.

Be forewarned: landlords are very wary of expatriates' phone bills and will even discourage phone use by saying your calls will be tapped. I promised my landlady to use a credit card; she was skeptical but allowed me the use of her phone because she liked me (and my large monthly rent payments).

How To Pay Your Telephone Bill

All bills must be paid in full within 10 days. You must go in person to the post office and queue. You might enjoy this sort of "Soviet" experience once, but after that you will probably think of better ways to spend your days in Ukraine. You can send a housekeeper or office employee to stand in line for you and pay your bills.

SCHOOLS

For international families living in Kyiv, the city boasts several international schools. These are very expensive, but the majority of expatriate children attends one of them. Compensation packages for embassy and other foreign government personnel, as well as for

Western employees at some of the larger companies, include private tuition for their children.

For Ukrainian students, education begins at age six, and primary school lasts four years. Secondary school lasts seven more, although there are plans to add an additional one or two years. A diploma is awarded upon completion of ninth grade or ninth form. Those remaining in secondary school for the final two years are preparing to enter a university or technical college. There are also technical courses available upon leaving ninth form.

Instruction is now in Ukrainian with foreign language classes in Russian, English, and other languages. One high-school student described his difficulty in learning Latin, precisely because the instruction is in Ukrainian, formerly a foreign language in his native Kharkiv!

There are over a dozen universities in Ukraine. A third of these were established recently, and some are not yet accredited. College admissions are competitive. Stories of bribes are common, but many students earned their places. The level of education in Ukraine is very high and may be one of the best incentives for considering doing business here. Ukraine also boasts high computer literacy. Kyiv was considered a center for computer programmers in the Soviet era, and its software industry is booming now. One new concern is that some of the best talent is being lured abroad, where salaries are more competitive.

Observations from a Peace Corps Volunteer

From 1999 until mid-2001, Elsa Shartsis was a U.S. Peace Corps volunteer in Lutsk, in southwestern Ukraine. Her assignment was teaching in a Ukrainian university, and she described for me impressions and explanations of various Ukrainian university terms. I thank Elsa profusely for allowing me to include some of her stories in this edition. As a result, all readers may benefit from her experience and careful observations.

Elsa's intention was not to openly criticize any one person or institution. She praised the many bright, hardworking, helpful, and academically rigorous people whom she encountered, and this included students, teachers, administrators, and professional people. They inherited from the Soviet era a creaky educational system that looks very corrupt from a Western perspective and is apparently fairly low on the priority list in terms of reform.

Lutsk is a city of 218,000 people and includes several public and private universities. Elsa taught in a state school, with some 12,000 students, 1,500 teachers and 19 faculties. About 500 students were "post-diploma" students. These students already had a bachelor's or specialist's degree, but they were studying for a second degree in another field because they wanted to change jobs. Obviously, these were older than the typical students, who are usually about 17 and just out of secondary school, when they enter university. There are more female students than males studying at the university.

There were about a dozen blind students at this university, who studied by means of readers and tape recorders. There were a few wheelchair-bound students, who are required to attend classes, pick up assignments, and confer with teachers for only 40 days per year. The rest of the time they study at home. Disabled access is rare in Ukraine, and this university was no exception.

On admission, students are assigned to a group that will stay together until graduation. There are few, if any, elective courses, so group members move together through the curriculum and more or less share the same experiences. Various teaching techniques and university practices reinforce this group spirit. Strong, lifelong friendships result, and many students find spouses within their group. Cohesion, mutual support, and teamwork are stressed, often to the detriment of individual effort and independent thinking.

Admissions. There is no standardized admission test like the ACT or SAT. Instead, every university writes and administers its own admission tests. This takes place during July, and the teachers write, administer, and score the tests. The word "faculty" here means an academic division, e.g., the law faculty, rather than the staff of teachers. So university admission depends on how well an applicant does on a test that is written, administered, and scored by the same person or small group of people who determine whether or not to admit them.

Tuition. A student who does not do well on admissions tests may still be able to enter a state university by paying tuition, or may pay to enter a private institute or university. Consequently, many students (and their parents) assume good grades, promotion, graduation, and a diploma can be bought. It is not necessarily related to an individual student's actual academic performance and/or decent behavior in class. Students with this attitude are difficult to teach, but there is real pressure on teachers to put up with them because every institution is trying to stay in business and every student counts.

Free education. There are free schools on all levels, including state-run universities. Students are admitted according to how well they do on an admissions test. As students, they receive a stipend from the state, the amount of which depends on a student's grade point average. The stipend is very low and not enough to live on. Parents must still support their children attending university. It is common for food parcels to be sent to students not living at home.

At Elsa's university, about 60% of the students paid tuition, whereas in Soviet times no students paid. The nonpaying (scholarship) students receive a stipend from the state of 17 UAH per month, unless a student received all 5's (see following section on grades); then they receive 25 UAH.

Also, tuition rates vary according to the faculty. The law faculty, followed by international relations (where Elsa taught), was the most expensive. The university had six hostels that cost 40-50 UAH per year to live in. The dormitories were reputed to be crude, and they appeared to be so from the outside. Elsa heard that most students chose to rent space in someone else's apartment to living in the dorms.

Most students were locals, so some lived at home with their families. Other students came to Lutsk from "the village" and had to find a place to live in town. "The village" is a generic term that means an agricultural community. The term has nothing to do with size, but with its residents' occupations. A village is a community, of any size, where most of the residents are involved in farming.

Course/Grades/Marks. Course refers to a student's year of study, as opposed to a class, which is a topic of study lasting for the semester. Marks that are given range from 5 to 1, with 5 the highest. This was the scheme used for pre-university marking too, but that was recently switched to 12 through 1, where 12 is the highest mark. Some observers regard this as a meaningless complication. Until now, the 5-scale university grading system has been very vulnerable to outside influences. Marks are universally inflated and usually bear little relationship to reality.

Exams. Most exams are oral and rather informal. About a month before the exam, the teacher gives students a list of 20 or 30 topics. These may be as general or detailed as the teacher chooses. Many of these lists are essentially course outlines, so giving the lists is superfluous if the students have come to class and taken notes. The teacher then prepares a series of cards or papers, each with questions or brief exercises on a topic. These are stacked, print side down, like a deck of cards. On exam day, four or five students enter the exam room and each picks three or four cards at random, then sit down and prepare answers to the questions on the cards, using no notes or notebooks and presumably not consulting each other. This last point is highly unlikely as students find it practically impossible to work alone. In Elsa's lectures, her students automatically consulted each other, by murmuring to each other in Ukrainian or Russian, whenever she called on someone and asked a question.

During most exams, each student is called on to recite. If a student doesn't do well on a card, and the teacher wants to take the time, the student is allowed to draw another card and try again. Elsa believes

224

that this is an okay, but she chose to give an American-style exam, including true and false questions, short answers and long essays, all preprinted and to be answered in writing on the exam paper. The dean discouraged this because copy paper was so expensive—he kept it locked up in his office—and university copy machines were inadequate. Elsa offered to supply the paper; the dean agreed, then supplied the paper himself. The exam proved extremely difficult for her students, because many of them spoke English well but wrote English poorly. There's a rule that any student who wants to improve a poor exam mark can have another chance. Elsa retested many students orally, and most of them significantly improved their grades.

Elsa also described the not-so-subtle directives that certain students receive high marks. Elsa called this *Ukrainska otsinka inflatzia*, or Ukrainian grade inflation, and it was a bitter pill to swallow. Her close university friends explained to her that Ukrainians are still stuck with the Soviet educational system, which is no longer really free. Students are desperate for good grades so that they can stay in school, and there is the sliding scale, based on exam grades, for financial assistance. The phrase "intellectual honesty" is largely unknown.

One of Elsa's students was: "a perfect cipher of a guy who was barely articulate or literate in any language, often absent and inattentive when he's present. His one plus was that he looked like Marlon Brando in *A Streetcar Named Desire*." He was one of the students who had to receive high marks because his father was close to the dean.

Another quaint custom was that no teacher would dare to give a student a low mark if he or she had established a series of high marks in the first year or two. That would spoil the student's record. So even if a student bombed on an exam, a look at the transcript, in which each teacher—not a registrar—records final grades, might dictate that the true grade cannot be recorded. Students would only receive marks consistent with those higher ones already in the book. As a result, most students with average-to-low marks early on won't stay in school because they can't afford it and so drop out. So who's left? Lots of students with consistently high marks, many wildly inflated, coasting along on their infrastructure of first- and/or second-year marks, possibly of political origin.

There are no standardized tests in Ukraine. All entrance exams are done by the individual school, some of which are more prestigious than others, and presumably some more academically rigorous and honest.

Bribery/*blat*/corruption. This is as pervasive in the university system as it is in other Ukrainian institutions. A degree does not command the respect that it does in other parts of the world. Professional confidence in a person depends more on personal knowledge and friendship than that person's CV or academic history.

Universities as political weapons. In Elsa's experience, it was not unusual for a university rector to cancel classes and direct students and teachers to attend a political event, sign a petition, vote, vote in a prescribed way, or otherwise perform some public, political act.

Professional schools. Doctors and lawyers do not go to medical school or law school per se. Rather, at about age 17, right out of high school (called secondary school in Ukraine), a student is admitted to the law faculty or medical faculty of a university. Medical students graduate in five or six years.

Upon graduation, the medical students must find a job. These are almost invariably institutional. There are very few independent practitioners. Further professional education is on-the-job training and the rare opportunity to study abroad.

University Degrees. A bachelor's degree is awarded after four years; after an additional year, a specialist degree; after another year, a master's degree; after another year or two or so, plus a thesis and publication, a doctorate.

***Starosta*.** Every group has a student monitor, or *starosta*, appointed by the head of the faculty, who is responsible for presenting the record book to the teacher at every class and for doing other odd tasks as requested. They also function as the group spokesperson. To be so appointed is an honor for a student and theoretically they must exhibit exemplary behavior and have high marks to be eligible. However, Elsa said some of her monitors were not helpful.

Credit books. Upon enrollment, each student gets a credit book, a passport-sized special notebook in which the student records each course taken, with dates, the mark (or pass/fail) earned, and the professor's signature. It's really a transcript but in the student's possession, not the registrar's. If a student loses it, he or she has to reconstruct it. This is very difficult, as the student has to track down each professor and ask them to reenter the information. Credit books mean that the professor can see each student's complete university record at a glance, and this might influence the mark in a given course. Contrast this with other countries where professors know little or nothing about the past performance of students enrolled in their courses; a student's grade is never based on grades earned in other unrelated courses.

Student activities. Any excuse for a party! Discos were all the rage with Elsa's students, with the requisite head-pounding music and strobe lights. Students enjoyed planning and attending these parties, usually in connection with a national holiday or academic milestone. Ukrainians love singing, skits, and all sorts of music. They seemed able to put on a performance at any time. Some of the faculty-sponsored events, performed during class time and somehow related to course work, seemed especially juvenile for university students.

Student study habits/learning habits/class deportment. This was real, true culture shock for Elsa as an teacher from the United States. Students were absolutely glued to one another and did not think or act independently. Everything was a group effort, even taking exams. Elsa tried to impress upon her students early on that she wanted to observe American conventions in the classroom, including American test-taking rules. She even reduced these to three basic rules: don't talk, don't look at another student's paper, and don't consult any notes or notebooks. As for classroom decorum, she tried to deal with the "interruption" problem by explaining the idiom "to have the floor" and asking for respect for whoever had the floor, either herself or a fellow student, by not interrupting. This required much tactful reinforcement but was moderately successful.

Elsa's faculty was housed in what was formerly a hostel but was later nicely *remonted* with fresh paint, floors covering, blinds, new furniture, and adequate lighting. However, the acoustics were awful and the worst possible design for classrooms—long and narrow with the whiteboard (which was an absolute necessity for writing words and terms or drawing diagrams to show relationships and cartoons) at the front, narrow end. Most students tended to cluster toward the back of the room. Elsa had to talk above the bouncing noise of constant murmuring, plus extraneous noises from the corridor and a construction project next door.

Elsa taught in English, and her students were more or less fluent in English. Every student in her faculty had to take two foreign languages and her students, with few exceptions, had chosen English as their primary foreign language. However, when students didn't understand her, they turned to their classmates for explanation. Elsa tolerated this during lectures, not exams, while she encouraged students to ask her if there are any questions. But she didn't allow other students to jump in when she called on a particular student. To Elsa this was a rude interruption, but to her Ukrainian students it was fulfilling a group obligation.

Elsa also tried to physically separate students at exam time. This worked more or less well, but there was a built-in limitation: standard classroom furniture consists not of individual desks but of long benches and long desks to match, accommodating four to six students. So, inevitably, two or more students on a bench might start with empty space between them, but by the end of the exam they were sitting shoulder to shoulder and communicating at will. To a Western teacher, these students were cheating. Most students could not observe her rules, and there was much verbatim duplication of exam answers.

Front row student. This is a wonderful Ukrainian expression, meaning a serious, interested, attentive student, who wants to block out distractions and learn as much as possible. Elsa had many of these, with the rest of her students wanting to sit at the back of the room. Finally, Elsa gently but firmly started to require that the front seats be filled first, so that students would be clustered in the front of the room rather than the back. Elsa wished she could have had a room with movable individual seats so that they could have gathered in a circle.

Elsa's twin students. Elsa taught a set of identical twin sisters, who were very attentive and respectful students (and physically beautiful too). They dressed alike and stuck together always. They sat together, touching and murmuring, at every one of her lectures. During the final exam, Elsa asked them to separate, indicating that one of them should move to a seat several rows away from her twin. No one moved, so Elsa asked again. Finally one twin got up her courage and asked "Why?" At last, one of the twins very slowly gathered up her things and moved. Elsa feared that she had traumatized these twins in the name of academic rigor! But, in fact, both sisters did very well and did not "cheat"—at least with each other.

Asking questions in class. This is very unusual and stems, Elsa believes, from the Ukrainian university teaching style. Here professors stand at the podium and deliver lectures, sometimes reading them, and that is all. No questions are asked, and there is no interaction, no discussion, no digressions, no visual aids, and no exchange of opinions. There are no course textbooks and few reference or research materials. Libraries are skimpy and woefully outdated. So course content comes straight from the professor with no other input. What the professor tells the students is the course.

Questions from students have very little role in this scheme. Elsa encouraged questions on any topic and stressed that there were no stupid questions. Elsa lavishly praised those who ventured to ask questions. On many occasions, no one spoke throughout an entire lecture despite her best efforts. Then, after the bell, while packing up her briefcase and most students were leaving, several students would converge on the podium with, you guessed it, their questions. Elsa always answered them, remarking that these would have been good questions to ask in class so that all students could hear both the question and answer. During the next class, she would repeat each question and answer to the whole class, without identifying the student who asked it. This always elicited further discussions. Elsa was fully aware that many students might be reluctant to publicly ask questions because they were afraid of making an error in English.

HERE'S TO HEALTH

Pre-Departure Health concerns
It is a good idea to consider purchasing SOS or Medevac insurance before you leave. It's cheap and provides peace of mind. If you are the holder of an international student identity card, the annual fee includes SOS insurance. This is medical evacuation insurance. In the event of a medical emergency, you will be flown to the nearest acceptable medical center. This does not mean the United States, Canada, or Britain. It will more likely be Vienna, which is where I was flown for a dental emergency in 1995. The company was very professional, and I highly recommend this insurance. Basic SOS coverage does not pay any hotel, hospital, or other medical expenses—it is purely for last-minute evacuations. There are, however, other plans that will cover medical costs. (Check out http://www.internationalsos.com).

AIDS testing is a requirement for permanent residence in Ukraine. You can have your test results translated into Russian, which will be easier than into Ukrainian. The document should also be signed and stamped by a medical professional. The more official the document, the better for working with Ukraine's bureaucracy.

The Center for Disease Control provides up-to-date information about immunizations at http://www.CDC.gov

Hospitals and Medical Care

I've heard lots of stories about the necessity for Ukrainians to bribe their doctors. Clearly, most foreigners will use the Western clinics if given half a chance. The American Medical Center now offers dental care in addition to its standard medical services, and new facilities for dental and medical care are continuing to crop up. Of course, not all of these are created equal. I would suggest that you check with your friends or call the staff nurse at your embassy for recommendations. Again, in the event of dire emergencies or should local treatment be unavailable, your SOS insurance will provide necessary medical evacuations.

If you are sick, be prepared for unsolicited references to herbal and homeopathic remedies. My suggestion is to hear the ideas out. Some of the remedies may be worth trying.

Pharmacists or chemists are called *apteka*; think of the word "apothecary" where you can buy most medicines without a prescription, assuming that they are available. There are several quasi-Western-style pharmacies, including one Swiss joint venture on Passazh off Kreshchatyk.

An Aside: The Good News About Hospitalization

In 1996, some of the government officials with whom we were working were accused of corrupt practices. In one day, four arrests were made in the Ministry of Agriculture. The head honcho disappeared, and we heard no news of him for several days. It turned out that he was fine, and just recuperating in the hospital. In Ukraine, you cannot be arrested if you're hospitalized!

SHOPPING GUIDE

Grocery Shopping: Western-style and Local-style

Grocery shopping is another area where the dollar/*hryvnia* economic zones may be more clearly defined. Most ordinary Ukrainians do not

Photo: Meredith Dalton

Bessarabskiy Rynok off Khreshchatyk in the heart of downtown Kyiv.

have the cash available to patronize the Western grocery stores or pricey restaurants, certainly not on a regular basis. Instead, they frequent the state grocery stores with their simple but now plentiful food. There was even a disdain, in a distinctly Soviet, almost anti-material way, for Western grocery stores and the Ukrainians who frequented them. This seems to be changing somewhat, as more restaurants are opening, and many are more affordable than in the past. Ukrainians are also taking advantage of the supermarkets, whereas few had interest in their "mom-and-pop" predecessors.

As an expatriate living an expat life you'll also shop in the local stores. A *hastronom* is the state equivalent of a grocery store. It typically carries local pasta and dairy products. You may have to queue here three times to buy your products: in the first queue you will select the product and request a receipt indicating its price; you will then pay at another counter where the receipt is marked as paid; in the final queue you will hand over the receipt in exchange for your purchased goods. This is also the practice in pharmacies and lots of other stores. Sometimes you will not receive a receipt at the first step; you'll ask the price, then tell the cashier how much your item costs. She gives you a receipt for that amount, which you trade for the item.

You might prefer the *rynok* to the *hastronom*. *Rynok* means "farmer's market." Here you won't be dealing with all these silly receipts; you will pay the seller directly. I love to hear the sound of clacking abacus beads in some of the *rynok* stalls.

The *rynok* is where you and your fellow Ukrainians can buy cheese, eggs, a wide range of sausages, as well as most vegetables and fruit. Don't worry if you forget to bring plastic bags as you can always buy one from the many old women who sell them. The bag designs are generally wholesome: flowers, smiling couples, children or their beloved pets predominate, but the occasional half-clothed beauty sneaks her way into the available choices. While standard backpacks are much sturdier, some folks recommend that you carry plastic bags like a local and blend in more.

The Western stores also carry fruit and vegetables at premium prices. These were probably your best source for imported cheeses, frozen entrees, smoked salmon, soup mixes, pasta sauces, olive oil, Irish beers, and expensive gin—essentially many of the food products the expat community was desperate for. The more recent arrival of supermarkets have attracted Ukrainians in a big way, and more than the smaller Western grocery stores ever did. Shipments are also more reliable, so I advise expats to now relax.

For everyday shopping, often your housekeeper can help. She can negotiate good prices, but I've also been refused certain items that were not a good buy, according to my housekeeper, even though I requested and needed them.

The *univermag* (say ***ooneeverMAHG***), from the Russian *universalny magazin*, or universal store, is a department store selling

Photo: Meredith Dalton

TSUM department store is the Kyiv equivalent of Moscow's famous GUM.

select groceries, hardware, household appliances, clothing, children's toys, and other goods. Modeled after Moscow's celebrated GUM, for *Gosudarstveny* (State) *Univermag*, TSUM, for *TSentralny* (Central) *Univermag*, was its equivalent in Ukraine and in all Soviet cities. All the cities in Ukraine still have one. In addition to selling egg crates and duvet covers, you can find sweet chocolates, sweet Soviet champagne and Crimean champagne, alongside corkscrews, batteries, light bulbs, videotapes, coffee grinders, small appliances, dishes, watches, and much more.

Kiosk Culture and the Free-Standing Vendors

During the early post-independence era, kiosks sprouted like mushrooms in the cities around metro stations, train stations, on major thoroughfares, as well as in the underground passageways. These kiosks were one of the earliest forms of post-communist private enterprise. In many places, the government has cracked down on the number of street vendors.

Originally, "kiosk," referred to Soviet billboards that displayed newspapers and Communist Party propaganda, as well as opera and theater schedules. Today's kiosks resemble glass and metal sheds. Magazines and sundries are sold, but food and drink items are the most common: imported cookies, juice, European beers alongside Kyiv's Obolon and Slavutych, and a wide array of vodkas and imported spirits. There are even plastic cups of vodka covered with aluminum foil lids and Russian Stolichnaya vodka in cans. Kiosks selling non-food items such as inexpensive watches, jewelry, and Chinese knock-off Swiss Army knives are often found in the underground passageways.

Alongside kiosks both at and below street level, vendors set up stands using portable tables, stacked fruit crates, or boxes. Their array of food and cosmetic products is often the same as that carried by the kiosk vendors. Mars and Snickers bars (sometimes past their expiration date), imported bubble gum, shampoo, inexpensive caviar, olive oil, and razors are typical items. Kiosks tend to sell to non-perishables, or at least those items with a shelf life of several months, whereas freestanding vendors are more likely to sell perishable fruits and vegetables, eggs, or the odd plastic bag of milk.

Separate stands, as well as kiosks, are devoted to books, bootleg videotapes (mostly in PAL VHS format), or bootleg compact discs with typos on the photocopied notes. It is also easy to find CD-ROMs that include huge libraries of bootleg computer programs. The joke that China has only one registered copy of any Microsoft product seems equally valid here. However, that joke became less funny when in 2001, first the United States, then Europe, threatened sanctions against Ukraine if it could not reign in its escalating pirate industry in CDs and videotapes.

There are also vendors who set up small tables for selling batteries for calculators and watches. You can also find stalls specializing in shoe repair, watch and clock repairs, locksmiths, film developing, etc.

Shopping for Clothes and Cosmetics

Benetton came early to Ukraine and today has stores in Kyiv, Odesa, Lviv, and elsewhere. Guards used to be posted outside Kyiv's Kreshchatyk store to control what were sometimes artificial queues (à la Hard Rock Café in various locales)—intended to create a sense of excitement. (Guards are still posted indoors in most supermarkets, clothing and electronic stores.) In the past, most foreigners moving to Ukraine could expect to save a lot of money insofar as impulse shopping for clothing was concerned. Today, far more options are available, though most foreigners still prefer to bring in from the West the clothes that they will need.

For a small fortune, Italian shoes were available early on at Fendi, and new places are cropping up. For example, Bally is now on Kreshchatyk. I always advise bringing boots from home, as well as sensible shoes for pounding the pavement. Know that whatever shoes you bring will be ruined by trampling the streets. An extra supply of pantyhose is also a good idea. Shoe polish and a small sewing kit proved handy for me; these are available but convenient to bring if you already have them on hand. Shoe repair is generally easy to find throughout the city.

Cosmetics have become big business in Ukraine, with Lancôme, Avon, Mary Kay, Yves Rocher, and other products now available. Prices are high, but the women of former Soviet republics are a good market opportunity after years of greedily devouring the slick pages of cosmetics advertisements found in then-contraband *Cosmopolitan* and *Vogue*. There are Russian-language versions of these publications, as well as many popular Russian and Ukrainian fashion magazines. (There is also *Playboy* in Russian.)

Hair Salons

There are state salons, worth at least one visit. How good are your language skills? And don't be scared off by the older women with henna or even bluish Soviet hair dyes if all you need is a simple cut. I knew a USAID worker who would only get her hair cut when she left the country, which seemed extreme. Now it most certainly is, as there are now Western-style salons available. Others feel more comfortable with the hotel hairdressers, who are used to Western clients with their sometimes limited language skills and their Western demands. Like so much other advice, talk to friends, both expat and local.

I went once to a haircutting school, right off Kreshchatyk near Passazh, recommended by my office assistant. We had to wait a long time because the woman we wanted was booked up. I ended up with a young male hairdresser, who boasted he could cut my hair faster than any cut I had had in the United States. I told him that being the fastest was not the most important point when it comes to haircuts, but speed seemed to him a more interesting challenge than heeding a client's request. The cut was fine. I think I let down "the fastest haircutter in the East" by my lack of salon knowledge. He certainly knew a lot more about American hair products and styles than his first American client! But I guess I'm not a great judge on this topic. I also had a woman come to my apartment once, but I wasn't too pleased with her blunt scissors or the haircut.

Gifts for Friends and Family

The *Berezka* (say *beriOZka* in Russian, meaning "birch," or *berizka* in Ukrainian) stores, from the Soviet days were the hard currency stores where only tourists shopped, because it was illegal for Soviets to own foreign currencies. This also limited contact between foreigners and local citizens. *Kashtan* (meaning "chestnut") is what these state stores were called in Ukraine, seemingly appropriate given the number of chestnut trees lining Kyiv's Kreshchatyk Avenue. In addition to very limited food items like sweet Soviet champagne and chocolates, these stores sold tourist items like *matrioshky* (nesting dolls) or Russian lacquer boxes, both of which were well known in the West. The days of the *Berezka* are over, although you may see *Kashtan* stores in Ukraine. In my experience, these have been uninteresting post-communist stores.

For most souvenirs, first visit Kyiv's winding, picturesque Andriyivskiy Uzviz (or *Spusk* in Russian, meaning "descent") where you'll find artists and vendors selling their paintings, ceramics, handicrafts, and jewelry. Small statues of Lenin and other Soviet memorabilia such as badges, military medallions, and stamps are also available. There are the famous lacquer boxes from the four celebrated Russian centers Palekh, Fedoskino, Mystera, and Kholui, as well as Ukrainian variants. Be wary of stenciled designs or transfers—if you choose to buy these, you clearly should not be paying the price for the hand-painted boxes. The brightly painted wooden spoons and candlesticks make good small gifts.

The ubiquitous *matrioshka* doll, popularized as typically "Russian," has distinctive Ukrainian variants. These are most easily

Photo: Meredith Dalton

Look for Sasha on Kyiv's winding Andriyivskiy Uzviz —he'll cut you a good deal if you mention yours truly.

identified by their Ukrainian costumes and musical instruments. There are also *matrioshky* clearly developed for the Western market—dolls featuring Bill Clinton, Michael Jordan, and the Chicago Bulls have been especially popular in recent years.

You can also buy hockey jerseys with the Cyrillic CCCP; the names of the more popular players are on the backs. You can also find Kyiv Dynamo T-shirts. This was one of the foremost football (soccer) teams in the Soviet era and remains extremely popular today. Other T-shirts are clearly designed for the Western market: their quality is gradually improving as their designs become more varied. On the Uzviz, you can also find inexpensive, military hats.

239

Like samovars, be wary of buying old icons, as it is illegal for any objects made earlier than 1945 to leave the country—customs officials take this seriously. If you buy post-1945 art and plan to take it out of the country with you, you'll need to have receipts for the objects, and, of course, there are separate forms that you will have to fill out and additional taxes to be paid. This applies to art, not souvenirs. Ask for details at the time of purchase.

If you can carry them home safely, I would recommend buying *pysanky*, the Ukrainian eggs that are first blown empty and then dyed with rich colors and in painstaking detail. The figurative and more common abstract designs, including modern and traditional patterns, are truly fantastic. Eighteen of 24 survived one of my harder trips, and the rewards were well worth the hassle.

Amber jewelry, actually from the Baltics, is another popular gift item. There is also a much cheaper amber-like product; ask to see both so that you may distinguish between the two. Also pay attention to the fine Ukrainian embroidery—table runners, placemats and napkin sets, and small wall hangings. Wonderful wooden boxes with inlay of diamond-shaped straw are uniquely Ukrainian, as are the beautiful wooden plates, carved or painted with abstract and representational designs. I gave my mother a lovely miniature *bandura*, similar to the painted balalaikas one finds in Russia. The *bandura*, a Ukrainian folk instrument from the lute-zither family, is a work of art in itself, even if never played.

There are several good shops in Kyiv for Ukrainian souvenirs. One is these is located near the Pushkin metro stop at 23 Chervonoarmiyska Vulytsya (Red Army Street), recently renamed Velyka Vasylkivska. It offers a wide selection of traditional Ukrainian shirts with embroidered collars. If you want a decorative plate, souvenir shops have larger selections than you might find on a random stroll down the Uzviz. Shop around. But the standard rule of souvenir shopping prevails: if you find something you really want, buy it now. It may not be there when you go back for it.

On the grounds outside St. Sofia's Cathedral, there are two souvenir stores; one specializes more in Russian souvenirs, the other in Ukrainian. In these, you can buy many of the same objects you'll find on Andriyivskiy Uzviz or in the other Ukrainian souvenir shops.

Art for Sale

In many of the former Soviet museums, the ubiquitous elderly woman who stands guard will turn on and off the lights as you enter and exit each gallery. The museums of Ukraine cannot compare with the spectacular wealth of St. Petersburg and Moscow, but there are many worth visiting, including some off the beaten path. Ukraine has significant fine arts, folk art, and ethnographic collections; don't forget the collections housed in the monasteries as well as the churches.

The fact that Ukraine's treasure trove of fine arts is diminishing is especially disturbing. Given the absence of money for salaries and operating expenses, the survival of both the performing and fine arts is at risk. Every major city has an opera house, but how will ballet and opera survive without improved economic conditions? During the Soviet era, the arts were supported by the state. Today, that support is gone, yet philanthropy is at best an incipient concept in Ukraine.

Museums may be suffering even greater losses than the performing arts due to limited funding. Unscrupulous museum directors claim that a lack of money for salaries or maintenance in the post-Soviet era justifies selling selections from their permanent collections. Taken to extremes, money for salaries and everything else won't be needed when there is no longer any art to venerate and conserve.

In the West, the process of deaccessioning art from permanent collections is well-established and at times necessary. However, these museums follow rigid guidelines: deaccessioning funds, for example, should be used exclusively for new acquisitions. We can rule out this possibility in Ukraine today, but will staff members really benefit or are a few individuals lining their own pockets?

These works of art are not sold via art auctions or public sales, but clandestinely to private collectors.

In 1998, one of Copernicus's invaluable volumes was stolen from the National Library in Kyiv. Only four such volumes were ever produced, and the theft of this priceless treasure is vexing. According to museum officials, a uniformed man came into the non-lending library and requested the Copernicus volume and five other works. The staff didn't question him, presumably because he wore a uniform, which connotes clout to many in the former Soviet Union—and often instills fear. The man examined the books and left them on the table. He returned a second time, however, there were only five books remaining after he left. He had escaped past two guard stations with the irreplaceable volume. Some have wondered whether library officials had, as they claimed, no advance knowledge of the theft.

For Those Who Travel a Lot

You may want to carry either a portable iron or steamer if you travel a lot. Small, inexpensive hairdryers designed for traveling have dual-voltage settings—those made by Conair are very convenient. You may also want to bring one of the small, dual-voltage hot-water heaters for preparing tea or instant soups; again, remember to use bottled water or well-boiled tap water. Franzus, among others, makes inexpensive travel products that can be used with 110 or 220 voltage; you don't need a converter, but you will need to bring adapters so that the plug will fit the local outlets. You can find all these products before you go in stores catering to travelers, or you can wait save some weight and buy these in Ukraine. Products purchased in Ukraine obviously won't need adapters, but they will also be heavier than products specifically designed for travel.

Ukraine uses plugs with two straight, round pins (type B). I suggest attaching adapters to your laptop computer and other appliances in advance, so you will have them when you need them. You can buy these at TSUM but bring at least a couple with you.

When shopping for converters, buy the better ones that have two settings. CD players and most small appliances can be used with the lower setting, and printers will require the higher frequency/voltage (1500). Laptops and video cameras only require a two-pin adapter.

Travel Agencies

Several years ago I heard that Intourist had retained its pro-Russian bias, meaning not especially pro-Ukrainian, and was also infused with Intourist-speak (or *tufta*). I don't know of expatriates relying on its travel services, but the agency lives on, and one would suspect that the dramatic rise in independent travel agencies will encourage Intourist to update its services as well. Perhaps it can be a good source of information for hikers and campers who enjoy traveling farther afield. I've met a few adventurous souls who enjoy trekking in the Carpathians, and western Ukraine especially has well-preserved castles and several monasteries worth visiting.

There are also many new private travel agencies that specialize in overseas travel. Check the listings in the *Yellow Pages* or the *Kyiv Business Directory*.

PUBLIC TRANSPORT

Flights

International flights to Kyiv are increasingly available from major European cities. British Airways, KLM, and Lufthansa are probably the best established carriers, but Malev, Lot, Austrian Air, Swiss Air, Air France, Sabena, and others have also arrived. Ukraine International alternates every day with Lufthansa from Frankfurt and is perfectly fine. Also, it is sometimes cheaper to buy international airline tickets in Ukraine, rather than abroad, due to associated taxes. This is true for buying domestic tickets as well.

Several domestic airlines now offer flights within Ukraine and the former Soviet Union. Ukraine Air was once the only option, and it struck me then as dodgy. The former Aeroflot airplanes were often grungy inside, and more than a bit frayed. One friend forgot to unbuckle his seatbelt to reach into the overhead compartment. *Nemaye problem* (or in Russian, *nyet problem*), the seatbelt merely moved with him as he stood up! With that said, the airline has not had any major catastrophes in recent years. Most Ukrainians don't tend to fly much because domestic prices are now too high. But for those who do, there are now more domestic carriers available.

Trains

The most amazing construction in and around Kyiv's Independence Square of 2001, in my opinion, was the new train station, which is far nicer than any train station I've ever seen in Europe or America. When you arrive by train in Kyiv, you can look outside and see a small church constructed on the very grounds of the train station— one friend said skeptically that this must surely be for show. Outside another window is a spanking new red and yellow McDonalds.

However, the people inside the train station look as dour as ever, and maybe this is because train travel has not yet improved. For the most part, all travel is overnight, although there is new competition in the form of luxury buses. Ukrainian trains run mostly on schedule, and they should since they are incredibly slow. Almost every train is an overnight one, even to travel short distances. You never know if you will be comfortable, freeze to death, or be overheated to severe headache proportions. But such is life in Ukraine. The ticket mafia once made it difficult sometimes to even get the ticket you needed, but it is now possible to buy tickets in advance.

Fortunately the old days of two train rates—foreigners and local—are over. Just to be sure, you might ask a Ukrainian friend to help you buy your ticket. Sometimes foreigners are still overcharged if someone thinks that they can get away with it.

You can still only buy tickets that include your starting point. You can't buy a ticket from Lviv to Odesa if you're in Kyiv, and this also means you can't buy three-way tickets: Kyiv to Lviv, Lviv to Odesa, and Odesa back to Kyiv. You can only buy one-way or round-trips.

The *providnytsia* (or male *providnyk*) on trains is like the *dezhurnaya* (floor mom) in hotels. One hears frequently that she is corruptible. What does this exactly mean? Is this how folks get robbed on overnight trains? Remember: if you reserve a berth and not the entire car, you can't control who shares the berth with you. There are sleeper cars for two or four people. I've been in both, and they are not all that different. If you are worried about your belongings, they'll be sealed shut beneath the lower berths. Also, bring the right sleeping clothes and slippers.

The *providnytsia* will come by and rent you your overnight sheets, which are not included in the price of the berth. She can bring you coffee or tea in one of the metal tea holders, both in the evening and in the early morning. Learn to travel like a Ukrainian: this means always be prepared for delays. Bring extra food with you as well as extra drinking water and booze should you want it. Toilet paper, hand wipes, and a Swiss army knife are always handy.

My earlier fears about sharing a compartment with strangers have lessened with time and experience. I probably prefer sharing with three strangers to one, although I'm not sure I would agree if the three were traveling together. But I have also never had problems. Often I have met charming traveling companions, but see my warning at the end of this chapter.

The Lviv Grand Hotel now owns a special car on overnight trains to Kyiv and Odesa from Lviv. This is a very non-Soviet experience. Many foreigners and wealthy Ukrainians are quite willing to pay the extra dollars for the décor, friendly service, and a clean bathroom! Not only will your bed be made before you depart (with a chocolate left on your pillow), you won't have to wake up to music blaring in your compartment. The Grand Hotel staff has apparently learned how to reduce the radio volume for its passengers.

Cabs in Ukraine

A key part of the Ukrainian experience is sticking out your arm (palm down) and hailing a cabbie—most often a driver headed in your direction, or he will take you there for the right fee. I say "he" because almost all drivers in Ukraine are males, with the exception of some tram drivers. Usually, you'll open the passenger door and state your destination. If he's interested, you negotiate the fare. Do this before climbing in. It's polite to climb in the front seat but always smarter to climb in the back. You may offend the driver by using the seat belt, but do it anyway.

The new, metered cabs cost slightly more than gypsy cabs, but are very comfortable and worth the price. Some people still prefer to negotiate these fares in advance when possible. If you choose to take a cab from one of the taxi ranks at the hotels, the fares will be significantly higher.

Sometimes you have no choice but to walk a few steps more to hail a gypsy cab. The longer you are in Ukraine, the less you will think about the dangers inherent in hailing a gypsy cab. This is certainly the case when you have no other options. For the most part, gypsy cabdrivers are good-natured, even when lost. It's when they insist on an unfamiliar "shortcut" that I get nervous, shift closer to the door, and speak up. The truth is I have never had nor heard of problems with gypsy cabdrivers.

My mother (of all people!) most enjoyed the tale of my gypsy ride that took place in Moscow, not in Ukraine. I include it here for the lessons I learned from the experience. It was very late, and my friend and I were having trouble hailing a cab when a van pulled up. My friend spoke to the driver and told me to climb in. I thought she would follow, but she was headed in another direction.

That night, I ignored the cardinal rule of never getting into a cab with more than one person. On this occasion, I was so relieved to find a willing driver that I foolishly let down my guard. Inside the van were two women and a man, all friends of the driver, it turned out.

I consoled myself that these women were there; naturally, they were the first ones dropped off. I moved closer to the door handle. The men were very courteous, and one offered me a cigarette, which I declined. "Menthol or regular?" he asked. "Juice or beer?" he continued, but he too was soon dropped off. I was able to relax a little. With me as the only passenger, the driver pulled off the road and turned off the engine. He took the bottle opener from his key chain and popped open a warm beer for me. He restarted the car, and I realized now that I was safe but silently cursed my foolishness. I had also failed to negotiate my fare in advance.

When the van pulled up to my door, I offered the driver a generous fare. He refused my money. He said that he was not a cabbie; he was going my way and wanted to help me out, especially because it was so late. It turned out that he and his companions ran a kiosk on the outskirts of town, which was where he got the drinks and cigarettes. Never since has a gypsy driver refused my money and, despite this driver's kindness, I have never since gotten into a cab with more than one man. Observe the rule of numbers, and be safe. Also, be wary of sharing elevators—I know an American who was assaulted and robbed on an elevator—trust any suspicious instincts that you have and act on them.

One night in Kyiv an American friend and I were simply unable to hail a cab. We found ourselves in a deserted area, so we opted to walk briskly to a better lit and more traveled road to find a cab. We were lucky. Public transportation ends sometime after 1 am, and a city bus, moonlighting as a gypsy cab, stopped for us. We were delivered home safely and in style!

City Transport

Dnipropetrovsk, Kharkiv, and Kyiv have metro systems, each with three connecting lines. Some of the stations are lovely Soviet structures (not always oxymoronic!), and while they may have lost some of the luster of Soviet times, vestiges of their glory days remain.

Photo: Meredith Dalton

Dynamo Station is a typical Kyiv Metro stop.

The Kyiv metro is reportedly one of the deepest in the world. It is said that all stations are on the same level, which is why it sometimes takes two excruciatingly long escalators to reach the metro itself. It is also designed to function as a bomb shelter should the need arise. One of the urban myths I was told was that construction of the Kyiv's metro continued uninterrupted even during the German occupation. The truth is that the metro opened in 1960. Another truth is some of the builders of the Kyiv metro were dispatched to clean up Chornobyl after the 1986 disaster.

The metro is an inexpensive form of transport. You buy a token (called a *zheton*), and drop it into the turnstile to enter the metro. At the base of each long escalator is a woman seated in a booth to see that there are no problems on the escalators. The rails and steps operate at different speeds, which means if you stand rigid from the beginning while holding the rails, your hands and body may not be aligned.

Public street transportation includes the *tramvay* (or tram), which are streetcars traveling on rails with electric wires overhead. A *troleybus* (say ***troLAYboos***) has wheels like a bus and is attached to two overhead wires. An *avtobus* is a bus. For each of these, you will need a ticket called a *talon,* sold in booklets or individually. There is an honor system aboard; you will stamp your ticket yourself in a small machine or pass it to someone closer to help you out, as frequently it is quite crowded. There are periodic ticket checks to make sure everyone adheres to the honor system.

While the tickets cost the same, there are separate tickets for buses and another for trams and trolleys. I was reprimanded once for using the wrong one, but a gallant Ukrainian spoke up for me, sternly admonishing the attendant that I was a foreigner, and that this was an innocent mistake. I wasn't fined.

You may also buy monthly passes that are available for purchase only at the beginning of each month. Passes are for use on the metro only, for ground transportation only, or for all forms of public transportation—excluding minibuses.

Jitneys or minibuses (called *marshrutnoe taksi,* in the singular, or simply *marshrutka*) are the latest arrival on the local transport scene. There is a burgeoning market for these vehicles that travel the city's most popular routes. Clearly more of these are needed, because the number of trams and trolleys has declined in the past couple years. People are also willing to pay a slightly higher fare for minibuses, as opposed to the other forms of public transportation. One reason is that there are fewer stops, and the minibuses are also less crowded. I've also heard licenses for these minibuses are reasonable. This bodes well for both the public and people trying to enter this market.

Lastly, an alternative to overnight train travel between Ukrainian cities are the sleek, new intercity buses that travel between the major cities every day. One-way fares as of early 2002 were roughly $10, and movies are shown en route and snacks are available for purchase.

DRIVING

Because I dislike driving, my first advice to everyone is "hire a driver." I'd opt for that in the United States if it was truly feasible— or in any other country for that matter. Most Ukraine drivers today strike me as erratic, but that may be a result of the number of cars competing for road space. Throughout all the cities, the number of cars has expanded vastly since the early years of independence. The streets clearly weren't made to handle the current amount of traffic, and as elsewhere in the world the situation only gets worse with time.

It is possible to rent a car in Ukraine, but would you really want to? Avis arrived a few years ago to compete with the smaller firms already here. Hertz is a more recent competitor. I understand that rates are much more reasonable than in the past. Whether you drive or are driven, you'll see drivers barreling down sidewalks. You'll also see U-turns in the most unexpected places, and more than once I've been in a car when traffic was headed in both directions in a single lane! With such erratic driving, pedestrians should always assume that the driver has the right of way. I know of several cases of people being hit, and I have heard of and witnessed bad car wrecks. Ambulances can be slow in arriving. You aren't supposed to honk your horn, but people do. The car alarms going off throughout the city more than make up for no horns.

I'm still surprised that parking is not more of a problem in the cities, especially given the rising number of cars. A painted yellow curb, yellow sign, or sign with a red X means "No Parking." A diagonal red stripe means "Temporary Parking only." Most hotels have parking lots, and there are paid parking lots around town. Shady types will try to charge drivers for what appears to be ordinary city parking; sometimes they're successful. There are now more parking attendants wearing company uniforms, which would seem more legitimate. But the most enigmatic to me is all the parking—in addition to the driving—on sidewalks! Naturally the drivers who remain near or in their parked cars can simply move on if necessary.

If you have a driver, this is a good opportunity to practice your Russian or Ukrainian or teach English, as the case may be. My driver knew where to get fire extinguishers, space heaters, and a 200-pound safe—this was in the days before the *Yellow Pages* became widely available. He also took my shoes to a friend for resoling, and it didn't cost me a dime, although I tried to pay. My driver ran other small errands for me, and he carried my groceries and heavy luggage. I am certain he would have done more for me had I asked. Occasionally he brought me nicknacks. But more than this, he was a friend and a sort of personal bodyguard, and he would escort me on foot at times when traffic or practicality precluded the possibility of driving. He also knew who paid his salary, and the concept of *blat* sometimes involves giving small gifts to your boss.

There are embassy staff who have shipped their cars to Ukraine. They clearly don't object to driving as I do. They also have red diplomatic plates, which means they won't be hassled by the dreaded traffic police. If your papers are in order, there isn't much of a problem. But I recall several occasions when my driver returned to the car infuriated that the officer expected a bribe when no rule had been broken.

Other license plates that won't be pulled over: the blue plates, which belong to cops; plates beginning with 000, which belong to members of the SBU, Ukraine's secret police or KGB equivalent; plates beginning with 999, 777, or 555, belonging to members of parliament; and cabinet ministers' plates, which showcase a crest with a number between 0 and 100. You get the idea.

In reference to driving, one friend remarked that Ukrainians are among the most patient and impatient creatures on earth. Think back to the Soviet era when people would stand in line for hours, sometimes without knowing what they were waiting for. But put them behind a steering wheel and immediately they must be in front.

In the old days, some traffic lanes were reserved exclusively for Communist Party officials. Today, license plates, and not the make of cars, confer special driving status, and they are not about to let their competitors with "common plates" get in the way. But it's not always clear that all the players, especially those with ordinary tags, know the new rules of the road.

Driving on Empty

It is a common sight to see drivers refilling their vehicles with extra gas carried in the trunk of their cars. It always made me think that rear-end collisions must be deadly. Our salaried drivers always drove close to empty, and while it bothered me, we only ran out of gas on two occasions. Because extra gas was in the trunk, it was only moments before we were on our way again. Out of curiosity, I frequently check the gas gauge when I climb into a gypsy cab. They're always the same—the needle is close to empty. Perhaps this is to prevent thieves from siphoning off their gas? Turning off the engine and freewheeling downhill isn't all that unusual either.

Prices for gasoline (*benzyn*, say **benZEEN**) are high by local standards, and there is no unleaded fuel. You won't see the queues from the old days. Still, gasoline is hard to come by, and Kyiv regulates the number of filling stations within city limits. Many gas stations are found on the outskirts of Kyiv, such as on the road to the airport. But drivers know where to find gas within the city.

Incidentally, the road to Boryspil Airport is in fact one of the best in the country—it was repaved in the early 1970s before U.S. President Richard Nixon's visit. It always reminded me of a Potemkin village, in this case, a smooth Soviet road fabricated to mislead a world leader. Nixon should have appreciated that irony.

Car Theft

Car plates in Ukraine identify where a car is registered. KV and many new variants with K on the plate indicate cars from Kyiv; one exception is KR, which is used in Crimea. LV is for Lviv; OD or OA for Odesa; and so on.

Sometimes one cynically wonders how many of the cars on the road are stolen vehicles. There are lots of Mercedes and Jeep Cherokees among the many Ladas and Zhygulis. The Jeeps are supposedly a popular target for theft. I heard of a Danish woman whose Jeep was carjacked several years ago. She was pregnant and thrown out onto the ground, but at least the thugs kicked her small daughter out as well.

Some Ukrainians are concerned enough about theft that they remove the wiper blades at night. Many don't bother to have radios, just as many people in other countries choose to buy removable radios for their cars. Car alarms and removable wheel-locking devices are commonly used as deterrents against car theft. One night I invited a friend's driver from Moldova to stay in my apartment, as there was some mix-up with his hotel reservation. The poor man couldn't sleep for fear of damage to his car, which he would be driving back to Chisinau the next morning. His concerns may have

253

been legitimate, or maybe they stemmed from the fact that both car theft and crime were reported to be high in Moldova.

General Safety Precautions

More than car theft, the greater concern, clearly, is personal safety. One of my colleagues described a horrible snow storm south of Kyiv as "the most harrowing road experience" of his life. He was visibly shaken and adamant that the trip could have been avoided or postponed. So many cars—close to 400 by newspaper accounts—ran out of fuel or were stranded that the army was called in to assist on that occasion. There was a genuine fear that people would freeze to death in their cars. Our colleague and his crew were able to drive through a tunnel carved out of the snow, but in fact this was not even on the road itself but off to the side. The lesson here is: don't drive, or let your driver proceed, if the situation is hairy. And ALWAYS INSIST on wearing your seatbelt, regardless of the weather, and even though you may even offend your driver. I always say it's the other drivers on the road I distrust.

Most accidents befall Ukrainians and foreigners alike due to adverse driving conditions such as unsafe roads or alcohol-related accidents. If you drive out of town, you will see fenced-in "car graveyards" on the sides of the highway. These propagandistic displays of hideously wrecked cars are meant to discourage unsafe driving practices.

CLUBS AND ORGANIZATIONS

For expatriates in need of moral support or business advice from other expatriates, there are several important organizations. Kyiv's International Women's Club caters more to the housewives of working expatriates than to working women, but both groups are represented. The American Chamber of Commerce and the British Ukrainian Chamber of Commerce are here, as are Alliance Française,

Photo: Meredith Dalton

Ukrainians and other nationals enjoying an American Independence Day.

Amnesty International, and Alcoholics Anonymous. Various religious organizations are also represented.

Some embassies host happy hours on a regular basis, and most celebrate their country's national holidays. Embassies of NATO countries occasionally invite citizens of other NATO countries to their social functions, provided that guests show their passports.

Being a non-club sort of person, I've always preferred occasional functions to club membership. But one club I have participated in is the Hash House Harriers. With chapters around the world, this has been dubbed "the running club with a drinking problem." In Kyiv, the Hash organizes biweekly runs—or walks for those choosing not to run. The Hash is a sort of scavenger hunt; participants have to locate the course through symbols made of ribbons or flour thrown in handfuls on the ground. When those around you locate clues, they shout them out so you need not worry about losing the group or the trail if you are falling behind. There are many arcane rules about behavior during the Hash. The drinking comes afterwards, to the accompaniment of silly and often bawdy songs. A lot of beer is drunk from plastic bowls, or Cokes for those who don't imbibe, and what remains at the end of the song ends up on your head. But it's all done in good spirits.

The Kyiv Hash provides a great way to see different parts of a lovely city replete with green spaces and to meet friends from the international community. There are also Ukrainian members, often introduced to the Hash by their foreign co-workers or friends. Most appear to be bilingual (or even trilingual), although sometimes Hash humor eludes them, just as their humor at times eludes many of us!

The Hash for the first-timers, a.k.a. virgins, is free; it's $5 thereafter. Give it a spin, even if neither running nor beer is your thing. Currently the Hash assembles in Kyiv on alternating Sunday afternoons at Eric's Bier Stube; the exact time varies according to the season. Generally, it's 1 pm in the winter and 2 pm in the summer. Odesa opened its own chapter of the Hash in 1999. Check Kyiv's O'Neals Irish Pub or the Mexican Restaurant for details, or visit the Hash's international website at http://www.gthhh.com.

ENTERTAINMENT

Restaurants and Nightclubs

New restaurants are constantly cropping up in Kyiv. You may not consider dining out as entertainment per se, but a lot of expat social life takes place at restaurants. However, it's difficult to give specific restaurant recommendations here, because venues change often. The variety of ethnic food available gets better all the time, and there are also more fast-food options. It used to be quite difficult to find good coffee in Kyiv, but the situation has improved greatly.

In the springtime, Kyiv takes on a vibrant atmosphere. With their white plastic chairs and colorful umbrellas, cafés sprout alongside city sidewalks, offering vodka, beer, and limited menu items. Many restaurants will set up tables outdoors, if possible.

Although Ukrainians don't dine out with the same regularity as the expatriate community, in any given restaurant there will be a mix of locals and foreigners. In the Western restaurants, you will see the more well-to-do Ukrainians, because for average Ukrainians, dining out is exclusively reserved for special occasions, and usually meals are taken in Ukrainian rather than Western restaurants.

The expatriate bar scene is alive and well in Ukraine and a great place to meet other foreigners. This network is easy to tap into and provides a familiar support mechanism that you may need and welcome periodically. Gay bars, advertising themselves as such, are also now showing up on the lists of entertainment options.

The nightclub scene may not appeal to everyone's tastes, but many foreigners find themselves (possibly dragged) into an all-night discotheque at some point. Chances are you paid a steep entrance fee and were frisked in the process. If the pulsating rhythms and heavy clouds of smoke don't immediately drive you away, sit back and watch the people. Here is a good opportunity to glimpse the younger Ukrainian set, especially those with some money to burn. You'll also likely see some expats trying to pick up some local beauties. There are also a growing number of nightclubs specializing in adult entertainment.

At some point, you may be invited to join a Dnipro boat cruise for dinner and drinking. The cruise is generally good fun and a pleasant way to see the city from a different perspective. On most night cruises, the top deck will function as a dance floor with disco lighting along with a DJ for at least part of the evening's entertainment.

Live music is frequently heard in the subways, where accordion music seems especially popular. Presumably for the best folk music, you should head to Lviv, although Odesa too has a long tradition of lively folk music. There are also casinos all over town, and some of the nightclubs have casinos, in addition to their dance floors and bar areas. As for big-time gambling in Ukraine, I've been told that there is only one thing worse than losing—and that is winning. If you do win big or show a lot of money while trying to do so, expect some thugs to start watching your movements.

Sports Facilities

Pool tables have long been available in several of Kyiv's more popular bars. Then bowling arrived several years ago, pleasing expatriates and locals alike, especially those tired of the capital's nightclub and bar scene. Incidentally, bowling alleys do have full bar facilities as well.

The first Western health club opened in Kyiv in 1998. The facility had standard weight machines and trainers to assist you, and aerobics classes were available on a regular basis. More health clubs have since opened, and there is a trend among Ukraine's middle classes who enjoy working out. Membership fees vary, depending on how exclusive the facility is. Some people prefer working out to socializing or being seen; for others, it's the reverse.

Lviv's exclusive Grand Hotel once again gets the credit for being the first in its class. It first established itself as Ukraine's best hotel back in 1992, and in 1998 it boasted the fanciest gym facility in the country. Its pool had a wave machine, and patrons swimming laps were surrounded by palm trees and singing canaries! At the same time, Lviv added a casino, a virtual reality club, and even a ski machine to its hotel complex.

Lastly, you can go cross-country skiing and horseback riding within Kyiv's city limits near the Hippodrome. Ask around about other venues. For those who want to go downhill skiing, they will need to head to western Ukraine, to the Carpathian Mountains.

Hidropark

By definition, many expat hangouts aren't places where you will encounter a true cross-section of the local population. You will,

Photo: Meredith Dalton

The water park at Kyiv's Hidropark.

however, find many Ukrainians enjoying more sedate environments like the numerous parks and green spaces throughout Kyiv. One of my favorite places is Hidropark, where Ukrainians go to relax. In the summer evenings and on weekends, the place is alive with activity. You will see all ages enjoying themselves; there's even an area where older folks congregate to gossip and dance to accordion music. There are several restaurants on the park's grounds. You may prefer to eat outdoors at one of the many *shashlyk* stands, enticed by the wafting smells of meat kebabs sizzling over hot coals. Elsewhere, couples move over to the dance floor as the night progresses and the speaker volume is turned up.

In the Hidropark you can stroll along the Dnipro's banks, swim, or sunbathe. Lounge chairs and small paddleboats can be rented. A water-slide is popular in the warmer months. An outdoor gym facility with lots of weight machines attracts bodybuilders in their tank tops. For children, there are old-fashioned outdoor amusement

259

rides. Vendors throughout the park sell ice cream, soft drinks, and standard alcoholic fare; you can also buy the popular dried fish that tastes as fishy as it smells.

Hidropark is a great place to wander and people-watch; and when you're ready to leave, you hop back on the metro because Hidropark is directly on the metro line.

Movie Theaters and Performing Arts

One of the newer trends in the world of Kyiv entertainment is the arrival of new large, upscale movie houses. The first one was located a few footsteps off Kreshchatyk, with many of the older theaters upgraded and ready to compete. The older Ukrainian movie theaters are large and often drafty. Unlike opera houses and most restaurants, they could not care less if you wear your overcoat inside—and you'll probably need it.

Refreshments and prices in these new facilities reflect their Western forerunners. The films include both Russian releases and the latest American and European films dubbed into Russian. Films in English are still shown at one of a couple of popular theaters in central Kyiv; these releases are generally recent but not currently playing overseas. Check http://www.whatson-kiev.com or the weekly hardcopy version of the magazine for the latest listings.

What's On is also an excellent source for finding out about live performances—bands playing in bars, classical music performances, dance, and theater. Current art exhibitions or openings are listed.

Kyiv's circus, opera, and ballet are must-sees when they are in season. They are generally closed in summer months. Ticket prices are very reasonable, and your support is frankly needed. Apart from the limited funding, there is the growing concern that Ukraine's most talented ballet and opera stars prefer to study and work in Russia (or elsewhere), where the schools are better established and so attract the better students. You will also have the opportunity, of course, to see various Russian troupes when they are traveling through Ukraine.

Bootleg Galore

You may buy bootleg videotapes on the street. The quality of dubbing is awful in some cases—sometimes a single voice translated all the voices into Russian, and snippets of English are still audible in the background. In the past you might find some videos that were copied by means of a hand-held video camera in a movie theater! You can guess the results. As for bootleg CDs, there may be no liner notes, and sometimes the album is entirely different from the packaging. However, you can generally listen to the CD before you purchase it, whereas videos are sealed. Because of the crackdown on bootleg recordings you might soon see a dramatic rise in the cost of available CDs and videotapes.

You might decide to buy a multisystem video-player that will read any video format; this is useful if you bring videos from abroad and also intend to watch locally produced films.

Cable television has finally arrived in Ukraine, which is good because until now a satellite dish was practically necessary for the foreigner's survival. If nothing else, news in English is always a relief, and the channels and films coming out of Europe are much appreciated.

English-language books are now available in Kyiv and elsewhere.

European Travel

Finally, take advantage of Ukraine's location if you can afford it. In most cases, you should be saving some money while in Ukraine, at least on some of your books, clothes, and general impulse buying. Then again, if you are dining out or barhopping a lot—and depending on how much your apartment costs you—your savings may never eventuate.

Many expatriates still claim that they have a psychological need to travel outside of Ukraine from time to time. For some of us, it's necessary—wherever we are living—to revitalize ourselves by getting away every three to six months, if only for a long weekend. Western

Europe is an easy flight from Kyiv and elsewhere in Ukraine, and both Turkey and Cyprus are other popular tourist destinations. Make sure, of course, that your visa allows for multiple entries into Ukraine.

SAFETY

Before settling in Ukraine, you might want to arrange for someone at home to have limited power of attorney in your absence. Get all your insurance papers in order. Consider getting an international driver's license in the event that you will want it for Ukraine or elsewhere. Leave most of your credit cards at home. Bring some extra passport photos just to be on the safe side, although they are easily available in Ukraine. Put a card in your wallet that identifies your blood type and any medical allergies. Maybe you want to bring some hypodermic needles that you know are sharp, safe, and unused?

I always try to avoid late-night arrivals whenever traveling, and check out hotel and apartment escape routes in the event of fire. Register with your embassy upon arrival. They will need a local phone number for contacting you in the event of emergencies at home, or should political evacuations become necessary. Your embassy will also want contact information for someone back at home who can be contacted should you need help of some sort.

Always lock your doors, and never answer the door without first asking "Who is there?" (*Khto tam?*) Teach your children to do the same. Make sure that neither they nor any babysitter ever says on the phone that you are not home. Only say that you are unavailable, and take a number so that you may call back.

Safety Precautions While Street-Roaming

In Ukraine, pay attention to your style of dress. Don't insist on standing out or talking too loudly. Make a habit of surveying your surroundings, watch your jewelry, and beware of pickpockets. Learn to identify the most familiar car makes.

Carry your ID, green card, and/or copy of your passport with you as you roam the streets. I never had any problems, but I know men, especially younger ones with darker skin, who had problems with the transit police. Like the traffic police waving their batons at unsuspecting drivers, the police can demand to see your papers without giving a reason. Their selection of when, why, and who they stop is random (but less random if your skin is dark).

Always assume that the driver has the right of way or will seize it. There is growing courtesy toward pedestrians, but with the sharp increase in cars, impatient drivers are also out in full force.

Be careful on all those granite steps, especially after rain or when they are icy. Watch the pavement for missing manhole covers, and look overhead for rotting balconies and unruly icicles. People have been killed by falling icicles, and the weight of snow and ice led to the collapse of the portal by the main post office in 1989, just off what is now Independence Square. Eleven people died.

It's not all gloom and doom here, just an ounce of prevention. By staying alert, you'll also notice a lot more around you.

Safety Alert

One spring evening just after dark, a close friend and her male companion, who had been enjoying an evening stroll outdoors, had a horrible experience after buying vodka from a kiosk vendor. The only thing my friend could figure out later was that the vendor must have slipped a drug, probably rohypnol, into their glass of vodka. Their mistake was not leaving with their bottle as soon as they purchased it. Rather, they let the kiosk vendor serve them in plastic cups and even join them in a drink.

The woman recalled being dizzy; she and her friend remembered nothing else until later back in her apartment. The vendor had come home with them. Neither could recall either walking the short distance to the apartment or inviting the vendor into the apartment. She later recalled going in and out of consciousness, which supports the rohypnol theory. In the morning she awoke to find out that she and her companion had been robbed. She had also been sexually assaulted. She never contacted the police or her embassy. When asked why she didn't at least notify the *Kyiv Post*, she would only say she regrets not doing so. She wanted me to include her story here so that this kind of incident might be avoided in the future.

The United States Embassy in Kyiv has reported similar offenses involving drugs; there are also stories of people being drugged and robbed on trains. For example, one reader strongly recommends never accepting food or drink from people on trains. A young guy sharing her compartment offered to bring her tea. It was laced with a narcotic that slowed down her heartbeat to an almost fatal degree. The lesson here: be wise and be wary of accepting drinks from strangers. But I warn you, it won't always be easy.

Chapter Six

DOING BUSINESS IN AND SURVIVING UKRAINE

Several points in earlier chapters bear repeating here. Ukrainians don't like to be called Russians any more than Southerners in the United States like being called Yankees—or Scots being called English. The name Ukraine may originate from a Slavic word meaning "borderland," but that doesn't mean it is one any more. Nor is it Southern Russia or Small Russia. Ukrainians today prefer the name "Ukraine" to "the Ukraine" as the latter suggests to them a geographical region, presumably under the yoke of another country. Ukraine's history is a troubled one, and Ukrainians are both proud and at times divided.

Left-Bank Ukraine and Right-Bank Ukraine continue to exhibit marked differences in language, history, and customs. Time will tell us whether these differences become too divisive and how nationalism will prevail. From the outside looking in, Ukraine appears to be more united 10 years after independence was won, and economically stronger than at any point during the last decade.

Ukrainian independence proved intoxicating for the country, but its implementation has not been easy. However slow reforms may seem to outside observers, these are under way and will not be revoked willingly. Meanwhile, satellite television and Internet access have changed lives and redefined Ukraine's borders in today's "global village."

Much of what can be said about modern Ukrainians is equally applicable to modern Russians, at least those from Russia's western regions around Moscow and St. Petersburg. Russia and Ukraine in the early 21st century may exhibit more divergent paths. Ukraine's challenge now is to work within its own borders, while striving to be a good neighbor. But these are my opinions.

Ukrainians say they tire of expatriates who occasionally treat them as if they are a vanquished people. Ukrainians are certainly not that. However, my fascination with Ukraine is often matched by my frustrations. Those who accept the challenge to work in Ukraine must consciously strive to work within its perplexing, undulating parameters. Accept that your advice and opinions will not always be welcome and that friendships reign supreme. You as the foreigner are perceived as being rich, money issues should be trifling, and your attitude toward graft is rather naive. Corruption is cultural and as ingrained as excessive drinking. The Ukrainian government and the Ukrainian people are not, however, one and the same. All this has been said before, but it cannot be ignored. Some slide too deeply into harsh criticism and accusations; then it is surely time to leave Ukraine.

TEN YEARS AFTER INDEPENDENCE

Jet-skis on the Dnipro, takeaway sushi, the arrival of Ukraine's first five-star hotels, and the opening of a Kyiv juice bar are among the many positive faces of a new Ukraine. Computer programming wizards, young fashion designers, an emerging Ukrainian film industry, and renovated churches and monuments all seem to reflect Ukraine's economic growth of the past two years. In fact, the year 2000 marked the first year of positive growth since independence. Granted, some Ukrainians will tell you that these recent changes are 90% façade and 10% genuine economic achievement.

As I continue to revisit Ukraine, I am optimistic for the gradual and evident changes that I have seen in the seven years. But I also listen to the real experts like Steven Pifer, a former U.S. Ambassador to Ukraine and now Deputy Assistant Secretary of State in the Bureau of European and Eurasian Affairs. In late 2001, Pifer spoke on the remarkable internal transformations taking place within Ukraine. But he also warned that the country still suffers from an overly intrusive state, pervasive corruption, and deficiencies in both transparency and in the rule of law. These are serious charges. Scandals such as the possible government involvement in the murder of journalist Heorhiy Gongadze in 2000 and subsequent lackluster investigation have eroded Ukraine's reputation in the West.

It is clear today that Ukraine looks increasingly to the West, while its geography, history, and culture are inextricably linked eastwards. The challenge, of course, will be to strike that elusive balance between the two.

FAVORITE SAYINGS

Throughout this text, I've mentioned several popular sayings. Here are a few (some repeated) that are very relevant to life in Ukraine:
1. *At home do as you wish, but in public do as you are told.*
I said earlier that this was an improvement on "When in Rome..." because it underscores the existence of two different, yet overlapping,

worlds. You need to know something about both the private and public worlds, especially if you intend to do business here. Establishing solid relationships, especially business contacts, requires that you navigate a steady path between these two worlds.

2. *We pretend to work, and they pretend to pay.*
This was a cynical—or realistic—perspective of working within the Soviet system. You will encounter Ukrainians who still maintain this perspective, but you cannot assume that this is always true. You will no doubt find many different profiles of working Ukrainians.

3. *May he live on his salary!*
This Soviet curse is linked to the previous saying. It underscores the gross inadequacy of most salaries both in the Soviet and post-Soviet eras. Scrimping is a way of life for most Ukrainians, and filching is a common problem in the workplace. Often companies keep extra office supplies under lock and key, even though no one wants to have to do this. Similarly, people say that you can tell which industries or businesses are located in nearby towns by the products being sold on the side of the road. Do remember, however, that this does not necessarily imply theft. Stories about workers being paid in products are legion—those who can convert these into cash are the unsung heroes of Ukraine's gray, as distinct from black, economy.

Further, for some Ukrainians, moonlighting may be one option for supplementing paltry incomes; however, underemployment is more likely the case. That bureaucrats abuse their positions of power by demanding bribes to perform their tasks as public servants is partly a result of pitiful salary levels, but not a justification.

4. *More men are drowned in a glass than in the ocean.*
Any questions?

5. *There is no disputing a proverb, a fool, or the truth.*
I'm not sure if this last one is for the cynics or the healthy skeptics.

ATTITUDES TOWARD MONEY

Those coming to Ukraine to do business should be aware of the various attitudes toward making money. Making money used to be considered inherently evil, and this perspective surfaces in some of the anti-Semitic sentiment. Historians have cited cases where Jewish landlords seized the key to the church as a mortgage or they allowed peasants to run up huge debts, and then demanded immediate repayment. Similar tales recounted swindling or stealing property from drunken peasants. Jews (and other foreigners in the cities) were also accused of using inaccurate weight measures in their businesses (just as people today complain that some scales at the *rynok* are weighted in the seller's favor). Armenian Christians were accused of practices frequently ascribed to Jews but were never so vilified. Georgians were commonly the butt of Soviet jokes involving money, and the Georgian *spekuliant*, meaning a speculator or simply a person who makes money, still retains derogatory nuances.

During the Soviet era the concept of *uravnilovka* established equal pay for the same work regardless of effort, resulting in what some foreigners have bemoaned as a culture of "good-enoughness," rather than one that pursues excellence. A friend offered the example of mixing cement in freezing temperatures as recounted in Solzhenitsyn's *One Day in the Life of Ivan Denisovich*. Ukrainians themselves have expressed dismay and even embarrassment at the shoddiness of certain Soviet products, and improving quality standards is one of the incentives today to adopt (or adapt) Western practices.

Younger generations have a decided economic advantage in independent Russia and Ukraine, because they are psychologically equipped to make the leap to free-market thinking. Some have traveled abroad (primarily to Europe) and most are learning foreign languages. In particular, English is recognized as the most valuable foreign language. These Ukrainians are especially attracted to the West and want to see Western business practices adopted. They also want to be seen as European, not as East European. For this to happen, Ukraine will have to change: the widespread corruption that exists today must be reduced dramatically.

TIPS FOR BUSINESS SUCCESS

Dress

Westerners should wear business attire to all business meetings. This means conservative suits for men. Avoid lighter colors as to some people this indicates a lazy or unreliable person. Do not remove your suit jacket without asking first. Generally follow the lead of your Ukrainian counterparts or hosts. Of course you will remove hat and overcoat. Women should dress conservatively and even femininely.

If possible, dress in layers in an effort to combat the sometimes oppressive centralized heating or the freezing offices you might encounter. This is true not only for winter but also for spring and fall. And don't forget your umbrella.

Business associates and pickpockets will pay attention to the shoes that you wear. So should you polish them or not? Expect in any case that the soles will quickly be ruined by the grime and pounding the city streets. For business purposes, I generally stick to simple black flats, and I pack a ziplocked bottle of shoe polish in my suitcase when traveling.

Food and Drink

Chances are very good that whenever you visit someone's office for a meeting, you will be served a demitasse of highly sweetened Nescafé or a cup of black tea with sugar on the side; chocolates or a few cookies should also be available. If there is mineral water on the table, you should finish any open bottles that are near you before you open a new one. If you are hosting the meeting in your office, you should likewise provide coffee or tea and cookies.

Depending on the nature of your meeting, you might be served alcohol, always accompanied by at least a small bite to eat; open-face sandwiches are also likely in this case. However, in most office settings, you shouldn't expect more than a few toasts. In a banquet setting, it's another beast entirely.

Business breakfasts are still unusual and won't be initiated. However, if you propose the idea, it will not be declined. Business dinners rarely include spouses.

Smoking Happens

The joke is that there are two sections in every Ukrainian restaurant: smoking and chain smoking. It doesn't mean that you will succumb, but you must be aware of its prevalence.

People will also smoke during your business meetings. You may be offered a cigarette, but rarely will you be asked if you mind someone else's smoking. And you should not respond yes if asked. It's merely a courtesy because you are a foreigner, and this is where *vranyo* is necessary—irrespective of your position on smoking.

Business Card Formalities and Tips for Meetings

Arrive on time for all business meetings and dinners. Never shake hands across a threshold, and always remove your gloves first. Men will initiate handshakes with women. Kissing on alternate cheeks three times is not an uncommon greeting.

To all meetings, you will need to bring an abundance of business cards, printed in English on one side and in Ukrainian (or Russian if you insist) on the reverse. Do not underestimate the importance of the exchange of business cards and be respectful of this ceremony that officially kicks off most meetings. Even if you speak Russian in your meetings, Ukrainian is the politically correct language. Thus, if you are also doing business in Russia, why not carry two sets of business cards? Your company's name, address, contact numbers, and email address should be standard on business cards. For Ukraine and Russia you should also include your degrees after your name, with your company title or position printed below in the standard manner.

The person who called the meeting will proceed with summarizing the reasons for the meeting. There will probably be some small talk at the beginning, but unless you are meeting with established friends, don't expect more than perfunctory niceties. Don't ask personal questions or give any details about yourself or your family that seem to indicate any sort of problems. Moreover, you should be aware that, as you form closer alliances with your business contacts, some will feel responsible for your problems in-country, just as most of us hope that foreign visitors to our own country will have a good experience and depart with a favorable impression. Be careful not to overburden Ukrainian business acquaintances and friends with your problems.

Bring an ample supply of letterhead stationery, although some variant should be easy enough to generate these days, given all the fonts and formatting features available on word processors. When writing letters in Ukrainian, the phrase "Respected" is used as opposed to "Dear..." Envelopes are addressed in inverted form, beginning with the city, country, and zip code on the top line, followed by the address below, and finally, the recipient's name on the bottom line. ·

In most cases you will be working through an interpreter, and this requires extra time and organization of your thoughts. You should probably begin the meeting by apologizing for not speaking Russian or Ukrainian. Then you should summarize your points before you go into specifics. To wrap up your meeting, you should repeat your main points and suggest topics for future consideration. This will include, of course, any subjects that were inadequately resolved in the current meeting. All this naturally takes longer than conducting meetings in a single language. In fact, it will take more than twice the time, given the needs for interpretation, repetition, and clarification. That your Ukrainian counterparts are often loath to make decisions is another issue altogether.

Also, you may notice during your meeting that, like the people you encounter in the streets, your Ukrainian counterparts or hosts don't tend to smile much. Don't interpret this as a sign of anything. Joviality in meetings may be viewed as inappropriate and even insincere, although people will lighten up once a meeting has ended.

Never call someone *tovarish*, meaning "Comrade," and diminutives are discouraged in business situations where ideally patronymics are used. Rather, diminutives should be reserved for close friends. Protocol is that you show respect to age and rank.

Avoid a hard-sell technique, which will not be well received. You should stress your desire to make a contribution to Ukraine, rather than your desire to quickly repatriate profits. At the same time, don't be deceived: your Ukrainian counterparts want to work with you because of your foreign currency (as well as technical expertise).

Foreigners should expect excruciating delays—never expect to waltz into town, sign a contract in short order, then fly out. Negotiations are always lengthy. You will also encounter red tape that boggles the imagination—you'll wonder at the need for all the official stamps, bells, and whistles. Some foreign firms refuse to work in Ukraine for these reasons, but if you intend to stay here, you should accept the system, as it is unlikely to change any time soon.

Most Ukrainians are unaccustomed to playing the role of decision-maker. Still, some of those whom you encounter will be dictatorial and authoritarian. For them, admitting mistakes might be quite difficult. Ukrainians have typically preferred to think as opposed to respond or act; better yet, they may try to pass you on to someone else. For this reason, you should always strive to work with the most senior person available to you. In theory, this should save your firm some time. Your company should also utilize its senior people whenever possible, as older businessmen (and I mean men) are considered more experienced and preferable. Sometimes the young whippersnappers put forward by consulting firms can be an affront to their Ukrainian counterparts. Relationships take time, and Ukrainians want to work with a steady counterpart, rather than be shuffled among various consultants flying in and out of town. Thus, whoever is selected should not be changed mid-course if possible. It's a matter of respecting one another.

Ukrainian women are expected to be unassertive, although this doesn't mean you won't encounter some very assertive women. Women are still undervalued in Ukrainian society and in business relations. Foreign women are treated with considerable respect, but this might prove equally frustrating in light of the standard sexist treatment toward Ukrainian women. Equal pay doesn't exist in this male-dominated society, but there are increasing numbers of women in important roles. Today the vast majority of Ukrainian women work, although the wives of the New Rich do not.

In business situations Western men should not flirt with Ukrainian women, although Western women should be prepared for men who may flirt with them. Don't take this seriously if it happens. Also, because Ukrainian men are afraid to not be gentlemen, some foreign women might use their femininity to their advantage. In all cases, expect that your cigarettes will be lighted, your coat removed, and doors opened for you.

Business Telephones

All business must be done in person, but you'll need a phone because existing phone lines are insufficient and the quality of lines poor. Even if you can get through, often you'll reach a busy signal on the other end. With a *mobilniy telefon* (mobile phone), you can alert people when you are stranded in traffic, although you should always plan for delays. People give out their cell phone numbers and leave their phones on. It's not uncommon to be given home numbers, in which case it's okay to contact people there. This is partly done because it's sometimes hard to get through on the office phone lines.

Hiring Local Staff

Upon arrival in Ukraine, hire a driver and a translator. Recognize that the most valuable staff members have added value in general information: how to get around red tape, where you can get keys duplicated, purchase a fire extinguisher, notarize a document, and so on. While Kyiv's *Yellow Pages, Golden Pages,* and the *Kyiv Business Directory* are available in bilingual versions and useful, people rely most heavily on friends and staff for suggestions. (See the later section on Finding Equipment for a caveat to this.)

You will also need to hire an accountant and have access to a knowledgeable attorney.

Protocol for Interpreters

Always place your interpreter next to you, but look at your counterpart, not at your interpreter. Refrain from making statements such as "Please tell him..." Organize your comments in advance, and pause frequently to give your interpreter a chance to translate. Avoid slang and jargon, including sports analogies, which may be misinterpreted or simply translate poorly.

Never say anything in English that you don't want understood by everyone present. You might also assume that telephone lines are tapped. No paranoia here, but take necessary precautions.

When hiring interpreters, look for those who love languages and especially this career field. Many interpreters want to use their language skills as a springboard to other positions, especially in a Western company where salaries tend to be significantly higher. Over time some interpreters slip into their desire to speak for themselves, rather than serve as the mouthpiece for another person. I have encountered interpreters who, after repeated conversations, were eager to demonstrate their familiarity with the subject and sometimes pre-guessed what was about to be said. This is not the purpose of an interpreter and can only lead to inaccuracies. Words will literally be put in your mouth, and if you don't speak the particular language well, you may never know it. As authoritarian as it may sound, one needs an interpreter who speaks only when spoken to and then translates as accurately as possible.

Some interpreters tend to sanitize more awkward conversations, and this is not desirable either. You may want to work with several interpreters to identify one with whom you have a better rapport.

There are some related cultural issues. I have encountered a few expatriate men who were uncomfortable traveling out of town with female interpreters. We have also had interpreters who were cowed by some of the frankly intimidating higher officials in the Ukrainian government. Your firm or team will not want to project an image of being easily intimidated.

My company initially decided against setting strict guidelines regarding interpreters drinking alcohol at business functions. But excessive alcohol intake on several occasions resulted in a revised policy that strongly discouraged interpreters from drinking on the job.

Finally, it is always a good idea to have someone in your party take notes of the meeting. Ideally, this will be someone who understands both languages and can monitor the accuracy of the translation.

BUSINESS HOURS

Occasionally, the operating hours of a business will be changed without notice. This can be frustrating to say the least. Generally, shops and some restaurants post their operating hours near the entrances, but for unknown reasons, doors will close for extended, unannounced periods throughout the day, such as for an office birthday party, or a store will close for lunch in the middle of the day precisely when many of its customers want to do their shopping. For the most part, the hours posted will be accurate and shouldn't hamper planning your day's schedule. The standard posted business lunch hour is from 1 to 2 pm.

BUSINESS MATTERS

Opening a bank account used to be hazardous to your mental health. The process of withdrawing your money was a personal hassle, even risky, and expensive. Top this off with the service mentality that was then clearly lacking in banks. Much of these issues have improved, although the paperwork involved in opening business accounts is largely the same as in the past.

Without question, you should be in contact with Ukrainian accountants and lawyers—prior to your arrival in Ukraine. They can advise you and your firm on specific needs, such as setting up bank accounts, registering your company, complying with local labor and tax laws, and following standard hiring practices. Few firms from the West would consider hiring in-house accountants on a full-time basis, particularly for small, start-up enterprises, but this is often a necessary first step for doing business in Ukraine. Hiring an interpreter would be a close second, followed by a car and driver. Some firms might opt to hire a Ukrainian lawyer as in-house counsel, particularly in the firm's earlier stages, rather than retaining the services of a larger law firm.

RENTING VERSUS BUYING

Many Westerners view buying office space in Ukraine as an investment (or risk) that they would prefer to avoid. The laws have changed, so purchasing office space may become more popular. Obviously, not all apartments make suitable office locations, for example, many companies operate their businesses out of residential apartment buildings. One would never purchase such an apartment to be used as office space, although it is possible to buy and operate businesses on the ground-floor level of many residential buildings. Again, you should seek the advice of knowledgeable lawyers, accountants, and real estate professionals. You may choose instead to negotiate a lease that allows for substantial renovations to the space.

Office space available for rent ranges from fully modernized, Western-type offices at very steep prices to residential flats, unfurnished or sometimes partially furnished, depending on the arrangements made with the landlord. By contrast, most residential apartments (except for the most expensive ones) are rented fully furnished, which simplifies the furniture issue for expats, who will be spending only a couple years in Ukraine. If you have leased office space or a residential apartment that is partially or fully furnished, it is always a good idea to append to your contract a list of included furniture items in the event of any disputes. This should be standard practice, but it is not.

Location, location, budget. Companies will naturally choose office space according to their firm's specific needs. For example, will your new business have a lot of foot traffic? Is there sufficient parking available or will people arrive via public transportation? Businesses must also remember that some parts of the city have better phone lines, and this may influence your company's location decision. Fortunately, today there are many real estate agents who can provide you with the most current information and price lists.

Lastly, there are buildings throughout the city—I've heard up to 10%, but this seems excessive—where there are neither meters nor monthly utility charges. These were set up this way during the Soviet era, and currently there is no incentive to make any changes.

OFFICE EQUIPMENT AND SUPPLIES

You can find reasonably priced computers and generally overpriced office supplies and furniture at various places. Your best options are to ask other expatriates, check the listings in the *Kyiv Business Directory* (or equivalent) or ask your local staff. The third option has a caveat: be wary of kickbacks to your staff for directing sales to their friends at particular stores. This may not be important to you so long as the price and/or quality is right.

Microsoft Word is the word processing program that people in Ukraine know and use. You'll need the Russian or Ukrainian edition and/or fonts for any software programs that you use.

INTERNET AND EMAIL ACCESS

The Internet is alive and well in Ukraine, particularly in the larger cities. The greatest challenges include access to sufficient phone lines and the quality of these lines when available. Efforts are under way to solve these problems. In some areas you can purchase telephone lines from UTEL. They are expensive, but you won't spend years on a waiting list.

Email services are widely available now, even America Online (AOL) has local access numbers in Kyiv, Odesa, and elsewhere. You do have to pay a surcharge above the standard monthly fee, so I would advise this only for people whose business takes them in and out of Ukraine on a regular basis.

Like the costs for mobile telephone usage, Internet fees have significantly reduced. There are many local Internet providers, allowing you to choose a plan that makes the most sense for your anticipated needs. Internet cafés are also available in the major cities throughout Ukraine.

COURIER SERVICES AND MAIL

DHL, Federal Express, and UPS are now available in Ukraine. They are expensive but do a good job. I was very pleased with DHL, whose staff was well trained and courteous. Check to see which companies provide services and fees matching your needs both within and outside Ukraine.

In addition to basic services, the Ukrainian post office sells phone cards and accepts payments for utilities and telephone bills. You may also send telegrams and faxes and place international calls from here.

JOINT VENTURES AND LOCAL PARTNERS

There is no simple answer to this problem. I say problem, because I know of cases where a joint venture was more or less required for entry into a Ukrainian market, but the foreign investor in the end got the short end of the stick, and sometimes ended up with no stick at all. Identifying the right partner is half of your challenge, and one of the foremost reasons for investing time in your relationships is to locate this ideal person or organization who will help you with the second half of the challenge—to (further) unravel the byzantine Ukrainian business world. Naturally, should you meet someone who seems too eager, trust your instincts.

MAFIA

To me, it's a bit like excessive drinking. If you think you have a mafia problem, you probably do. Think safe sex and safe business all the way. At the same time, don't let the foreign press or your friends who are unfamiliar with the territory dissuade you. If you've done your homework, and this means extensive research including due diligence, proceed with caution.

SO CAN YOU MAKE IT?

Expect to make a faux pas now and then. Ukrainians recognize culturally sensitive foreigners and tend to forgive them readily. A few important themes are worth repeating.

Learn the Language

Bring your Russian and Ukrainian phrasebooks and pocket-sized dictionaries. You will also find these for sale in Ukraine, but you will want to familiarize yourself with basic phrases before you arrive. Plenty of these are available for learning Russian phrases and a few for Ukrainian. I recommend purchasing these in both languages, because they are cheap and chances are good that you will encounter both languages. If you are headed for western Ukraine, you should concentrate on Ukrainian over Russian. Because all students are now taught in Ukrainian, this will influence eastern Ukraine in time.

Do Your Research

Read up on the history of Ukraine; buy a guidebook or two. A list of recommended books on Ukraine and the former Soviet Union are included in the *Further Reading* section at the end of this book.

Research Current Events via the Internet

Start with the *Kyiv Post*. This English-language newspaper is available online at http://www.kpnews.com. The paper version is available weekly in Kyiv at popular expatriate hangouts and is free.

The Kyiv Business Directory is also online. The online version operates essentially as a phonebook. The telephone number of a firm is provided by category (e.g. car rental, then Avis), but no additional details are given. The paper version is better, including a good, pullout map of the city, a brief history, and lots more information. Try to find this when you arrive in Kyiv; sometimes it is made available for free in select restaurants, supermarkets, hotels, and at the airport. Hotels typically charge $5. It is updated quarterly. You can call the

281

company directly to find out how to get the latest copy at (044) 573–8393 or 573–8353.

Also available in Kyiv are several yellow page directories. One is called *Yellow Pages*, another is called *Golden Pages*. These are also available in select bookstores and at hotels.

For regional current events, try *The New York Times*, *The Financial Times*, *The Economist*, and sometimes *The Wall Street Journal*. Check their websites for more information regarding subscription rates and online access. *The Eastern Economist* has detailed information and their website tells you how to order it. *Interfax News Agency* is a news source faxed to subscribers on a daily basis. These last two are more expensive than most of the above suggestions and also more specialized. They may well be worth the cost depending on your needs.

SUBJECTIVE TOP TOURIST SUGGESTIONS

This is not a guidebook, but here is my "top 10" list, which you'll notice really stretches the concept of 10 numbers. Some of the ideas are lumped together unfairly. It all depends on how much time you have. Even if you are not posted in Kyiv, you will probably have the opportunity to visit Kyiv where most of the following are located.

- The Monastery of the Caves/Pecherska Lavra and St. Sofia's Cathedral/Sofiyivskiy Sobor, both in Kyiv; Pochayiv Lavra in the Ternopil region in western Ukraine.
- An opera or ballet performance at one of several grand opera houses throughout Ukraine; a performance by the Kyiv Circus; and a football match showcasing Kyiv Dynamo.
- The Ukraine Museum of Folk Architecture, outside of Kyiv in Pyrohovo.
- Hidropark and Andriyivskiy Uzviz, both in Kyiv.
- Babi Yar and the Chornobyl Museum, also in Kyiv.
- Try out the various forms of transport: a train ride to Lviv (perhaps contrasted with a return in the Grand Hotel's car?); a race up the

Potemkin steps in Odesa; a ride on a tram, trolley, bus, or new minibus; a ride on Kyiv's or Kharkiv's metro; a luxury bus ride to any of Ukraine's cities; a gypsy cab ride; and a stroll down Kreshchatyk on the weekends when vehicular traffic is restricted.

- An (expensive) night on the town starting with a typically Ukrainian dinner, followed by a visit to an expatriate hangout, and ending up in an all-night discotheque or nightclub.
- A Sunday with the Hash House Harriers and a Dnipro boat cruise with friends.
- A visit to a Ukrainian home or *dacha*. Consider yourself honored to be invited.
- For those seeking adventure off the beaten track, there's skiing in the Carpathians, medieval ruins and castles in western Ukraine to explore, underground caves in Crimea, and Yalta's celebrated Swallow's Nest—the picturesque castle perched high on a cliff overlooking the Black Sea.

UKRAINE IS NOT YET DEAD

Two points always come to mind when I speak about Ukraine. First, Ukraine is not for everyone. Many Ukrainians are dissatisfied and eager to emigrate. Many foreigners are eager to see a part of the world they've been missing—then flee. Second, Ukraine is not Russia, despite strong links between the two countries.

Russia's financial and consequent social crisis in the summer of 1998 had significant and dire ramifications for Ukraine. Initially, Ukraine fared somewhat better than Russia in the aftermath of this crisis because the international investment community was extremely slow to invest in Ukraine. Russia to Ukraine's east, and Poland, Hungary, and the Czech Republic to the west, have received considerable investment and attention. Ukraine, by contrast, has received principally international aid since independence. Frankly, much of this had to do with Ukraine's arsenal of nuclear weapons (now relinquished) and nuclear power plants, including Chornobyl.

The start of the 21st century has seen positive economic growth recorded for the first time in independent Ukraine, but the endemic corruption and daunting bureaucratic hurdles remain. My advice for doing business in Ukraine includes many caveats. To succeed in and enjoy Ukraine demands knowledge of its many cultural traditions, its peculiarities, and its strengths and weaknesses. The focus in the present text is on customs and etiquette. Your decision to further explore business in Ukraine at this juncture must be predicated on solid business research and personal circumstances.

Specifically, you must decide if Ukraine makes sense for you and your family, and your company must decide if Ukraine makes sense in the long run. If it doesn't, more than likely it won't for the short term either. Companies must further consider the specific business, legal, and political issues relevant to the work that they aim to do.

My purpose is not to sell you on Ukraine but, rather, to share observations of expatriates working in a variety of situations.

While much of Ukraine's wealth derives from her celebrated soil, Ukrainian post-independence agricultural production dropped to less than half of what was produced in Soviet years. At last there are positive improvements in this sector, yet the concept of a market economy is still far from being implemented. More than a few reliable and savvy resources have stated matter-of-factly that no foreigner should attempt to enter the oil and gas industries in Ukraine, where personal safety may be an issue. Obstacles in the banking and financial sectors reinforce this. Consequently, few foreign businesses are willing to enter Ukraine under current conditions. Tax laws must be improved to entice more than a handful of adventurous entrepreneurs.

At times, it is overwhelming to grasp the magnitude of areas of Ukrainian life demanding improvement. Yet it is equally important to recognize the incipient changes that have been implemented since independence 10 years ago. Current issues include, but are not limited to: coal mine safety; nuclear reactor safety; air traffic control;

airport, road, and rail construction; conversion of coal-powered plants to gas; military reform; security and defense conversion; telecommunications; development of independent media; civil society; rule of law; observance of human rights; elimination of trafficking in women; reform of the criminal justice system; the development of political parties and grassroots organizations; fair elections and participatory political systems; reform of the tax and bankruptcy codes; pension reform; local government and finance reform; improved labor-management relations; labor statistics; tax accounting; customs reform and border controls; international trade and foreign direct investment; entrepreneurship and small business development; banking; promotion of agricultural development and non-governmental grain storage facilities; private land ownership and real estate markets; public health and hospital management; education and training; tourism, and so on.

So am I gung-ho on Ukraine? Ukraine is a land of opportunity, and its neighbors to the west, in particular Poland, Hungary, and the Czech Republic, have exhibited tremendous progress. However, none of these countries was a Soviet Republic. (None avoided the Soviet sphere of influence, either.) Furthermore, despite the promising successes of these former Eastern Bloc countries, it is more apt to compare Ukraine to Russia.

Today, Ukraine's future looks bright—but it remains very tentative. Wiping out several generations of communist mentality appears to be less of an obstacle than initially suggested. But it might still take several generations to reign in the mounting mafia and corruption charges.

Ukraine's singular strength is her 48-plus million people rather than her under-producing soil. The population is declining, and social ills that have escalated since independence have converged on Ukraine practically in lockstep with democratic reforms. Genuine reforms must be implemented at the highest government levels. This means President Kuchma and his clan.

Ultimately, my greatest hope for Ukraine's entry into the 21st century rests with the young, entrepreneurial set, which tends to be young, well-educated, and ambitious. These are members of Ukraine's emerging middle class—the new risk-takers in their society.

The example of the Internet perhaps offers an analogy for the near future in independent Ukraine. Worldwide, the Internet seems to be teaching, not just Gen-Xers but multiple generations, that change is accelerating, and those who are not willing or able to adapt quickly will be left behind. In Ukraine, the beneficiaries of this thinking are largely limited to the younger and more flexible citizens.

Expatriates wishing to remain in Ukraine for an extended period should have respect for Ukraine's history and strive not to judge so harshly the obstacles facing Ukraine in this transitional period. It is important to examine Ukraine today in light of some 2000 years of history. Ukrainians today have no interest in becoming another United States, and I certainly don't want that for them. What do they want is to be a part of the new and vibrant Europe. Eastern European connotes the status of stepchild. Ukrainians are Europeans, and changes in their thinking reflecting this are today visible and palpable.

I will close as I began this text. Ukraine is not for the meek. Ukrainians are not meek, they are a proud people with a troubled history. They are survivors and deserve far better than they have fared. For true entrepreneurs and mavericks, there are exciting opportunities in this country whose great people sing aloud:

Ukraine is not yet dead, nor its glory and freedom,
Luck will still smile on us brother-Ukrainians.
Our enemies will die, as the dew does in the sunshine,
and we, too, brothers, we'll live happily in our land.
We'll not spare either our souls or bodies to get freedom
and we'll prove that we brothers are of Cossack kin.
We'll rise up, brothers, all of us, from the Sian to the Don,
We won't let anyone govern in our motherland.

The Black Sea will smile yet, Grandfather Dnipro will rejoice,
Yet in our Ukraine luck will be high.
Our persistence, our sincere toil will prove its rightness,
still our freedom's loud song will spread throughout Ukraine.
It'll reflect upon the Carpathians, will sound through the steppes,
and Ukraine's glory will arise among the people.

CULTURAL QUIZ

SITUATION ONE

When visiting a Ukrainian home, it is inappropriate to:

A bring nonalcoholic drinks.
B bring cakes and cookies.
C give two flowers to the wife of the host.
D give three flowers to the wife of the host.
E give flowers to the wife of another.

COMMENTS

Alcoholic and nonalcoholic drinks, cakes, cookies, and flowers (yes, to the wife of another) are all appropriate gifts. Just make sure that you bring an odd number of flowers since even numbers are reserved for funerals: (C) is unacceptable here.

SITUATION TWO

In business meetings,

A it is appropriate to serve alcohol without a small bite to eat so long as alcohol is not served before noon.
B it is appropriate to serve alcohol without a small bite to eat so long as everyone is seated.
C it is appropriate to serve alcohol without a small bite to eat so long as everyone clinks their glasses together in toast.
D you must always serve alcohol with a bite to eat.

COMMENTS

(D). If possible, you should serve tea and coffee with a bite of something, but it is imperative to serve a small bite to eat with alcohol.

SITUATION THREE

A woman should not sit at the corner of the table, as superstition says:

A she will not marry for seven years.

B bad luck will be brought upon all the guests at the table.

C all her money will fly out the next open window.

D a woman should be seated at the head of the table.

COMMENTS

(A). She will not marry for seven years.

SITUATION FOUR

At all but one of the following, you will check your coat in the coatroom upon entering:

A upscale restaurants.

B movie theaters.

C opera houses.

D ballet performances.

COMMENTS

(B). Movie theaters were traditionally large and drafty, and the moviegoers kept their coats on. This may change with the arrival of large, Western-style movie theaters. In that case, expect to receive a dirty look if your coat lacks a loop for hanging!

SITUATION FIVE

The second largest city in Ukraine is:

A Kharkov.

B Kharkiv.

C Odesa.

D Dnipropetrovsk.

E Lviv.

F Donetsk.

COMMENTS

The answer is both (A) and (B): Kharkov is the Russian name for the city and the one most often heard, while Kharkiv is the Ukrainian name, and technically this is the proper name. In this book, I use the Ukrainian spelling though Russian is overwhelmingly the language of the streets here. For the capital city, I use Kyiv, not Kiev.

SITUATION SIX

To export 19th century art (e.g. an icon) from Ukraine, you will need

A   to pay a bribe.
B   your own personal jet.
C   to register the art, pay a fee, and receive the official stamp to show the customs officials upon exiting the country.
D   to trade in your conscience.

COMMENTS

This is a trick question. Only (C) is definitively wrong. Since it is illegal to export items made before 1945, you cannot go through legal channels, pay a fee, and receive an official stamp.

DO'S AND DON'TS APPENDIX

DO

- Check your coat in at the opera and at restaurants. Many places won't seat you if you insist on keeping it with you.
- Avoid tap water.
- Remember the rule: boil it, cook it, peel it, or forget it.
- Bring business cards, preferably translated into Ukrainian and/or Russian, as well as English.
- Learn the Cyrillic alphabet. It takes very little time to do so and will enable you to read simple signs.
- Bring small gifts when invited to people's homes.
- Remove your shoes when inside people's homes.
- Avoid cabs when you see the driver accompanied with a friend. This could be a setup.

DON'T

- Admit smoking bothers you, if someone is kind enough to ask.
- Shake hands over a threshold.
- Shake hands with your gloves on.
- Whistle indoors.
- Keep your hands in your pockets.
- Sit on steps or on the ground.
- Sit at the corner of a dining table.
- Give flowers in even numbers.

Refer to the chapter *Ukrainians and Foreigners* for do's and don'ts regarding superstitions, etiquette, and gestures. See the chapter *Socializing, Food, and Drink* for drinking do's and don'ts.

GLOSSARY

aeroport	airport
apteka	pharmacy (chemist)
avtobus	bus
avtovokzal/avtostantsya	bus station
bank	bank
bar	bar
benzyn	gas/petrol
benzokolonka	gas station
bulvar	boulevard
byblyoteka	library
chai	tea
cholovychiy/muzhskoi (Russian)	men's
do cebe	pull
fabrika, zavod	factory, plant
hastronom	grocery/food store
hazeta	newspaper
horilka	vodka
hotel	hotel
kafe	café
kasa, kasir	cashier
kava	coffee
khlyb	bread
khymchistka	dry cleaners
knihi	bookstore/books
kovbasa	sausage
kvyti	flowers
laskavo prosimo	welcome
magazin	shop
maslo	butter
metro	metro, subway

moloko	milk
myaso	meat
mylytsya	police
ne fotografuvati	no photography
ne paliti (kuriti)	no smoking
nebezpechno	danger
nema vikhyd	no exit
nema vkhoditi	no entrance
obmyn valyut	currency exchange
overezhno	caution
ovochi frukti	vegetables and fruits
pamyatnik	monument
perekhyd	pedestrian crossing
perykarnya	hairdresser
pyvo	beer
ploshcha	square
poshta	post office
posolstvo	embassy
prospekt	avenue
remont	construction/repairs
remont godinnikyv	watch repair
remont vzuttya	shoe repair
restoran	restaurant
riba	fish
rynok	market
sik	juice
sir	cheese
smetana	sour cream
stantsya metro	metro/subway station
suvenyri	souvenirs
taksy	taxi
telefon	telephone
tramvai	tram/trolley

troleybus	trolleybus
tualet	toilet
unyvermag	department store
unyversitet	university
vikhyd	exit
vino	wine
vkhyd	entrance
vokzal/stantsyya	train station
vulitsa	street
vyd cebe	push
vydkrito	open
vzuttya	shoes
zaboroneno	forbidden
zakrito	closed
zhurnal	magazine
zhynochiy	women's

CALENDAR OF FESTIVALS
AND HOLIDAYS

January 1	New Year's Day
January 7	Ukrainian Christmas
January 14	Old New Year's Day
March 8	International Women's Day
May 1 and 2	Labor Day
May 9	Victory Day (World War II)
June 28	Constitution Day
August 24	Independence Day
November 7	October Revolution Day

Ukrainian Independence Day in 2001 marked Ukraine's 10th anniversary of independence. The Soviet tradition of appeasing workers on selected holidays continues in independent Ukraine, and probably too much state money is spent on Independence and Labor Day celebrations.

The other big celebration during Soviet times was October Revolution Day. Technically, it is no longer observed, but often it has been hard to ignore, because it continued to be celebrated for so many years. Declining attendances suggest that this holiday will receive little more than nostalgic attention in future years.

From the communists' anti-religious standpoint, January 1 was the most important holiday, and when gifts were exchanged. "Old New Year's" is unofficially observed by some on January 14, or more likely the celebration of Old New Year's Eve. Expect no work in Ukraine from Western-observed Christmas (I've heard it derogatorily called "Catholic Christmas") until after Ukrainian or Orthodox Christmas.

Early May is also filled with holidays. May Day is Labor Day (International Workers Day), followed by another holiday on May 2. It is quite common for Ukrainian holidays to last two days instead of one. This second day was explained to me as a day to recuperate from the previous day's drinking, but in reality it often became a day to continue to binge, carouse, and play. May 9 is Victory Day, celebrating the end of World War II—very important in the former Soviet Union where so many lives were lost in the Great Patriotic War. A new holiday, since 1996, is Constitution Day, held on June 28.

It is also not uncommon for the government to start a holiday weekend early. Friday and Saturday may be declared the official weekend to follow a Thursday holiday; then it's business as usual on Sunday!

International Women's Day is treated as a sort of egalitarian Mother's Day; the difference is that all women are congratulated, not just mothers. On this day, there will be parties with flowers, champagne, fruit, and chocolates. Traditionally, men give flowers to women.

Flowers are also given, on a much smaller scale, on March 1, which is considered the (unofficial) first day of spring. Other seasons start at the beginning of their respective months.

April 1 is April Fools' Day in Ukraine. Odesa is known for its April 1 festivities, with its milder, seaside climate and a longstanding reputation as the Ukrainian center of humor and fun. April 1 is not one of the officially recognized holidays, but there is a joke that May Day in Ukraine is International Workers' April Fools' Day.

RESOURCE GUIDE

Much of the information on available goods and services, health matters, home and family, entertainment and leisure, transportation and communications, media and language education, and business is now available online. You will also find that the more popular sites are included as links on many websites. Most of the information here relates to Kyiv, and, to a smaller extent, Lviv and Odesa.

http://www.ukrbiz.net provides information in English, Ukrainian, and Russian. For additional yellow pages in English or Ukrainian, check out the UkraiNet *Yellow Pages* at:

http://www.ukrainet.lviv.ua/yellow/pages.htm

BUSINESS RESOURCES

The Ukrainian Business Directory (**http://www.inf.kiev.ua/nptu/index.html**) is online only in Ukrainian. You should also check out **http://www.kievphones.com/index.e.html**.

Go to **http://www.lviv.org/eng/index.htm** for information specifically about Lviv. This site currently has lots of spelling errors in Its English version, but their English is nonetheless far better than many expats' Ukrainian! The information appears to be updated regularly.

Daily Life

Go to **http://www.ukemonde.com** for information on religion in Ukraine and about Ukrainian émigré communities; **http://wu-wien.ac.at/groups/ukraine_hp/pics/subway.gif** for a great subway map of Kyiv; **http://www.subwaynavigator.com** for a metro map of Dnipropetrovsk, Kharkiv, or Kyiv (or a number of foreign cities); **http://www.whatson-kiev.com** for entertainment in Kyiv.

http://www.expatlife.kiev.ua is a website designed for expats living in Ukraine. **http://www.budgettravel.com/ukraine.htm** has links that can help you find information about embassies, consulates, and tourist offices in and outside Ukraine, as well as visa requirements; pre-entry vaccination requirements, and medical advisories. There is also information on cities, regions, and provinces of Ukraine; telephone usage; transportation to, from, and within Ukraine; travel agents; credit cards; time; weather; maps; flags, newspapers; accommodation; tourist attractions such as museums, churches, and activities such as shopping, casinos, hiking, cycling, internet cafés. Also check out **http://www.geocities.com/jeffkiev** for up-to-date links to *Kyiv Post*, *What's On* magazine, the U.S. Embassy in Kyiv, and the Ukrainian Embassy in Washington D.C. This site also contains links to a logistics company, visa assistance, restaurants, tourist sites, a suggested reading list, as well as information on gay Ukraine and gay Kyiv, as well as Gala Radio in Kyiv. Links to radio stations throughout Ukraine can be found at: **http://www.internetradioindex.com/ i-probe/ip_radio_5h.html**. For Radio Lux in Lviv, go directly to **http://www.radiolux.lviv.ua/world.ram**.

ONLINE NEWS

The *Kyiv Post* is available online at **http://www.kpnews.com**. Another online news magazine is **http://www.ukraine-observer.com**. The *Ukrainian* is a magazine available in Kyiv and posted on the Internet a month later at **http://www.theukrainian.kiev.ua**.

http://www.aimnet.com/~ksyrah/ekskurs/russlink.html has a long list of links to Russian and former Soviet Union web resources, for example, websites created for Ukrainian émigré communities in Canada, Australia, Chicago, Florida, etc.

Also, for information about all the ex-Soviet countries, check out **http://src-h.slav.hokudai.ac.jp/link/index-e.html**. For Ukraine specifically, you can go directly to **http://src-h.slav.hokudai.ac.jp/eng/ fsu/ukr-e.html**.

ADDITIONAL RESOURCES

One of the better Ukraine sites that's been around for a while and is quite comprehensive is: **http://www.brama.com**.

http://www.ukrainebiz.com/Articles/ukraine_regions.htm is a site giving good synopses by region, including geography, population, industry, history and culture, foreign economic relations, agriculture, transport and communication, economy, etc.

http://www.cia.gov/cia/publications/factbook/ Pick your country of choice, including Ukraine.

For the chiefs of state and cabinet members of foreign governments, go to: **http://www.cia.gov/cia/publications/chiefs/** and again pick your country of interest.

For maps of Ukraine, go to: **http://www.lib.utexas.edu/maps/ukraine.html**

For an English/Ukrainian/Russian/Polish/Belarusian dictionary try: **http://www.slovnyk.org/cgi-bin/dictview.cgi?i=en_US**

For a list of various hotels in Ukraine (with prices) visit: **http://www.allrussiahotels.com/hotels.nsf/(Country)/Ukraine!OpenDocument**.

If you discover other websites that you find particularly useful, please contact me at **Meredith.Dalton.wg93@wharton.upenn.edu** with your suggestions.

FURTHER READING

Suggested Introductory Reading

The following three books make for good reading as an introduction to Ukraine and Russia.

Traveling Companions by Friedrich Gorenstein, trans. Bernard Meares (New York: Harcourt Brace Jovanovich, 1991). This is an interesting fictional account of two men who meet on an overnight train in Ukraine. The playwright protagonist tells his tragic life story by interweaving tales of the occasional simple pleasures amidst the larger, bitter experiences in his Ukrainian village. He recounts the horrific German occupation that initially he believed might prove superior to life under the Soviets. After the war, life continued in its bleak fashion under Stalin and included a seven-year sentence in a labor camp. Gorenstein's tale is hard-hitting all the way but told in compelling storyteller fashion.

Imperium by Ryszard Kapuscinski, trans. from Polish by Klara Glowczewska (New York: Vintage Books, Random House, 1994). Kapuscinski is the Polish journalist who has written extensively on Latin America, Africa, the Middle East, and the former Soviet Union. This is a very readable, if meandering, text wherein Kapuscinski recounts colorful vignettes from the disparate Soviet republics. This composite profile reminds us that the various cultures with their separate histories and cultures were never fully subsumed by the attempted wholesale Sovietization.

In Search of Melancholy Baby: A Russian in America by Vassily Aksyonov, trans. by Michael Henry Heim and Antonina W. Bouis (New York: Vintage Books, Random House, 1989). This is a fast-paced and enjoyable autobiography by a dissident writer who emi-

grated to the United States in 1985. The author's observations, along
with his comparisons and contrasts between America and the Soviet
Union (but really Russia) are compelling.

Russian History and the Soviet Peoples

A History of Russia by Nicholas Riasonovsky (Oxford University
Press, 5th edition, 1993). This is one of the classic college texts and
a good standard reference source.

Russia and the Soviet Union by Warren B. Walsh (Ann Arbor:
University of Michigan Press, 1958). From my grandmother's collec-
tion, still one of the better overviews of Russian history just after
Khrushchev's denunciation of Stalin.

The Russians by the Pulitzer Prize-winning correspondent Hedrick
Smith (New York: Ballantine Books, revised 1984). I always recommend this as one of the best examinations of Soviet life during the late
Brezhnev era. Smith was traveling to Russia and speaking to the
Russian people long before most Westerners had access. The people
he met were often too scared to give him their home phone numbers,
if they were so lucky as to have a phone. Read this great book, then
follow up with Smith's sequel, *The New Russians* (New York: Avon
Books, revised 1991). This brings us up to date through Gorbachev's
reign and the final days of the Soviet Union. The Avon edition was
updated to include the failed coup of August 1991.

David Remnick's Pulitzer Prize-winning *Lenin's Tomb: The Last
Days of the Soviet Empire* (New York: Vintage, updated 1994)
describes life during the breakup of the Soviet Union. Recommended
in all circles, it is an excellent book to throw in your suitcase. Many
contend that Remnick is the best American writer on Russia today.
Remnick's most recent book, *Resurrection: The Struggle for a New
Russia* (New York: Vintage, revised 1998), is also highly praised.
Life under Gorbachev and Yeltsin in the early to middle 1990s is his
focus here. Unfortunately, no book exists to explain the leadership in

post-Soviet Ukraine, but the above four books by Smith and Remnick are invaluable for understanding Ukrainians and Soviet history.

The Dream that Failed: Reflections on the Soviet Union by Walter Laqueur (Oxford University Press, 1995). This is another account of what went wrong in the later years of the Soviet Union. The text is more academic than the above book, and does not focus on personal testimony per se, but it is useful for those readers in search of insightful political analysis.

"The Russian Question" at the End of the Twentieth Century: Toward the End of the Twentieth Century by Aleksandr Solzhenitzyn (New York: Farrar, Straus and Giroux, 1995). This was written by the famous dissident writer and intellectual, best known for the weighty *Gulag Archipelago* and *One Day in the Life of Ivan Denisovich* (always highly recommended).

Russians in the Former Soviet Republics by Paul Kolstoe (Bloomington, Indiana: Indiana University Press, 1995) is useful for statistical purposes. Conflicts in Crimea and Transdnistr are touched upon.

Ukrainian History

Ukraine: A History by Orest Subtelny (University of Toronto Press, third edition 2000) is an excellent history of Ukraine. Others also recommend *A History of Ukraine* by Robert Paul Magocsi (University of Washington Press, 1996). Magocsi also wrote *Ukraine: A Historical Atlas* (University of Toronto, 1986); this is a valuable source of history as reflected through Ukraine's changing borders.

Kiev: A Portrait, 1800–1917 by Michael F. Hamm (Princeton: Princeton University Press, 1993) is useful for history and information about the capital city and its inhabitants, and the book's photo reproductions are a welcome addition to the text. The history of Jews in the capital city is also well documented.

Others include: Anna Reid's *Borderland: A Journey Through the History of Ukraine* (Westview Press, 2000); and Andrew Wilson's *The Ukrainians: Unexpected Nation.* (Yale University Press, 2000)

The Black Sea

Black Sea by Neal Ascherson (New York: Hill and Wang, 1995). This great book traces the region's long and complex history from the time of Jason and the Golden Fleece until the fall of communism. This unique study of the Black Sea highlights its bridges between European and Asian culture and provides insight into both past and current tensions.

Stalin and the Terror/Famine

There are many books now available on Stalin. *Stalin: Breaker of Nations* by Robert Conquest (Penguin, 1991) is a very readable account from the author who has written many related books. One of these is on the famine, *The Harvest of Sorrow: Soviet Collectivization and the Terror-Famine* (Oxford University Press, 1987), and several are on the Great Terror, including *The Great Terror: A Reassessment* (Oxford University Press, 1987).

For another account of the famine, see Myron Dolot's *Execution by Hunger* (New York: W.W. Norton and Co., 1987). Both this and Conquest's books give very detailed histories of the 1932–33 famine, deliberately engineered by Stalin as a means of bringing about Soviet collectivization of Ukraine.

Jews and Babi Yar

The Jewish Traveler: Hadassah Magazine's Guide to the World's Jewish Communities and Sights, ed. Alan M. Tigay (New York: Jason Aronson, revised 1994). The book provides great information on Kyiv and other cities throughout the world.

Babi Yar: A Document in the Form of a Novel by A. Anatoli (Kuznetsov), trans. by David Floyd (New York: Farrar, Straus and

Giroux, 1970 uncensored version of 1966 censored version). This is a fascinating book on several levels. Currently out of print, the later version shows text that was censored by the Soviet government. The author was a young witness to the events and determined then that he would record his horrific memories as a testament to those who were killed here. Contrary to some accounts, the author was not Jewish.

Soviet Women

Soviet Women: Walking the Tightrope by Francine du Plessix Gray (New York: Doubleday, 1990). This is a very informative book that helps to explain both the plight of Soviet women and the sexist culture in which they still find themselves.

How We Survived Communism and Even Laughed by Slavenka Drakulic (New York: Harper Perrenial, 1992). Written by a Croatian, this is one of the great books about Eastern European life, especially for women. Contrary to its title, this book is not a humorous account, but I highly recommend it.

Contrast *Moscow Days: Life and Hard Times in the New Russia* by Galina Dutkina (New York: Kodansha America, 1996) with Jennifer Gould's *Vodka, Tears and Lenin's Angel* (New York: St. Martin's Press, 1996). Dutkina is a Russian woman (born 1952) who describes post-Soviet life as lived by so many contemporaries. Gould is a young Canadian Jew whose expatriate lifestyle and privileges rings true for another section of the population.

Chornobyl

Here are three books that I suggest for information on the world's deadliest nuclear accident (to date):

Chernobyl: The Forbidden Truth by Alla Yaroshinskaya; trans. Michelle Kahn and Julia Sallabank. (Lincoln: University of Nebraska, 1995). This was written by a Ukrainian journalist who fought for several years to publish material on Chornobyl. Such discussion was prohibited in the aftermath of the disaster and a criminally punishable offense.

Journey to Chernobyl: Encounters in a Radioactive Zone by Glenn Alan Cheney (Chicago: Academy Chicago Publishers, 1995). The American author was in Ukraine when the Soviet Union dissolved. He traveled illegally into the radioactive zone to talk to pensioners who had returned there against the orders of the government. He also spoke with Kyiv residents about their personal experiences immediately following the world's deadliest nuclear disaster.

Also by Cheney is *Chernobyl: The Ongoing Story of the World's Deadliest Nuclear Disaster* (New Diocene Books, Macmillan Publishing Co., 1993), a more statistical account that lacks the strong narrative component of *Journey to Chernobyl.*

Vodka

A History of Vodka by William Pokhlebkin, trans. Renfrey Clarke (London, New York: Verso, 1992 translation of 1991 text). From a Marxist historian's perspective, this book documents the history of vodka in the Russian Empire and presents compelling arguments for government action to curtail the rampant alcohol abuse that has long plagued Russia and the former Soviet Union, especially since World War II.

Travel Guides

In general, you are far more likely to find information on Russia than Ukraine. Sometimes Kyiv is still thrown into travel books on Russia, since it was the third largest Soviet city and historically the "mother of Russian cities."

Lonely Planet Russia, Ukraine and Belarus (Lonely Planet Publications, second edition 2000). The best generic guide available. I highly recommend bringing a copy with you.

Fodor's Moscow, St. Petersburg, Kiev (Fodors, 3rd edition, 1997). This book covers only these three cities, but it is also worth bringing along for the Kiev (sic) section.

For information specific to Ukraine (which is extremely rare!), look for *Hippocrene Language and Travel Guide to Ukraine* by Linda Hodges and George Chumak (New York: Hippocrene Books, third edition 2000). This is more of a language than travel guide.

Kyiv: Sightseeing Guide and *Lviv: Sightseeing Guide* ("Centre" d'Europe Publishing House, 2001) are both excellent guides with many good photos. (For information on both of these bilingual guides, contact the publishers at (322) 723–566, fax: (322) 727–671 or http//:www.centrevr.lviv.ua.)

(Russian) Etiquette and Customs
The following books are all quite helpful:

From Nyet to Da: Understanding the Russians by Yale Richmond (Yarmouth, Maine: Intercultural Press, revised 1996).

The Russian Way: Aspects of Behavior, Attitudes, and Customs of the Russians by Zita Dabars with Lilia Vokhmina (Lincolnwood, Chicago: Passport Books, 1995).

Put Your Best Foot Forward Russia: A Fearless Guide to International Communication and Behavior by Mary Murray Bosrock (International Educational Systems, 1995).

Ukrainian Cooking (and Customs)
There are various books on Russian cooking, many expanded to include the best of Ukrainian and Armenian recipes, since these were sometimes adopted as Soviet cuisine. I recommend *Festive Ukrainian Cooking* by Marta Pisetska Farley (University of Pittsburgh Press, 1990). In addition to recipes, old folk traditions are recorded.

Dissident Humor

Jewish Humor: What the Best Jewish Jokes Say about the Jews by Rabbi Joseph Telushkin (New York: William Morrow and Co., 1992). This is a great book in many respects, although clearly the dissident jokes are most relevant. One of the strengths of this book is that the author always presents his jokes in a didactic context.

Language and (Ukrainian) Phrasebooks

Bilingual dictionaries are readily available in the country. If you want to buy one before you go, Russian language dictionaries are always easy to find, and Ukrainian ones are becoming more available.

The Atlas of Languages: The Origin and Development of Languages throughout the World edited by Bernard Comrie, Stephen Matthews, Smaria Poinsky (Facts on File, Inc., Quarto, Inc., 1996). This is a great book for people who are interested in the interrelations between various world languages and their roots.

Lonely Planet Ukrainian Phrasebook by Jim Dingley and Olena Bekh (Lonely Planet Publications, 1996). This and the Ukrainian language book produced by Rough Guide are small enough to fit in your coat pocket. I would recommend that you bring one with you.

For phrasebooks in Russian, you will have many more choices. Barrons publishes one that is also pocket size, and which I especially like, called *Russian at a Glance: Phrase Book and Dictionary for Travelers* (Barrons Educational Series, 1991).

Business Information

Whereas books on doing business in Ukraine are very difficult to find, there are more books on doing business in Russia. *Doing Business in Ukraine*, edited by Adam Jolly and Nadine Kettaneh (London: Kogan Page Ltd, 1998) is a recent book on Ukraine, which includes a lot of upbeat business propaganda. Published before the 1998 crisis, it presents a rosier picture than actually exists, but it is still useful.

The Mafia

Comrade Criminal: Russia's New Mafiya by Stephen Handelman (New Haven: Yale University Press, updated preface 1995). The best source of information available on the subject.

Folk Traditions

Evenings on a Farm near Dikanka by the famous Ukrainian writer Nikolai Gogol was originally published in the mid-19th century. Gogol's appreciation of his country's folk traditions is reflected in this book.

Ukrainian Music

World Music: The Rough Guide, edited by Mark Simon Broughton (Rough Guide Publications, 1995), is a great book for all sorts of world music, as the title suggests. A 1999 revised edition is available.

THE AUTHOR

 Anne Meredith Dalton first visited the Soviet Union in 1982 while attending the University of Edinburgh in Scotland as an exchange student. She received both a bachelor's and an master's degree in art history from the University of Texas in Austin. The focus of her master's thesis was Russian and Ukrainian art of the early 20th century. After serving as curator and director of the Oklahoma City Art Museum, Meredith entered the Wharton School of the University of Pennsylvania as an MBA candidate. During the summer of 1992, she interned in Moscow with the Russian Privatization Institute funded by financier George Soros. After receiving her MBA, she joined a DC-based consulting firm specializing in USAID contracts. This work, combined with previous experience trading commodities and financial futures, landed her in Kyiv, Ukraine, beginning in 1995. The project in Ukraine was designed to assist grain exchanges in the development toward a viable market economy. The establishment of forward and futures contracts for wheat and other agricultural commodities remains a top priority in Ukraine, formerly hailed as the breadbasket of the Soviet Union.

Meredith was born in Richmond, Virginia, and lived in various places before her family settled in Oklahoma City in 1971. She continues to travel frequently.

You may contact her with questions or comments via: Meredith.Dalton.wg93@wharton.upenn.edu.

INDEX

fashion 92–93
flag 63
food 173–85, 207–8, 231–35, 270–71
    fast-food 185
Franko, Ivan 58

G

gestures 89
gifts 82, 156–7, 238–40
glasnost 32, 43, 78
Gorbachev, Mikhail 32, 44, 132, 133, 165,
    167, 170

H

hair salons 237–38
health 230–31
    hospitals 231
history, early 34–38
homosexuality 96–97
hospitality 87, 156–58, 162, 173, 188
hotels 205–6, 207–9

I

immigration procedures 195–96
independence 17, 18, 21, 68, 266, 267
insurance 196, 230
Internet 96, 279–80, 281
interpreters 273, 275–76
Intourist (travel agency) 205, 243
Islam 52

J

Jews 13, 15–16, 41, 97–99, 102,
    130–31, 269
    history 52–57
joint ventures 114, 280
jokes 120–41

K

Kharhiv 9–11, 16, 22–23, 61, 72, 142, 247
Khmelnytsky, Hetman Bohdan 20, 40–42,
    52, 93
Krushchev, Nikita 24, 44, 132

Kuchma, Leonid 13, 14, 17, 34, 47, 285
Kyiv
    climate 15
    history 34–39
    profile 68–72
    spelling of 22
Kyivan Rus 13, 19, 34, 51, 52, 66, 165

L

language 12, 15, 17, 19, 22–24, 25, 57, 69,
    116, 117–18, 141–55, 275 76, 281
    grammar 143–45
    greetings 145–46
laundry 215
lawyers 80, 204, 275, 277–78
Left-Bank Ukraine 12, 16, 21, 66,
    142, 266
logistics companies 213
Lviv 17, 21, 23, 41, 53, 58, 61, 63, 65, 128,
    142, 205, 257

M

mafia 25, 46, 67, 83, 103, 114, 201,
    280, 285
mail 280
marriage 94, 95, 123–25, 191–92
Monastery of the Caves 35, 49, 60,
    165, 282
monuments 42, 54–56, 58, 60–62, 71
mortality 15, 91

N

names 152–54
    patronymics 151–52
national anthem 14, 64, 286–87
nationalism 17, 21, 58, 108, 128, 190, 266
nekulturniy 84–85
New Rich (New Russians) 68, 74, 103,
    137–41, 210, 274
nuclear energy 33–34
nuclear missiles 33–34

O

Odesa 16, 22, 53, 72, 142, 205, 257